PENGUIN BOOKS

CALIFORNIA DREAMING

Lawrence Donegan was born in Scotland in 1961. He was educated at St Modan's High, Stirling.

After a short, unproductive spell studying politics at Glasgow University, he became the bass player with Scottish pop group the Bluebells, who had a number-one single with the infuriatingly catchy 'Young at Heart'. Donegan later joined Lloyd Cole and the Commotions – once described by a gullible French journalist as 'the most well-read group in the history of rock'.

He is a freelance journalist, writing for the *Guardian* amongst other publications, and is the author of the bestselling *Four-iron in the Soul*, and of *No News at Throat Lake*, both published by Penguin.

Lawrence Donegan currently lives in California.

California Dreaming

A smooth-running, low-mileage,
cut-price American adventure

LAWRENCE DONEGAN

PENGUIN BOOKS

PENGUIN BOOKS

Published by the Penguin Group
Penguin Books Ltd, 80 Strand, London WC2R ORL, England
Penguin Putnam Inc., 375 Hudson Street, New York, New York 10014, USA
Penguin Books Australia Ltd, 250 Camberwell Road,
Camberwell, Victoria 3124, Australia
Penguin Books Canada Ltd, 10 Alcorn Avenue, Toronto, Ontario, Canada M4V 3B2
Penguin Books India (P) Ltd, 11 Community Centre,
Panchsheel Park, New Delhi – 110 017, India
Penguin Books (NZ) Ltd, Cnr Rosedale and Airborne Roads,
Albany, Auckland, New Zealand
Penguin Books (South Africa) (Pty) Ltd, 24 Sturdee Avenue,
Rosebank 2196, South Africa

Penguin Books Ltd, Registered Offices: 80 Strand, London WC2R ORL, England

www.penguin.com

First published by Viking 2001
Published in Penguin Books 2002

1

Copyright © Lawrence Donegan, 2001
All rights reserved

The moral right of the author has been asserted

Set in Monotype Bembo
Printed in England by Clays Ltd, St Ives plc

For Maggie

Babowsky: Give me an honest price, not one of your 'special deals'.
Salesman: Of course, Mr Babowsky . . . now, how much are you willing to pay?
Babowsky: There ya go . . . you're doing one of those hustle numbers.
Salesman: I'm just trying to get an idea of how much you're willing to pay.
Babowsky: Four dollars . . . I want to pay four dollars.

Tin Men, screenplay by Barry Levinson

'The slaughterhouse of failure is not my destiny.'

The Greatest Salesman in the World by Og Mandino

Acknowledgements

Thanks for help and support to Jonny Geller, Tony Lacey, John Hamilton, Jane Gelfman, Hazel Orme, Hugh Shiels Jnr, Andrew MacNab, John Colquhoun, Denis Campbell, Ian Whittell, Steve Nash, Douglas Kean, Jeremy Ettinghausen, Zelda Turner, Donald Walker, John McAteer, Francis Diver, Colin Macnab, Caroline Macnab and not forgetting (how could I?) John Philliben.

A professional never sells anyone anything. He gets people *happily involved*. I know this instinctively now but there was a time when such a self-evident truth of salesmanship would never have occurred to me. I read it first in a book I bought at a flea market for tenpence, *How to Master the Art of Selling* by Tom Hopkins. I was trying to bridge the cultural chasm between the Velvet Underground-loving, Wim Wenders-worshipping, sixteen-year-old me and my step-father George, a double-glazing salesman with a forty-a-day habit.

Don't get the wrong impression. I loved George. He was a decent man – still is, come to think of it – but, as the family counsellor put it, we had trouble 'connecting'. He couldn't under-stand why I dressed only in black and wore eyeliner. And I couldn't understand why whenever I asked him at the dinner table, 'Would you mind passing the bread, George?' he would always say some-thing like, 'Would me passing the bread best suit your needs right at this moment, Lawrence?'

Tom Hopkins enlightened me. Page thirty-eight, the Porcupine Close: 'The porcupine is the technique of answering a prospect's question with a question of your own that allows you to maintain control and lead on to the next step of your selling sequence.'

Suddenly the verbal gymnastics and obsequious manner made perfect sense. The My Dear Old Mother Close, the Benjamin Franklin Balance Sheet Close, the Alternate Advance, the Uh-Price Non-Technique, the stolen minutes exercising his 'smiling' muscles: they were sales techniques. George wasn't doing any of them to reinforce my juvenile conviction that he was an oily, middle-aged loser. He was only practising his techniques. He was trying to master the art of selling. He was following his dream – a better life for himself and his family, me included. I was ashamed of myself.

Thereafter, I never rejected an advance from a salesman, or headed for the exit when he started to explain why the Hotpoint WM769 washing machine was a better buy than the Zanussi FJ167W (a faster spin cycle, since you ask). I hated being pestered when I was out shopping as much as the next person. But now I understood. It wasn't the salesman's fault he was so annoying. He was only doing his job. He was only trying to get me happily involved.

I thought about Tom Hopkins and my stepfather and the misplaced contempt I once held for all the world's salesmen on my first Sunday afternoon at Orchard Boulevard Pre-Owned Autos. It was just after 6 p.m., the busiest time of the day. The sunbathers who had spent the day at the Pacific coast beaches twenty miles to the west had all stopped off on the way home to look at cars. I was standing in the glorified cubbyhole we called the Automobile Sales Office.

The room was divided in two by a chest-high counter. On one side two men were seated on a raised platform. Frankie Reames looked like the former bass player in the Beach Boys but the sunny smile and sunnier disposition were deceptive. He was the original Asphalt Warrior, a legend in the business. Once upon a time he was the best car salesman in northern California; nowadays he was the used-car manager. Al Davison didn't have a title or a nickname. He was the Clint Eastwood of the partnership; droll, weathered and mysterious. Al was fifty-five years old, black and a Vietnam veteran, which must have been excellent preparation for the life he was living now.

On the other side of the counter, ten salesmen were re-enacting the evacuation of Saigon. The air was thick with sweat and urgency. Every arm was reaching out across the desk. In every fist there was a sheaf of paperwork or, as every one of these bawling, desperate people would have it, a *car deal*.

Helicopter gunships were quieter than Sunday evenings at Orchard Boulevard Pre-Owned Autos.

'AL . . .'

'FRANKIE . . .'

'Fifteen hundred down, three hundred a month . . .'

'He wants a stereo . . .'

'FRANKIE . . .'

'. . . and he wants the wheel alignment done . . .'

'HAVE WE GOT A FUCKING DEAL?'

'Look at this credit history . . . the guy . . . he don't pay nobody, the schmuck . . .'

'STOP *fucking* SWEARING in the sales office.'

In the midst of the chaos stood a solitary member of the general public, who was under the mistaken impression that this second-hand car dealership had promised a free paint job for the 1989 Honda he'd purchased earlier in the week.

'Unbelievable, just unbelievable, you dirty cheating bastards,' he screamed, as he was escorted outside by Pete, our part-time receptionist and full-time body-builder.

Al Davison stopped pecking at his computer keyboard. 'Jeeeeesus.' He started massaging his temples in a failed attempt to make everyone in the room disappear. Sensing his partner's despair, Frankie Reames stood up on his seat, began flailing his arms and demanded everyone's attention. The room went quiet momentarily, awaiting the managerial announcement.

'*I'm the captain of a pirate ship,*' he cackled, then ruffled Al's silver hair. 'Don't worry, pal, it's all beautiful.'

The racket resumed, though Frankie remained standing on his chair. From his vantage-point our eyes met. I was tucked away at the back of the throng, a black hole of timidity in a roomful of thrusting personalities. I'd had a torturous day so far, unable to strike up a conversation with any customer that went further than: 'Hi, I'm Lawrence, your salesman. Can I help you today?'

'No.'

Hopefully my luck was about to change. The boss bathed me in his best 'Sloop John B' smile. 'Lawrence, that's a nice green shirt you're wearing. It's good to see you in here. What can we do for you?'

'Don't laugh,' I said, my words betraying a lack of confidence

Tom Hopkins would instantly have diagnosed as fatal in a salesman, 'but I think I might have a car deal.'

Orchard Boulevard Pre-Owned Autos – The Orchard, as it was known – wasn't the kind of place you visited if you liked to make your automotive purchases in luxury surroundings. You didn't get half an hour to 'think about it', not unless you had a cattle prod handy to keep the salesman away. Complimentary cappuccinos were not part of the service (although a salesman might buy a customer a Pepsi or find their kids a balloon if he thought they were buying). If someone wanted that kind of treatment they should have wandered across the street to the plate-glass and polished chrome of the BMW store, or driven down to the Lexus dealership, or Toyota and Mercedes, where the female greeters had white teeth and short skirts, and the carpets hadn't been ground down by a thousand years of grit.

No, The Orchard was strictly business, as any passer-by might have guessed from the architecture. You could buy an office like ours in the classified ads in the *San Jose Mercury News* for a few thousand dollars. I believe the technical term is 'kit home'. Judging by the flaking green primer paint and creeping wood rot this was one of the original prototypes.

Mostly, the car deals were done inside, in one of the six sales booths and the sales office. The furniture was fire-sale chic, the wall-hangings strictly operational – '*The State of California Does Not Allow For a Cooling-off Period On Any Automobile Purchase*' . . . and so on.

Then there were the staff. The salesmen hung out on the porch, taking the shade under the awning, smoking, watching for customers and swapping tales of car deals that might have been.

Back in the sixties, this car lot was an apple orchard. Later it was turned into an unlovely asphalt square, big enough to accommodate 250 vehicles of varying price and roadworthiness. At 75 degrees, it was hot enough to burn my pale, unprotected Celtic skin but 'just perfect' according to everyone else. In the summer, on afternoons when the weather forecast was for 90 degrees, the temperature gauges on the display cars hit 105. The solitary concession to the unbearable sun was a red and blue striped canvas tent at the rear of the office, but the only time it was used was when Frankie treated the staff to pizza and salad for lunch on Saturday. It was too far from the action. Not even Tom Hopkins could sell a car sitting back there.

The very best salesmen preferred to bake in the heat, like Ernie. This was called 'working the line': you stood among the cars, waiting for the customers to park on the street, and then made your move. Most car dealerships run a rotation system – where the salesmen take it in turns to speak to customers – but Frankie preferred the old school 'open floor' approach. First man to the customer 'owns' that customer. He liked it because it kept his salesmen hungry. Very hungry, in some cases.

The secrets of being a success at a place like The Orchard were timing and disguise. Never hesitate, otherwise another salesman will take your customer. And never bull-rush a customer, otherwise you'll scare them away. Ernie was a master of disguise. He pretended he was counting cars, then hit the introduction with energy. 'One, two, three, four, five . . . *Hey, folks*, welcome to Orchard Boulevard Pre-Owned Autos, my name is Ernie, I'm your salesman today. Goodness, madam, that's a sexy dress.'

It sounds corny but, trust me, it worked. The place might not have looked like the Taj Mahal but it did more business than most places on the boulevard. Two hundred and twenty cars in a month, one of the highest volume used-car dealerships in northern California (note the 'one of': a working knowledge of semantics was another useful asset at The Orchard).

The rule was sell them quick and cheap, then move on. If a customer knew what they were doing when they shopped there they just might have a good deal. If not? Well, at least they'd get a half-decent car, smog-checked and safety-tested to the standard required by the State of California Department of Motor Vehicles (DMV). We didn't sell wrecks or roll back the odometers. That type of unscrupulous behaviour was legislated out of existence in the early 1990s. Just as well, really: before then, buying a car at The

Orchard was like having a bit part as a victim in *Jaws*. Here's a story I heard on my first day:

In Spring 1990 a customer walked on to the lot looking for a four-door saloon with a manual gearbox. The car had to be red. The salesman found one that suited and together they went off on a test drive. When they came back the salesman asked if he liked the car. 'Sure, I love it,' the customer said. 'The only problem is the gear-box – it only has four gears. I'd like five gears, you know, for that extra acceleration.'

'No problem, sir,' the salesman replied. 'Why don't you go get yourself some coffee for ten minutes and I'll get a fifth gear fitted for you?'

When the customer disappeared, the salesman unscrewed the gear-stick knob on the customer's car and replaced it with one taken from a five-speed manual parked on the other side of the lot. The customer was delighted, especially as the dealership agreed to foot the three-hundred-dollar cost of having the extra gear fitted.

The following morning the phone rang. 'How's the car?'

'Great, but I've got a problem with the fifth gear – I can't find it.'

'Don't worry. This happens a lot when you fit a supplementary gear. Give it a couple of months and it will work itself in.'

But I digress. Ernie was the best at running the line, though he didn't sell the most cars at Orchard. That accolade belonged to Mickey 'The Legend' McDonald, a rosy-faced Alabama native with the physique of a battered bed-settee. McDonald wasn't as quick on his feet as Ernie but was intimidatingly sharp and had an ability to distinguish between the casual shopper and the cast-iron buyer that was, frankly, supernatural.

Those two, along with Mal Lindsey, a former college football player who looked like he'd stepped off the set of *Porky's*, and an El Salvadorian immigrant called Jorge Fernandez, were the 'stars'. They made more money than everyone else, seldom went a day without selling a car and took all the lunch breaks and holidays they wanted.

Everyone knew that the bosses couldn't afford to lose good

salesmen. If you sold a lot of cars, you were expected to act as if you owned the place. Mickey, for instance, worked three or four days a week instead of the required six. Mal, meanwhile, took one hour out of his day to construct, then smoke, a cannabis reefer as big as Babe Ruth's baseball bat. Jorge's principal indulgence was swearing in Spanish at English-speaking customers who refused to buy cars.

Beneath this top tier were a handful who had been in the business for years and clearly knew what they were doing. Sam Ritzenburg, Al Buzwatti, Bhagwan Naresh, Jack Nasseri, Hughie Breeker and Raul Cortez were never in any danger of walking off with the Salesman of the Month award but they made a decent living. Every once in a while they could afford to eat sushi for lunch.

More used to Burger King were the salesmen on the bottom rung. Juan, Wayne, Jackson, Stevie and Tony 'The Tank' Tognazzini – my best friend of three days' standing – were younger than the others. They'd been in the car business for just a few months, or in Tony's case a couple of weeks. They were called 'Greenpeas'.

The salesmen who weren't selling cars tended to stick together so at least I'd had the chance to exchange a few personal details with this last group. Stevie had got the job through his father, who ran the line with Frankie back in the early 1980s. He was nineteen, played in a thrash metal band and was a fan of an obscure, unlistenable Scottish punk band called The Exploited. Juan had a brown belt in an unpronounceable martial art. Jackson had a dagger tattooed on the inside of his left thigh. Tony's last job was as a manager at a retail garden centre but he left when the Internal Revenue Service inspectors moved in at two hours' notice.

You've already met Pete, our receptionist. When he wasn't escorting incandescent customers off the premises, he brought a rudimentary order to the office. Three days a week, eight hours a day, he sat at his desk just inside the floor-length glass doors, eating Safeway's mixed fruit salad and answering the phone. Once every hour he stepped outside and did a hundred push-ups.

None of these people was a saint, some probably had a criminal record, but they were streetwise, sharp and, for the most part, friendly. I liked them. In time I might have liked them a lot more but first I had some questions: who were they? What had brought them to Orchard Boulevard Pre-Owned Autos? Did they enjoy being despised by the general public? Why were they working for a guaranteed wage less than they could earn flipping patties at McDonald's (sales commission is extra, of course) when most of their contemporaries were cooped up in a cubicle at some Silicon Valley high-tech company pulling down ten thousand a month, plus stocks? No doubt the answers would come – if I kept my job long enough.

Oh, yes, I almost forgot. Finally, there was me: the New Guy or, as I'd recently been christened, Scotty. What had brought me to Orchard Boulevard Pre-Owned Autos on this Sunday evening? I'll tell you that later. All you need to know right now is that ever since I'd started working there I'd been dying inside.

Mark Swann wasn't my customer to start with. I inherited him from Bhagwan Naresh, who must have been suffering a temporary crisis of confidence – or perhaps just couldn't be bothered – because five seconds after he'd shaken Mark's hand he left him standing on the lot and headed in my direction.

'Greenpea,' Bhagwan hissed, 'come and talk to this guy. I can't get on with him at all, he's a strange fellow. His name is Mike.'

I hesitated, scared that my seemingly natural talent for repelling customers would make my more experienced colleague think even less of me than he already did, which wasn't much in the first place. 'No, it's okay.' I waved him away.

'Come on, trust me, it's a car deal. He wants a Lexus.'

I trotted after him, like a schoolboy being escorted down to the headmaster's office. 'Mike. This is Lawrence. He's my deputy assistant floor manager.'

I'd been in the car business only seventy-two hours but already I knew this much: when you are introducing another salesman, always tell the customer he is about to be placed in the capable hands of a more senior sales professional. The implication is that he is such a valued customer he deserves superior handling.

Bhagwan smiled, maliciously. 'Good news, Mike. He's our Lexus specialist.'

'The name's Mark,' Mark said, with a smile like a broken mousetrap. I suspect he wasn't impressed, or even taken in, by my fictional job title.

'You know about Lexus?'

I said nothing but moved my head in a fashion that might conceivably have been construed as a nod, or possibly a shake.

'This car here, the engine, a V6 straight or a four-cylinder? And it does have traction control, doesn't it?'

'Which car, the white one or the black one?' I was playing for time. The truth was, even if I'd just spent three days ploughing through the entire Lexus engineering workshop catalogue I still wouldn't have known what he was talking about. You see, I know nothing about cars. In the end, I threw myself on his mercy.

'Mark, I'll be straight with you. I'm not a Lexus specialist, I'm not even an assistant deputy sales whatever the other guy said I was. I'm just Lawrence, a salesman.'

The next thirty minutes is a blur. All I remember is that Mark was deeply impressed by my honest approach. He wanted a car with leather seats and said that his wife would pickle his testicles if he spent more than eighteen thousand dollars. I recall trying to forge a meaningful bond by insisting that we had quite a lot in common. It turned out that he, too, had been a car salesman before he got a proper job. Not only that, we were both wearing the same Nike running watch and, er, that was it.

Still, we struggled through a stilted conversation while he drove the car along Orchard Boulevard and out on to the freeway. He'd picked out a white Lexus with '$25,000' plastered across the top right-hand quarter of the windscreen. It was easily the most upmarket car I'd ever travelled in, smooth and comfortable, and as we zipped up the freeway at 85 m.p.h. I could tell he liked it. He was already taking mental ownership.

The first minutes after returning from a test drive are the most crucial moments in any sale. This is where the customer, if he's interested in buying, sets his bargaining position, and the salesman begins to close the sale.

'What do you think?' I asked, as Mark slammed his door shut.

He thought for a moment, then shrugged. 'It's okay, I suppose,' he lied.

This exchange exhausted my entire repertoire of closing questions. I stood there, dumb as a cardboard box, while Mark fingered hairline scratches on the paintwork and made unflattering remarks about the resale value of used Lexus saloon cars. Eventually, he realized that I was defenceless in the face of his Olympian negotiating technique.

'You want to go inside and see if we can make a deal?'

I nodded eagerly, and galloped after him. I was excited, nervous, although as we headed across the asphalt towards the office something occurred to me: I'm the salesman, wasn't I supposed to say that?

'A car deal?' Frankie jumped off his seat. 'Let me see what you've got,' he said, his demeanour changing in an instant from buccaneer to bank manager.

The office cleared, as quick as sea mist in the sun, until there was only me and Bhagwan. His sudden interest in what was going on might or might not have had something to do with the 12½ per cent commission on gross profit he'd make if he wrestled the deal from me and finished it off. The radio was turned down low but I could still hear 'Kashmir' by Led Zeppelin.

'Let me take care of this, Mr Reames. Mr Reames, let me take care of this.' Bhagwan was a Pakistani of aristocratic bearing and almost impossible prettiness. He had a habit of addressing everyone as Mr, presumably as a post-ironic statement of his contempt for the servitude inflicted on the Indian sub-continent during years of colonial rule. Under normal circumstances I would have been with him every step of the way, but not today: this was my car deal and he was trying to steal it. Bastard.

Fortunately, Mr Reames was having none of it. 'Butt out, Bhagwan, this is Lawrence's deal. He's doin' okay so far,' he snapped, grabbing the paperwork. 'How much is he offering?' He didn't wait for a reply. '*Eighteen* thousand?'

Beside him, Al looked appalled, as if the front axle had just fallen off his brand-new Chevy truck: 'Fuuuuuuck.'

Reames ignored him, tapped a few keys on his computer, then took a green marker pen and began writing in capital letters: 'THANKS YOU FOR YOUR OFFER. FOR LAWRENCE'S FIRST DEAL. OKAY AT $18,000. FINAL PRICE.' He underlined 'first deal'.

This was embarrassing. I'd spent the last thirty minutes trying to pass myself off as a car salesman. Admittedly, the façade was gossamer thin but where was the sense in letting the customer know he was dealing with a rank amateur? Frankie sensed my awkwardness. 'Don't worry about it. Trust me, it'll work,' he said, benignly. 'Look at the discount I've offered him.'

Seven thousand dollars off, without even a twitch of a struggle. I couldn't wait to tell Mark the good news.

I'd left him sitting in the sales booth furthest from the office. The corridor was filled with the babble of negotiation. He was now standing in the doorway. 'You'll never believe this, Mark,' I began, raising my voice to make myself heard over the rattle of the air-conditioning unit.

I sensed that he was less enthusiastic than he'd been when I left him. As soon as I had started talking he glanced at his Nike running watch. 'God, is that the time?' he said. 'I've gotta go.'

I ignored this and showed him what Frankie had written. 'Look. Fantastic, eh? Eighteen thousand, the price you wanted.'

It would take a team of research psychologists working round the clock for a year to figure out what happened next. As it turned out, eighteen thousand wasn't the price he wanted. Or, rather, it was and it wasn't. Not that he wanted to pay more but it just seemed, how did he put it? 'Too cheap. Too quick.'

A witty retort leapt into my mind – 'I could charge an extra couple of thousand and keep you here until sundown if you like.' – but not until three weeks later. The best I could manage at short notice was a contemplative, 'Mmmm.'

'Why's it so cheap?'

'I dunno, Mark. Because we like you?' I said, unconvincingly.

This hesitation lasted for another couple of minutes, until his resistance hardened into outright hostility. Eventually, he said, 'You know what, Lawrence? I don't think I'm going to bother with this right now. I need to go home and eat and talk to my wife.'

I was devastated, confused, bewildered. Five minutes ago I was ninth-tenths of the way towards selling a 1995 Lexus E300 for eighteen thousand dollars. Now I had nothing and all because I'd got the customer exactly what he wanted.

'But you said you'd buy it if I got you the price you wanted.' My eyes were glassy with emotion. 'I got you the price and now you're telling me you don't want to buy it. Where's the logic in that?'

At this Mark Swann, the dirty son-of-a-bitch, laughed in my face. 'Lawrence, relax, don't worry,' he said, with the ease of an experienced salesman. 'It's the car business. There is no logic.'

The first time I went to the United States I was the twenty-one-year-old bass player in a Scottish pop group called the Bluebells. We were about to embark on our first (and last) North American tour. Inexplicably *The Rolling Stone History of Rock and Roll* fails to record this landmark event but it was a life-changing experience for me. It was 2 December 1983. Unfortunately Concorde had been booked out by the cast of *Dallas*, so we travelled economy on an Air India flight out of Heathrow, landing at JFK airport in the early evening. There were no screaming girls on the observation decks awaiting our arrival.

The truth was, your average American couldn't have picked the Bluebells out of a police line-up had we been sporting masks and swag bags. This didn't matter, however, because we had our very own sugar daddy, a legendary record-company executive called Seymour Stein. A few months earlier he'd turned up a gig we played at a north London polytechnic. We had, as his assistant later put it, 'blown the big guy's socks off'. He immediately decided to release our record in North America on the Sire label – home of the Ramones and Talking Heads at that time, please note – and agreed to provide financial support for an extensive concert tour.

Needless to say, this was not the Rolling Thunder Revue. We travelled in a mini-van, eight of us – including roadies – packed alongside our equipment, except when the overnight drive between gigs was judged by our tour manager to be unmanageable (i.e. anything over 1,500 miles). On the rare occasions this happened, we flew on obscure, dangerous airlines called CheapAir and DeathJet. Our daily spending allowance was five dollars each.

If this sounds like hell, think again. Without question the trip was the happiest three weeks of my life. I was in love with the United States, from my first sight of the Manhattan skyline to my last glimpse of Cape Cod through broken clouds as we flew home on Christmas Eve. Throughout it all there was scarcely a moment where my jaw wasn't resting on my chest in disbelief. The world had never seemed so big and alive.

I spent the first day wandering around New York. For some strange reason, I couldn't quite believe that everything I'd seen on television – the Empire State Building, yellow taxis, the apartment building where John Lennon was shot, people who said, 'Hey, buddy, get outta the way', police sirens that went *woowoowoowoowoo* and not *nee-naw nee-naw, nee-naw* – was real and not a figment of someone's imagination. But here they all were, life-sized and 3-D. Amazing.

We played a concert on the Lower East Side the following night, then drove to Washington DC. Again, I was incredulous: 'What? You mean Ronald Reagan really is President?'

The trip was just one glorious surprise after another. In Chicago, I went to look at the Sears Tower and ended up discovering a marvellous new invention called Chicken McNuggets at a McDonald's across the street. In Minneapolis, it was so cold the snot in my nose froze. When we got to San Francisco I met people with matted hair who walked around with dogs on strings. What's more, they really believed the Grateful Dead made good records. A week later in Atlanta, Georgia, there was the first recorded case in history of a woman who found me vaguely attractive and wanted to have casual sex with me in a motel room.

Naturally, the concerts themselves were something of a let-down after such adventures, though we did play at a nightclub owned by Prince *and* I later heard a rumour that Madonna – another of Seymour's disastrous new signings – came to see us in Los Angeles. In short, we failed to take America by storm. If we needed further confirmation of this sad fact it came on the last night of the tour when the club owner came side-stage during the gig and said, 'Hey, fellas, could you finish after the next song? People want to get up and dance.'

Can you imagine how hurtful this was, especially when we genuinely believed in our hearts that we were the new Beatles?

Two things happened when we got back to Scotland. One, I was sacked as the Bluebells' bass player because the record-company boss thought I was useless; and, two, I vowed to myself that one day I would return to the United States, not as a failed musician this time but as an explorer. Had my senses deceived me or was it really possible that colours and sounds and smells could be so vivid, that daily life could be so . . . so . . . breathtaking? If the answer was yes then I wanted to spend every day of my life in such a place.

I got over being booted out of the band within the hour (it helped when I discovered that the unemployment-benefit office paid twice as much as the record company) but I never lost my desire to live out my American Dream through every twist and turn of the next fifteen years.

Of course, living the American Dream is only possible if you live there, and living there is easy to dream about but a lot harder to do.

In the weeks after I was thrown out of the band I did a little research on the United States' immigration rules. It appeared that there were two routes: you could live a life of such abject poverty in a Mexican shantytown that you became desperate enough to throw yourself at an electric fence on the Texan border, hoping it had been temporarily switched off while the fuse was being changed; or you could throw yourself on the mercy of an avaricious immigration lawyer in New York. Both options were out of the question.

I spent the next few years doing the things that people do – falling in and out of love, buying a home, taking the driving test eight times, losing hair and teeth, being disappointed – and as time passed it became clear to me the I was no more going to begin a new life in America than I was on Planet Saturn. That was until a chance meeting outside the Waterstone's bookstore on Sauchiehall Street, Glasgow.

'Howdy, buddy! Lawrence *Donnnnegan*, howya doin'? It's *moi*.'

Andy Walker stood right in front of me, spread his arms wide like a goalkeeper and then did something that took my breath away. He hugged me. None of my friends – at least not the male Scottish ones – had ever hugged me. We didn't do that kind of thing, and the Andy Walker I used to know certainly didn't on the basis that 'only woofters hug each other'.

We hadn't seen each other for fifteen years. In the five seconds it took to struggle free of his grip I could tell he'd changed enormously. Just as well, really. Back then, Andy was supposed to be an engineering student but in his own mind he was really John Belushi in *National Lampoon's Animal House*. For reasons I'd never been able to fathom we got along famously. Perhaps it was because, inside, I secretly wished that I, too, was idiotic enough to drink a cup of my own vomit for a bet.

He was a different man. Now he looked like William Hurt in *Broadcast News*: tanned, good-looking, well-dressed and smooth. I felt decidedly shabby as we looked each other up and down.

'Lawrence Donegan, you rascal, long time no see. What are you doing with yourself these days?' His accent was distinctly transatlantic.

'A bit of this and that. Journalism mostly,' I replied.

'I haven't seen you on *The Letterman Show* yet. How's the rock and roll career?'

'You know . . .' I shrugged. 'Anyway, what are you doing with yourself?'

We went into the bookshop and had a coffee while he told me his story. Anthony Trollope's books are shorter than Andy's anecdotes so in the interests of brevity I'll stick to the highlights. He'd left university with the worst degree possible (they gave it to him just to make him go away, apparently), bummed around in London for a few months, then went to California, to Silicon Valley. There, he spent two years designing computer chips, became an engineering consultant and set up his own company. Now he was a chief executive officer, with eighty-five employees and brand-new offices in the heart of 'The Valley'. He was married, had three dogs, three cars and had just bought a house for a couple of million dollars. He seemed so fulfilled, so happy, energetic and positive, that the longer I sat there the more I began to feel like a loser.

Eventually, I said, 'God, I always wanted to live in America.'

'Why don't you, then?'

'What d'you mean?' I laughed, bitterly.

'That's what's wrong with this country.' I'd forgotten that in his more sober moments, the younger Andy bore more than a passing resemblance to Woodrow Wyatt. 'It's such a can't-do place. You gotta be positive, seize the moment, take your chances . . .'

'Ooh, er, listen to Oprah Winfrey.' I started to explain that I had responsibilities (I had none, really), that you couldn't just get up and leave a place on a whim. I'd spent three hundred quid on a season ticket for Celtic and there were still fourteen home games to go — I couldn't afford to waste money like that. Anyway, I wouldn't get a work permit.

'Don't worry about it,' he said. 'Come and work for me. I'll get you a visa, I'll get you a lawyer, a place to live. I'll get you anything you want.'

And that is how I came to land at San Francisco International Airport seventeen years and three months after I'd touched down in New York as a fresh-faced Bluebell.

Remarkably, getting there second time around was easier than I'd ever imagined it could be. Andy found me an immigration lawyer, who said he could help but it would cost me. When he told me how much, I thought he was joking — 'I only want to live there, not buy the place' — but it seemed that American lawyers don't do jokes.

'People are dying — literally *dying* in their hundreds every year — to get into the United States, Mr Donegan. Now, do you want me to go ahead with this application or not?'

I couldn't back out now, could I? In any case, Celtic were twenty points behind Rangers in the league, so there wasn't much point in hanging around. I filled in the forms. A couple of months later my passport came back, stamped with a United States entry visa. I had two years to find out if the America I'd first explored as a Bluebell was as great as I thought it was, or whether it had simply been the misguided fervour of a twenty-one-year-old let loose in a country where Budweiser was only forty-five cents a can.

By the time my bags were packed, I'd worked myself into a state of high excitement. I'd even managed to persuade my girlfriend Maggie it would be a terrific idea for her to give up an interesting, fulfilling career as a radio broadcaster and come to California for a couple of years where she could, as I so soaringly put it, 'do something else. Like what? Eh, I dunno . . . something . . .'

Luckily, her innate spirit of adventure more than compensated for the paucity of my rhetoric, as it always had. Fourteen years together had taught me she would try anything if it involved risk and the chance to have tanned legs all year round. A week later we had a party for all our friends and announced we were leaving. There was no going back now, not least because on hearing our news everyone immediately invited themselves to California for their summer holidays.

Andy found us a flat, in a small town called Los Gatos. 'It's right next to the office. You can walk to work every day.' I'd heard of Los Gatos. It was where the Brazil team stayed during the 1994 World Cup. Los Gatos. *The Cats*. Brazil '94. Cool. *Cool?* I was in California mode and it was still pissing down in Glasgow. God save us.

Getting through San Francisco airport was *Midnight Express II*, starring me. It turned out it wasn't just American lawyers who were humourless but immigration officers too. When I was asked, 'Purpose of visit, sir?' I smiled and said in my excitement, 'A great big adventure, Officer.' He fixed me with a cold stare and said, 'Stand over there, sir, please.'

Two hours and one chastening lecture about the inadvisability of abusing American hospitality later, we headed towards the Customs department where Eva Braun's long-lost daughter was immediately suspicious about the dozen boxes we'd sent over as air freight. 'What's in these goddamn boxes? Some of 'em weigh over a hundred and forty pounds.'

Frankly, I was beginning to wish we'd stayed in Glasgow. 'Books,' I said haughtily. Luckily, Maggie managed to put her hand over my mouth before my natural sarcasm kicked in.

'Happy reading,' she said, signing the release form.

Free at last, we picked up a hire car and drove south down Highway 101 towards Los Gatos. In keeping with the theme of the day, the journey was a tedious, frustrating, aching disappointment. California was supposed to be sun, beaches and wind-blown hair, not drizzle, concrete and traffic the way it is in movies when the end of the world has been announced and everyone's trying to get out of town.

It was dark when we arrived, so it was difficult to judge what Los Gatos looked like except to say it didn't look like south central Los Angeles. Our flat was near the town centre, on the first floor of an apartment block. The landlord was waiting for us when we got there with the exciting news that the neighbours had left out a bowl of fruit and some flowers for us. There was also a card, which showed a little cartoon pig waving a stars-and-stripes, that said, 'Welcome to your new home.'

The landlord's name was Thomas. He'd been to Scotland on holiday twenty years before and was clearly excited at meeting two people from such an exotic place. He'd taken the trouble to air the flat, had stuffed the fridge full of food and written down a five-page list of phone numbers that we might need, as well as some – like the one for the local *feng-shui* consultant – that we wouldn't.

Thomas was very helpful, although he did have an annoying habit of revealing the kind of financial details about himself and his family that you wouldn't even tell the man from the Internal Revenue. On the flat we were renting: 'We bought the place five years ago for a hundred thousand but I had it surveyed last month and it's worth two hundred and forty.' On his twenty-three-year-old daughter: 'She's making a quarter of a million bucks a year, and she got twenty-five thousand options at sixty-five cents each.' His son: 'I'm worried about him – he's driving a Porsche. It cost him sixty-five thousand.'

Was everyone in California so obsessed with money, I wondered, and if they were, how did they speak to each other in the comfort of their own home?

'Darling, can I give you a lift to the supermarket in my new forty-thousand-dollar car?'

'No, thanks, honey, I'm going to stay in and iron your new suit. It cost seven hundred and twenty-four dollars.'

We finally got rid of him after an hour, though not before receiving detailed instructions on how to get to his church. 'It's a very good place to worship,' he said, as I prised his bony fingers from the edge of our front door and shoved him out into the hallway. I wanted to tell him I hadn't worshipped anything since The Smiths broke up, but mindful that I'd pissed off every American I'd met since arriving I merely said, 'Great. Thanks.'

We woke at one o'clock the following afternoon, which wasn't part of the plan. The plan had been to get up as early as possible and begin ordering our lives. One of the great untold secrets about moving to a new country – at least, it was to me – is that you can't just turn up one day and pick up where you left off before. There is no before. Hence, there are bureaucracies to navigate and essentials of life to gather up, like a driving licence, cable TV and a telephone line, and a social-security number.

I called Andy to let him know we'd arrived safely. 'What are you up to today?' he asked.

'Nothing much. I thought we'd have a look round the town, then try to get our driving licences.'

'A driving licence?' He started laughing, like some cartoon villain who'd just tied the heroine to a railtrack.

'What's wrong?' I said, but he just kept on laughing.

When he finally got tired of the Dick Dastardly act we agreed that I would spend a couple of weeks bumming around – though he used some awful phrase you'd find only in a dictionary for businessmen, like 'getting acclimated' – and when I felt ready I'd come and see him about the job. 'I've got something in mind for you – you'll do great,' he said.

'You have?' Just then I felt a little shudder, the realization that this wasn't a holiday we'd embarked upon, it was real life. Quickly, I put this scary thought to the back of my mind and headed out with Maggie to explore our new surroundings.

Los Gatos was, well, out of this world. Not just pretty, or quaint, or fantastic, or wonderful, but just that: out of this world – *of another world*. Walt Disney World, or *Stepford Wives* World or Frank Capra's *It's A Wonderful Life* (the version where the town doesn't end up a dark and gloomy wreck) World. I read in a magazine a couple of months later that it was the eightieth most wealthy town in the United States, in which case the other seventy-nine must have been built by the property developers behind Xanadu.

Set snugly at the foot of a mountain range covered by redwood trees, every square inch of the town looked as if it had been scrubbed that morning with a toothbrush. The residential streets were lined with wooden houses built in Victorian times; the main shopping area had been lifted straight from Norman Rockwell. Most of the shops didn't sell stuff for real people. They sold Irish jewellery and plain pottery, which you painted yourself, and bicycles that cost four thousand dollars, and antique ball gowns – stuff people bought if they'd already bought everything else in the world worth buying and had now moved into the market for overpriced, worthless crap.

Hand on heart: in three minutes of wandering around Los Gatos I swear I saw more Porsches than I had in a lifetime in Glasgow. There was one car dealership in the town centre. It sold Ferraris and collectible Rolls-Royces.

As for the people? I'm no sociologist, and I hate to make snap judgements based on nothing other than blind prejudice, but the population appeared to be made up of twenty-seven Mexican landscape gardeners, one black guy who worked in the café on the main street and ten thousand rich white folks with nice tans and big white teeth. Everyone – except the Mexicans and the black guy – was walking around wearing a superior smirk. Honestly, if the town council ever considered a change of name it could do a lot worse than go for the honest approach and call the place Smug City.

At least the Department of Motor Vehicles (DMV) injected a measure of harsh, unpleasant reality into the community. A squat, claustrophobic building on the outskirts of town, this, Andy told me, was the place where everybody went to get driving licences, register their cars and so on. In fact, it was simply the place where everybody went to queue.

When we first walked through the front door I thought we had merely stumbled across a random mass of humanity. As my eyes became adjusted to the light it was possible to make out intertwining lines of people. The direction they were heading was harder to discern. The décor reminded me of a departure lounge in a Hungarian airport at which I'd once stopped off in 1985. The mood was equally downbeat. Everyone looked as if they were waiting to be measured for their own coffin.

The staff were all behind a long counter, each with a letter of the alphabet hanging above their head. It wasn't clear what this meant, nor was there anyone around who would tell you if it meant anything at all, so I joined the queue heading towards the letter D. Maggie went off and joined S queue.

I got to the front of my queue first, where I was greeted by Pete, the only happy person in the entire place. 'You're from Europe!' he exclaimed, as soon as I spoke.

I admitted that, yes, I was, and then he said, God, that was fantastic because he'd been to Europe only last year, to Italy, in fact – had I ever been to Rome and didn't I think the pigeons spoiled St Peter's Square? – and he and his wife could only stay there for four days because they were meeting friends in London – had I ever been to London? – and I said, yes, I had and that of course I thought Princess Di was gorgeous but by the way, Pete, is this the queue where you apply for your Californian driving licence?

'God, no,' he said. 'This is where you pay your parking tickets. Line F is where you pick up the form for your driving licence, and line P is where you hand it in once you've filled it out.'

Line F was short but, unfortunately, line P was longer than a conga line at a party for Bill Clinton's ex-girlfriends. By the time I reached the front counter I was tired, frustrated and very, very bitter. 'Here's my form, here's my American visa and here's my British driving licence. Can I have my Californian driving licence?' I barked. Then it occurred to me that if this was how miserable the DMV could make me in an hour how much work it would be if I *really* offended the people who worked here. 'Please.'

The man in charge of line P harrumphed. 'We don't just hand

these things out, you'll have to make an appointment to sit your driving test.'

'When can I do that?'

'When do you want to?'

'Any chance of doing it right now?'

'How does three weeks on Thursday sound?'

I could go on for months about how, behind all this bravado about whizz-bang, go-ahead capitalism, Americans are quite at home with inefficiency, obstruction and sloth. I could muse about how the Cold War was actually a battle between competing bureaucracies, not political ideologies, and that the one that produced better cars, not better customer service, won. I could list for pages the frustrations of trying to get a phone line installed when everyone working for the phone company has the brain power of an amoeba, as well as explain in detail why a business's automated telephone-answering service is not 'for your convenience' but for their convenience. But I won't. The memories are too painful.

However, I will say one thing. The DMV is a state-run organization, where public funding is limited and the staff are criminally underpaid. It's allowed to be a shambles. It doesn't have to make a profit. What excuse does the world's biggest Internet access company have?

'Well, thank you, sir. Everything seems to be in order,' the man from Customer Service said – once I'd got past the robot on the answering machine, that is. 'Now if I could just have your credit-card details.'

Pause.

'Pardon me, sir, but that's a British credit card. We don't accept those. We only accept American credit cards.'

'Why?'

'It's the rules, sir.'

'Sure, I understand. But why is it the rules?'

'It just is. Sir.'

Somehow, I found enough energy to put up token resistance. 'But hang on a minute. I read in the paper the other day that your company had just bought another Internet company for three hundred and fifty billion dollars. And now you're telling me that you can't accept a British credit card?'

Longer pause.

'That's right. Sir.'

'But, but . . . *why?*'

Longest pause.

'It's the rules, sir.'

In the circumstances I did the only thing any sane person could have done. I curled myself into a ball and sobbed quietly for the rest of the evening. Was this the same country that had so enthralled me when I'd first come here seventeen years ago? Was this the same place where everything had seemed so utterly possible? For the first time since I was booted out for being a crap bass player, I wished that I could wind the clock back and be a Bluebell again. That way at least I could have my old America back.

3

I didn't find what I was expecting at Andy's offices. This was supposed to be Silicon Valley but where were all the Porsches? What happened to the antique bonsai trees, the original Picassos and the Le Corbusier couches? Instead, there were Toyotas and bare grey walls. As for the cracked fruit bowl on the receptionist's desk, why was it filled with fun-size Snickers bars and not miniature gold ingots?

Call me paranoid, but I was sure the two receptionists were engrossed in a whispered conversation about me – 'And you know what? He doesn't even know the first thing about computers. He's just the boss's friend from Scotland' – when I arrived.

'I've come to see Andy Walker,' I said. 'My name is Lawrence –'

'– Donegan,' said one of the receptionists. She smiled wanly. 'Oh, yes, he's expecting you. Take a seat.'

I took a seat and a handful of Snickers bars. She was gone for ten minutes, which gave me time to gobble down the chocolate and chew over the following piece of information: in Silicon Valley – a fifty-mile strip of industrial real estate stretching from San Jose in the south to San Francisco in the north – sixty-two millionaires were created every day of the year. That's almost three millionaires an hour, or one every twenty-four minutes, including Christmas Day. 'The largest legal creation of wealth in the history of the planet,' claimed John Doerr, a billionaire venture capitalist responsible for launching many of the Valley's biggest companies.

If the wealth creation was legal, then the way people were spending this money was nothing short of criminally ostentatious. Take the case of Larry Ellison, founder of a software company called Oracle. According to that morning's newspaper, he'd just become the richest man in the world, supplanting Bill Gates of Microsoft. He was now worth $52 billion dollars, up from $37 billion last week and a meagre $13 billion last year. Tomorrow the stock market could fall and he'd be $12 billion poorer. But so what? He had more money than any man could ever spend – although, to give him his due, he was making a valiant effort at squandering the lot.

He owned three homes in the Valley, including a replica Japanese imperial palace that had cost $40 million, a pair of ocean-going yachts worth $85 million and enough antique sports cars to fill the starting grid at the Indy 500. He also had his own fleet of private jets and a bunch of aerobatic planes, plus three ex-wives to maintain in the palatial comfort expected by a billionaire's ex-wife. Then there were the plastic surgeon's bills. If the stories were true, scarcely a month went past without the dimple on Larry's chin inching ever nearer his forehead.

These days, Ellison preferred the vicarious company of blonde models. Did these beautiful women like to spend time with Oracle's billionaire founder because he had a sweet personality? Evidently not. His biographer entitled his book, *The Difference Between Larry Ellison and God: God Doesn't Think He Is Larry Ellison.*

I'd thought a great deal about what I was doing in Silicon Valley and had come to this conclusion: I didn't want to be the new Larry Ellison. Believe it or not, I wasn't bothered about making money. If I did, I wanted to be one of the mundane rich guys. In my Silicon Valley daydreams I'd make a million, just enough to go home to Scotland and buy a castle somewhere in Argyll, maybe a sports car or two.

I was lost, driving down the Mull of Kintyre in my open-topped Morgan, when the receptionist tapped me on the arm. 'Andy will see you now.'

She escorted me along a corridor strewn with half-filled card-board boxes. To the left there was a row of gloomy offices, like prison cells furnished with computers. To the right, an open-plan area had been divided into work stations by movable partitions. Two potted plants, the only decoration, looked anaemic in the thirty-watt light. There were lots of people around but, trust me, I'd been in noisier libraries.

Andy's office was quadruple the size of the others and bathed in natural light – the privilege of being the boss, I guessed. He had a painting of a Glasgow University building on the wall above one of his three desks. 'Come in, take a seat. Forgive the mess, we're moving to new offices in a few weeks,' he said, adding triumphantly, '*Bigger* offices.'

Presumably this would be to accommodate his burgeoning collection of business cards, of which he had thousands, all of them laid out in neat little piles across two desks. I stole a quick look while he answered the phone and was immediately overawed. I hadn't thought there were that many people in the world with the title Senior Vice-President (Digital Networking). Suddenly I felt giddy and confused, as if standing side-stage waiting to perform for the Queen, wondering what on earth I was doing there in the first place.

'You do understand that I know nothing about computers,' I said, nervously, as soon as he finished his phone call. 'To be honest, it's a triumph if I can get mine to start in the morning.'

He laid a hand on my shoulder. 'Don't worry. Everything's going to be all right. Now . . .' he grabbed a green marker pen and began drawing on the whiteboard that covered most of a wall '. . . we are a communication-systems company. We are developing the next generation of wireless processing chip. Do you follow me?'

He spoke without interruption for an hour. It felt as if someone had their hand on the back of my head and was holding me under water. I could hear sounds and make out shapes, but the world above me was muffled and indistinct. Occasionally, I would struggle free, break the surface and catch a glimpse of Andy, drawing on the whiteboard and talking excitedly – 'The core processor moves away from the paradigm of communication-specific designs to a more general industry-based application specific design' – and back under I would go.

When I finally came up for air, the whiteboard was covered in algorithmic equations and a bad drawing of a mobile phone. Andy stared at me then spoke, like a worried pedestrian comforting the victim of a car crash, 'Did you get that?'

'Of course not.'

He wasn't the slightest bit bothered by this response. 'Don't worry, you're a bright guy. All you have to do is learn what it is we do, grow to love it, then make everyone else love it. Trust me, this idea of mine is going to make everyone in this building a millionaire.' He smiled cockily. 'Except me. It's going to make me a billionaire.'

He started wiping away his squiggles. 'Trade secrets,' he explained, then turned to business. 'The starting salary for someone with your experience – i.e. none – is sixty thousand dollars a year, plus twenty-five thousand shares in the company.'

'Twenty-five thousand?' He mistook my astonishment for disgust.

'Okay, forty thousand. I understand how difficult it is to get good people in the Valley, these days.'

My heart started pounding like a Buddy Rich drum solo but, as casually as I could, I said, 'How much is the stock worth?'

Just as casually he replied, 'Difficult to say. Right now it's worth nothing. But if everything goes to plan, who knows? Maybe each block of ten thousand shares will be worth, mmm, I don't know, somewhere between one and ten million dollars.'

That was a lot of money. It was also a lot of caveats. 'And if it doesn't go to plan?' I said, not unreasonably.

He looked at me as if I'd just thrown up on his carpet. 'Don't be ridiculous.'

I'd arranged with Maggie that we'd go that afternoon to buy a car but Andy insisted that I stay at the office for a drink. It was the staff cheese and wine meeting, the only chance everyone got to socialize after a week spent thinking about all the money they might make one day. 'You'll get to meet some of the people you're going to be working with,' he said, escorting me along to the kitchen area.

'Hey, everybody, this is Lawrence, he's coming to work here. Lawrence, this is everybody.'

As I scanned the room my heart sank. I know you shouldn't trust first impressions but I'd never seen such a collection of social misfits since I'd stumbled into a roomful of evangelists at a hotel prayer meeting. Maybe it was the polyester clothing and pallid skin, or that everyone looked like the plain sheep of the family. I did the round of introductions, exchanging limp handshakes and dispirited conversation, and had my prejudices confirmed.

As happens at such occasions, people eventually organized themselves into little groups, each with their own informal discussion topic. In one corner a young, black-haired woman was holding court on the trials and tribulations of having her nails French-manicured. In another, someone with a German accent was explaining – to the utter bemusement of those gathered around him – why Munich 1860 was a better team than Bayern Munich. I ended up over by the nibbles, where the specialist subject was Kenny G.

'I've got front-row tickets for the concert next week,' someone said, to nods of envy from the rest of the group.

I almost choked on a raw carrot. 'Christ, you're going to a Kenny G concert? That'll be a good laugh.'

He looked at me as if I was something nasty he'd found in a cereal packet. The group fell silent. I felt obliged to fill the empty air. 'I mean . . . fucksake, Kenny G. You're a young guy. Come on . . . you're joking, aren't you?'

He wasn't. 'Sure, I know the latest record isn't as challenging as some of the others but *Breathless* is a classic album.' The fan club, judging from its sighs, was breathless in its admiration for *Breathless*.

Outnumbered, I gave up and went off to join the German football discussion group, only to find the subject had changed and now I was having to hold my own in a heated debate on the future of business-solutions technology, whatever that was. I felt myself slipping into a dark hole of depression. Was this it? Was this my future – the odd man out in *Revenge of the Nerds*? I was well aware that some of the world's smartest, most interesting and exciting people were working in Silicon Valley but it was also obvious that none of them was in this room. It was as if Andy had gone out and purposely hired these people for their lack of vitality. Sure, one day they might all be rich but who would want to be this rich and this tedious? And who would want to spend every hour of the working day with them?

As I left I shook Andy's hand, thanked him for helping me get to California and said I was looking forward to starting work next week. This last part, of course, was a bare-faced lie.

According to the National Automobile Dealers' Association there were 1,062,800 car salesmen working in the United States on the day Maggie and I went to buy our car. Just our luck to find the most objectionable one of the lot.

We decided to shop at Orchard Boulevard because I'd never seen such enormous stars-and-stripes flags – always a crucial element in any automotive purchase, I find – and because Maggie, who preferred a more scientific approach to such matters, had done a little research and discovered it had the biggest concentration of car dealerships on a single street in the entire United States. 'Seven thousand cars on sale every day of the week! Forty-five thousand satisfied customers every year!' the newspaper adverts screamed. I was willing to bet that not one of the forty-five thousand customers had been satisfied by Charlie.

All we wanted was a Volkswagen with low mileage and a reasonable price tag. 'I hate being hustled,' I said, when we got back from the test drive. 'Give me the best price, not one of your "special" deals, or unbeatable offers.'

Charlie ran his fingers through hair the colour of wet sand. 'Well, it depends on what you mean by best price. If you add the manufacturer's invoice, along with the dealer's mark-up and the sales tax . . .'

'Just tell me the best price.'

'Well, it depends if you want the luxury package . . .'

'Please.'

Charlie unfolded his arms, smiled benignly and said, 'Tell me this, Larry – it is Larry, isn't it? – how much would you like to pay?'

Who knows? He could still be standing there on the forecourt right now, babbling away about dealer mark-ups or waiting for my answer. I don't know. I never looked back as we headed up the street to another dealership, which was selling the same model for a thousand dollars less. There, we walked straight into Anthony, a nervous-looking teenager with a chin covered in bum-fluff. He didn't look old enough to have learned how to be a proper car salesman, which encouraged us greatly.

'We'd like to drive this car, Anthony, and if it works okay and you promise not to talk crap for an hour, we'll buy it from you,' I said, trying hard to sound like a no-nonsense shopper.

Once we'd shown him how to unlock the driver's door and jumpstart the flat battery, we headed off down the boulevard. The car drove perfectly, although Anthony wasn't able to tell us where the petrol-cap release was, or the spare wheel, or the windscreen-wiper knob. In fact, I'm not even sure he knew it was a Volkswagen. At last, someone who knew less about cars than me!

I was fully prepared to take advantage of my superior knowledge but when we returned to the dealership, alas, Anthony was ushered off the stage to be replaced by Charlie's more loquacious cousin, Mike. I was on the verge of walking out again when Maggie reminded me that we didn't have time to interview all of America's 1,062,800 car salesman until we found one we could love like a brother and that we needed a car that day. In short, Mike would have to do.

To my great surprise, he was courteous, helpful and a thousand times more interesting than a roomful of computer geeks. He even gave us a whole fifty dollars off the asking price. Not only that, he changed the course of my life.

Let me explain. When you buy a car in California there is a mountain of DMV paperwork to be completed, as well as computer checks to be made on the buyer's credit history. This work is done by the finance manager. The salesman is left to engage in small-talk with the customers and, far more importantly, make sure they don't change their mind about buying the car. We passed the time with Mike swapping abbreviated life stories.

As a teenager, he'd been more interested in baseball than studying. He left school in Albuquerque, New Mexico, with no qualifications. Even now, he was barely able to read or write. For the next couple of years he hung out with his friends on street corners, until one morning his father dragged him down to a car dealership owned by a family friend. 'I said I'd try it for a week. On the first day, I discovered I could talk to people. Ten years later, here I am in California – in the best place in the world, doing the best job in the world.'

He leaned back on his seat and put his feet on the desk. He caught me staring at his fake leather slip-on shoes. The sole and the upper were semi-detached, like the lips of a half-open mouth. 'You like them?' I could see through the torn stitching that he was wearing yellow socks. 'These are my selling shoes. I only wear them because it makes the customers think I'm not making any money.'

It was my turn now. I explained we'd arrived in California two weeks ago, that we were just settling in. I told him about the Bluebells, the job offer from Andy and the wireless processor chip, the terrible cheese and wine affair and the Kenny G fan club. I confessed I was having second thoughts. 'I guess what I'm looking for is . . .' I hesitated, embarrassed to use the phrase I wanted to.

'The American Dream?' he suggested.

'That's it,' I said. 'Stupid, isn't it?'

He tapped his desk with his index finger. 'The American Dream is here – right here on Orchard Boulevard.'

'What do you mean?'

'Put it like this. When you get out of bed in the morning, you can't bargain for your shoes, or the pants you're wearing, or the life you're leading. But you can come down here and haggle for a car all day long, and if you don't like the salesman, or his price, you can walk out the door. You know what that is?'

'A waste of a day?' Maggie said.

He pretended not to hear her. 'Undiluted capitalism – *America.*' He sat up straight, animated now. 'You want your fair share of the American Dream, buddy? Then you oughta be working as a salesman, not cooped up in front of some computer screen listening to Kenny G.'

The *New York Times* once reported that the average US citizen was subjected to 3,500 sales messages every day. Adverts, cold calls during mealtimes, estate agents, store girls spraying perfume, car salesmen; every 24.6 seconds of every day in America someone tried to sell you something. Selling was as much a part of the national impulse as, well, breathing. Admittedly, David Mamet said it more eloquently in *Glengarry, Glen Ross* but Mike was absolutely right: if I wanted my fair share of the American Dream – or, at least, if I wanted more than my fair share of the American experience – then it was patently obvious I should become a salesman. If I was to become a salesman, why not a car salesman? There wasn't a better job in the world, the way Mike told it. And from where I was sitting it looked easy – after all, it had taken him less than two minutes to persuade me to write a cheque for ten thousand dollars.

'Any jobs going?' I asked eagerly.

Long inured to my temporary enthusiasms, Maggie allowed herself a snigger at the very idea. She thought I was joking. She was wrong. I couldn't have been more serious.

Mike shook his head. 'We gave the last one we had to the kid who sold you the car, Anthony. It's his first day and he's made three hundred bucks commission. He's seventeen years old. He's never seen that much money in his life.'

I was happy we'd brought a little sunshine into Anthony's life but a little concerned too: if he'd made three hundred dollars' commission from us, how much profit had the dealership made?

Mike realized he'd been overly candid. 'Tell you what,' he said, changing the subject, 'you might want to try that place over there. I know they're always looking for salesmen.' He pointed across the six-lane boulevard.

I looked through the plate-glass window. On the roof of Orchard Boulevard Pre-Owned Autos a twenty-foot inflatable Godzilla was swaying in the wind, as if it had spent the afternoon in a bar drinking cocktails. It was wearing a grubby white T-shirt with MONSTER SALE splashed across the chest. It was hard to tell from a distance but the lot seemed deserted. Nor did it, at first glance, appear to be the epicentre of the American Dream.

What did I have to lose? I left Maggie waiting for the finished paperwork and for our new (well, second-hand 'new') car to be washed and polished. The instant I set foot on the lot a middle-aged black man came striding out of the office towards me. 'Hey, buddy,' he said, wrapping my hand in his enormous grip, 'my name's Hughie. We gonna make a deal today?'

'Sorry, I've just bought a car,' I said, apologetically. He let go of my hand. The smile went out like a blown light-bulb. 'I'm trying to find out about a job.'

He looked supremely indifferent. 'You're looking for Tommy, then. He's gone to McDonald's.' He walked up the steps to the office and held open the door. 'Come on in here and wait.'

There were six other salesmen inside, all huddled round the reception desk. They were listening as a younger salesman, his US Marine haircut dyed scarlet, made a phone call. 'This Ferrari you've got advertised in *Auto Trader*, sir,' he said. The others made strenuous efforts to stop laughing. 'I want you to know, sir, that I am very interested indeed in this vehicle.'

Two of the salesmen were now crawling around the floor like dogs, the others punching the walls in agony. The phone call went back and forth.

'Thirty-four thousand is a lot of money for a car that's been smashed up.' He went silent as the man on the other end of the phone explained why thirty-four thousand dollars was an excellent price for a yellow Ferrari with a front end like a burst accordion.

The salesman nodded. 'I take your point, sir, but tell me this . . .' He looked at the others, anticipating their approval '. . . what about if I gave you a top-notch blow-job? Would you give me a two-thousand-dollar discount?'

It took five minutes for everyone to wipe away the tears and straighten their ties, and another thirty seconds before someone noticed me standing by the door. 'Hey, buddy, you waiting to buy a car?'

I explained that I'd already bought a car across the street, that I was waiting to see Tommy about a job.

'You coming to work here?'

'Maybe.'

Apparently, I'd come on a quiet day – 'quietest day of the year' – but I should wait around until Saturday and Sunday, then the entire place would be rocking and rolling.

'How much d'you make last weekend, Ernie?' Hughie said.

Ernie didn't look up from the magazine he was reading. 'Two and a half, maybe three.'

I assumed he meant two and a half thousand dollars but didn't get the chance to ask. Just then Tommy came back with McDonald's for everyone. He was slightly older than the others, with shaggy grey hair and a belt-stretching stomach. He was wearing a black and red zipper jacket with a white lightning flash across the front. As the burgers were handed out, Hughie pointed at me. 'Hey, Tommy, this guy's here to see you. He's looking for a job.'

Tommy turned round, looked me up and down. 'You'll need more comfortable shoes than that,' he said, gazing at my hiking boots. 'When d'you want to start?'

This startled me. 'What about an interview?'

'You want an interview? Okay, then.' He took a huge bite out of a Chicken McSandwich.

'Have you ever sold cars before?'

'No.'

'Have you ever sold anything in your life?'

I dismissed the idea of lying. It didn't seem necessary. 'Not really.'

'Do you think you could?'

I smiled. 'Sure.'

He took another bite, looked at the others, who looked up from their french fries and nodded. 'Fine. Good. When can you start? Tomorrow?'

Normally I don't believe in signs – physical or metaphysical – but there was a notice on the wall by the reception desk, right next to plaque announcing Orchard Boulevard Pre-Owned Autos as the *Out!* magazine gay and lesbian used-car dealer of 1986. It was headed 'The Ten Commandments of Attitude'. I looked down the list. Number four said, 'You'll seldom experience regret for anything you've done. It's what you don't do that will torment you.'

I asked Tommy about on-the-job training and he brushed me off, saying, 'It's not a complicated job. Trust me, you're gonna sell cars, Scotty. You seem like a real people person.'

The traffic on the way home was slow. I was glad: it gave me time to think. I could take up Andy on his offer, learn everything there was to know about wireless processing chips. Who knows? One day I might learn to love my colleagues, even come to appreciate the special appeal of Kenny G. And at the end of it all maybe, just maybe, I would have a million dollars in the bank. Or I could work at Orchard Boulevard Pre-Owned Autos. I suspected I wouldn't make a million in the car business but I was utterly convinced I would discover the America I was looking for. That was the choice.

Maggie didn't say a word. She didn't have to. She knew, we both did, that there was no contest.

4

I was one of two salesmen who started work on the same morning. I spent hours thinking about what I was going to wear, finally selecting a pair of grey trousers, a mute blue shirt and a striped tie that had last seen action at a wedding three years ago. New shoes cost me $123. John, a former soldier from the Monterey peninsula, turned up in a golf shirt, thigh-length leather jacket and a San Francisco Giants baseball cap. It was 8.45 a.m. He was fifteen minutes late. At 9.37 a.m. he was gone.

Tony Tognazzini was thirty, dark-haired, overweight and, like all the younger salesmen, a designated balloon and lot-decoration specialist. He and I were sent to pick up a cylinder of helium and missed John's departure. 'Gone?' said Tony, when we came back to discover we were already a man down. 'Gone where?'

Mickey McDonald gave us a so-what look. 'Gone. Fired. Capped. Gone.'

'Frankie told him to get rid of the leather jacket and the baseball cap. He said it was the only jacket he had,' Hughie Breeker said, matter-of-fact. 'The guy didn't say another word. Just took his licence and left.'

'And he was late.' Mickey was sitting on the stereo speaker, his feet resting on top of the porch rail, his face in the shade. The sun was beginning to burn off the early-morning haze. 'The guy talked too much.'

This was true. You don't get to know someone really well in fifty-two minutes but John definitely talked too much: about his last job at a car dealership, about life in the army, about why it was dangerous to let other people drink out of your Coke can, about the Giants' vulnerability to left-handed pitching, and about how 'this place is quiet right now but, man, I can tell it's gonna be pumping at the weekend'. Now he'd never know.

'Who wants breakfast?' Hughie said. Clearly someone losing his job in the time it takes to blow up a few fistfuls of balloons had only a limited shock value. 'Coffee, anyone?'

'God, this business.' Mickey ran his fingers through his slicked-back hair and started laughing to himself. 'Fifty-two minutes. Do you think he'll get much of a pension?'

It being California, I didn't actually start work at the car lot the day after my 'interview'. It took almost two weeks of heartache and a skipload of paperwork.

You aren't allowed to sell cars in the state of California unless you have a vehicle salesperson's licence, and you can't get a sales licence if you are on the FBI's wanted list, which requires finger-print verification. I called the Los Gatos police station to ask for an appointment. 'We're so busy it usually takes four weeks,' a weary voice said.

I drove twenty miles to Stanford instead, to the university's police station, my stomach churning at the prospect of tangling once again with Californian bureaucracy. Things went smoothly, to start with. The police at Stanford don't have much to do apart from escorting old professors and drunk students home at night. They were delighted to have a visitor. One officer made me coffee, then took me down to a basement room where another took a photo-graphic record of my fingerprints. These were fed into a computer, which hooked up to another computer in Washington DC, which was hooked up to computers in every police station in the US.

'Fantastic machine, isn't it?' the cop said, while we were waiting.

Actually, it struck me as wildly excessive considering I only wanted to sell a few used Hondas but, mindful of the Californian bureaucrat's tendency to make your life a misery at the slightest provocation, I made a few approving noises.

'You're clear,' he said, as my snowy white FBI record came spewing out of the computer. He handed me a pink form, before uttering the dreaded words: 'Now just take this down to the DMV, have them verify it and they'll get you a sales licence.'

After a couple of days of lifting weights and a crash course in transcendental meditation, I felt mentally and physically strong enough to handle the DMV again. I joined a different queue this time but there was no escaping Pete. 'Oh, you're from Europe,' he said excitedly, as I pushed my passport and FBI form across the counter. 'I was on holiday in Europe last year.'

'I know,' I snapped, before he had the chance to engage me in another discussion about Princess Di. 'Is this where you get your vehicle salesperson's licence?' He shook his head, as if dealing with Forrest Gump. 'No, this is for temporary car registrations. You want Line V.'

An hour later I was a free man, fully licensed to sell motor vehicles in the state of California. In theory. All I had to do was wait for the US Postal Service to deliver my licence.

Even for someone well versed in the maverick ways of the Royal Mail, dealing with the US Postal Service is a mind-warping experience. Like every other state organization in California it's criminally underfunded. The staff are paid a pittance, the offices are tatty and the postal vans barely roadworthy. Anyone who has a package or a letter that needs to arrive the following day, or even the following week, would no more send it by the US Postal Service than they would by carrier pigeon. This, however, is not a source of national shame but a national joke, even among US Postal Service staff. 'Well, that's why they call it Snail Mail,' said the woman behind the counter, when I went to complain after five days of waiting.

I gave up in the end and spent a few days touring around northern California with Maggie. We went to San Francisco and stood awestruck at the smooth, rust-coloured span of the Golden Gate Bridge. We gasped at the world-breaking collection of tat for sale at Fisherman's Wharf. Why is it that the world's most famous tourist spots are also the world's biggest dustbins? 'This place is too beautiful,' I imagined the city planners saying. 'What can we do to make it ugly? I know. Thousands of pairs of Alcatraz pyjamas and chewing-gum on the streets. Bird shit, too, plenty of bird shit.'

A couple of days later we drove over the hills to Santa Cruz, a fading holiday resort on the Pacific coast. Maggie called it the town that time forgot – home to every hippie who had survived the acid holocaust. It is also a surfer's paradise, though not on the day we were there. We watched a dozen sorry surfers floating around on a flat, gloomy ocean in what was billed as the Cold Water Classic. I have attended livelier cremations. Bored stiff, we went on to Monterey, Carmel and Pebble Beach. I finally got to stand on the first tee of the world-famous golf course and ponder how stupid anyone would have to be to pay $325 for eighteen holes. To my utter dismay all the tee-times were booked.

My licence finally showed up after ten days. I was so excited I drove straight to the car lot. 'Great,' Tommy said, though in truth he looked underwhelmed at the news. 'Now you can fill in all these.'

He dropped an inch-thick pile of paperwork on the desk: tax-forms, immigration forms, new and used car and truck compensation plan, something called Form W-4(2000), a fidelity-bond application, insurance questionnaire, long-distance calls stipulation form, the company harassment policy form – which ran to eighteen pages and, as far as I could gather, outlawed everything but breathing, as long as it wasn't heavy breathing.

While I signed on the dotted line, Tommy filled me in on the pay and conditions. 'I'll pay you twenty per cent commission on every car you sell for me. If you sell me ten cars a month for two months, that'll go up to twenty-five per cent. Okay? I've got full health coverage, IPO, HMO, dental IPO. And we've got spiffs going all the time. You'll get a thousand-dollar draw every month, payable on the first and the fifteenth. The tenth is washout day.'

Washout day, IPO, HMO, spiffs? I didn't understand a word but I couldn't have cared less. I had arrived. At last, I was a used-car salesman.

While Hughie and Mickey went to get breakfast, Tony showed me around the lot with almost proprietorial pride. He'd only been selling cars for nine days but had already decided he'd found his true calling. 'I've got the personality for it. People like me,' he explained, and I suspected he was right. Dark-haired, rotund and permanently grinning, he was the kind of person it was impossible not to like. I concentrated hard as he pointed out the best cars and the cars not to sell to friends and close relations, then explained how the sales team was organized. Julius Caesar's legions weren't as hierarchical.

The salesmen were divided into two crews: A Crew and B Crew. Every month they competed against each other to see which could sell the most cars. At the head of each crew was a closer. We were never allowed to refer to a closer as a closer in front of customers because that would scare them away. He was a sales manager, unless you had lied and told the customer that you were the sales manager. Then he was the floor manager. All deals had to be approved by the used-car manager.

Tony and I were members of A Crew. Tommy was our closer. It was our job to line up the deals and get the customers into the sales booth. Tommy would then go in and hopefully convince them to sign on the dotted line. 'He's a good guy. Calm and quiet,' Tony said. 'Wait until you meet Sunny, the B Crew closer – he's crazy.'

Each crew had eight salesmen, subject to the boss not taking an instantaneous dislike to someone's leather jacket and firing them. The more experienced salesmen were paid 25 per cent cent commission on the gross profit from every sale – the difference between the amount the dealership had paid for the car and the price paid by the customer. New salesmen like Tony and me – the 'Greenpeas' – received 20 per cent.

However, the real money was made in competitions. There was a sales contest every week: who could sell the most cars; who could make the most gross profit; who could sell the cars that had been lying around the lot for months. First prize was usually around two thousand dollars, down to a couple of hundred for sixth place. Finally, there was the Blue Riband – the Salesman of the Month competition. Whoever sold the most cars got to drive the best car on the lot home every night for a month. But it wasn't just the car, according to Tony, it was the recognition, the fame, the name in lights!

'It's like winning the Oscars. Come and see this,' he said, waving me into the office, where the winners of every Salesman of the Month award since 1984 were immortalized on cheap, gold-coloured plaques. The names – Robbie McKendrick, Bob Canelli, Davie Smart, Fran Danasky – conjured up fast-talking sharks with comb-overs and checked jackets louder than a brass band. 'God, I'd love to be up there,' I sighed, and as I said this I was surprised to discover that I really, really meant it.

Breakfast arrived. We sat down at the wooden bench on the porch, four of us. We'd only just started eating when someone wandered on to the lot. I saw him first but Mickey leaped out of his seat.

'There's my guy back from yesterday.' He watched the customer weaving through the parked cars, then sat down again. 'On you go, Scotty,' he said, suddenly finding something in his french fries that needed more immediate attention. 'See if you can pop your cherry.'

'Me?'

'Go on,' Hughie said. 'It could be a car deal.'

It didn't occur to me to ask why no one else was interested in such a sure-fire money-maker. I wiped my hands on a napkin. This was it. My first potential sale. Trembling, I made my way down the steps and across the lot. 'All you have to do is keep talking,' Tony had told me, when I'd asked him the secret of selling cars.

The customer's name was Akram. 'Hello, Akram, I'm Lawrence,' I said, my sales patter immediately exhausted. Frantically, I tried to think of something else to say but as quickly as something came into my head I dismissed it as too corny ('This car is you!'), or too embarrassing, or too . . . well, too like a car salesman ('Hey, I'll get you the deal of a lifetime!').

Akram pointed at a silver sports utility vehicle. 'How much is this Land Cruiser?'

The price was on the windscreen. 'Thirty-eight thousand,' I said, puzzled.

He laughed. 'I know it *says* thirty-eight thousand. But what's the real price?'

This is exactly the kind of stupid, smart-alec remark I would

42

have made if I was him, but suddenly I felt as if I was in a verbal duel with Oscar Wilde. 'Hang on,' I said, scuttling back towards the office.

'Guys, he wants to know the real price.' I was panicking. 'What'll I tell him?'

Mickey stood up and stretched elaborately, as if he had a hundred years' sleep in his limbs. 'Tell him the real price is up his ass.'

Hughie took pity me on me. 'Come on.' He sauntered down the steps.

By now Akram was climbing over the seats. He'd found a couple of tears in the leather, a hundred scratches on the paintwork and ancient chewing-gum in the ashtray. There were so many scuff marks in the back it looked as if the last owner had been transporting sheep. 'I only want to pay thirty thousand,' he said.

This sounded to me like an overly generous offer. Hughie didn't give an opinion one way or the other. He closed the back door, rolled the chewing-gum into a ball and tossed it aside. 'There doesn't seem to be much point to me in worrying about the price when you haven't driven the car,' he said casually, then turned to me. 'Lawrence, get the keys and take Akram for a drive.'

This was fantastic. I couldn't quite believe I was caught up in a car sale where I wasn't the one who was buying. When I bought cars it was always the same simple formula. I would go to a dealership, spot a car in a colour I liked and look at the engine for a minute (though I didn't know what I was looking for). I'd take it for a drive and the salesman would tell me the price. I never had the gall to negotiate or search for chewing-gum in the ashtrays. I always caved in straight away when he offered me a full tank of petrol but no discount. This was different altogether. I felt as if I'd landed on some distant planet.

We went for a drive along Orchard Boulevard, then out on to the freeway towards San Francisco. Akram didn't say a lot, except to tell me how much was wrong with the car, which was everything as far as I could make out. Still, when we got back to the lot he was interested enough to have another look at the engine.

'This is the eight-cylinder, right?' he said. I ran off again to look

43

for Hughie, who refused to get out of his seat until I promised to buy him chicken tacos for lunch.

I left the two of them talking about eight-cylinder engines and carburettors and watched from the porch. There was lot of gesticulation, a lot of laughing, until they disappeared into the office. Tony was standing behind me. He leaned over and whispered in my ear, 'Scotty's got a car deal, Scotty's got a car deal.'

My thoughts were racing now. My first customer and already I had a car deal. I'd only been a salesman for a couple of hours. It had to be a record.

Mickey wasn't impressed. 'This guy's not in any danger of buying a car,' he said, as if that was the last word on the matter.

It was quickly becoming clear that the car business had more rules than golf. Tony explained another one: the salesman who talks to a customer first – the technical term is *'Up-ing'* a customer – is entitled to all the commission from the sale, *unless* he gets another salesman to talk to the same customer. Then the commission is divided between the two, even if the salesman who made the original approach didn't do any of the hard work. In short, Hughie and I would split the cash. But it didn't come to that anyway.

Five minutes later Akram was back outside, followed by Hughie and Frankie Reames, the boss. 'You want to pay thirty thousand dollars? That's less than I paid for the car,' Frankie was saying, incredulously.

'Yes, but I can buy the same car in Redwood City for thirty thousand.'

Frankie folded his arms and shook his head, like a nightclub bouncer turning back a drunk. 'Tell you what, you go and get me ten of them for that price and I'll buy them all from you.'

We all watched Akram walk off the lot, climb into his car and drive away. I felt bereft, as if I'd just lost my wallet. But just when I thought I was about to be sacked for being a miserable failure Frankie clapped me on the shoulder. 'Don't worry about that guy, Scotty,' he said, smiling. 'He's just a fucking mooch.' I had no idea what a mooch was but I could guess.

The excitement over, we spent the rest of the morning sitting around on the porch talking, about basketball, the weather, the deals everyone had made. Tony shouted out the make of every car that drove past the lot, from '67 Mustangs to top-of-the-range Mercedes.

Sam – 'Crazy Sam,' announced Mickey – turned up at eleven o'clock. He was about the same age as Mickey, in his mid-forties, but fifty decibels quieter. He bore an uncanny resemblance to Marty Feldman, which I guessed accounted for the nickname. Jackson, he of the scarlet hair and Ferrari phone call, was next. He'd brought a telescope to work. To pass the time he trained it on the women's hairdressing salon across the street. When a good-looking female appeared he handed it round so everyone could have a squint. I mentioned that my feet were already beginning to hurt, which prompted a heated discussion on the best kind of shoes for selling cars.

'Rockports,' Mickey said, showing off his, 'with two pairs of socks. You gotta wear two pairs of socks.'

It was obvious that Mickey's word on every subject was final, that he was our team leader. He didn't boss people round, he just talked over them. Words rolled out of his mouth like giant bowling balls, skittling people over. He rewarded their submission by being their friend for five minutes. Everyone wanted to be Mickey's friend not just because he was quick-witted and aggressive but also – I guessed – because they were hoping a bit of the magic would rub off.

'Give him five minutes with any customer,' Tony told me later, '*any* customer, and he'll sell them a car.'

Hughie, who'd been a masseur before he was a salesman, gave Mickey a back rub while Tony tried to garner some tips on selling cars from the Master.

'I ain't telling you guys anything, I said I ain't telling you nothing,' Mickey said, in his seductive southern drawl. He sounded like a cross between Bill Clinton and Foghorn Leghorn. 'If I did, you guys would sell all the cars and what would be left for me?' He was smiling but it didn't take a trained psychologist to know that he meant it.

This didn't seem like work. It was noon and the sun was directly above us, the sky a vivid cartoon blue. Already my pallid Scottish skin was being roasted. Jackson promised six months of the same. The world had never seemed more blissful. It felt like a lifelong holiday, as if we were all floating around on a yacht. Every once in a while someone walked on to the lot but they were either delivering something or trying to sell cars to the boss. What was the point in feeling guilty? Hughie said. You couldn't sell cars when you had no one to sell them to. Mickey went home at about one o'clock.

The salesmen on B Crew were due in at 2.30 p.m. but started drifting in at around two o'clock. Sunny, their closer, arrived on a Triumph motorcycle that was audible half-way to San Francisco. He was wearing leathers and a helmet that was only a swastika short of an SS captain's. He kicked off the engine. 'You lot sold any cars yet?' he growled, looking at us lounging around on the porch.

Hughie shook his head. 'Quiet as the dead, Sunny.'

'Didn't think so. *Losers.*'

Tony waited until he'd gone inside to get changed, then rolled his eyes. 'See what I mean?' he whispered. 'Crazy.'

Friday was sales-meeting day. The company that owned our lot had a new-car dealership just down the street, and once a week the salesmen from both showrooms met up. Attendance was compulsory, even if it happened to be your day off.

In theory, the meeting was for sales training and keeping employees up to date with the latest developments in the car business. In practice, according to the others, it was the boss's chance to boast about his latest new car or the round of golf he'd played at Pebble Beach the week before. Without exception, everyone said it was a waste of valuable sleeping time.

I, however, could hardly wait. I'd never had a job that involved attending proper meetings. It seemed so grown-up. I arrived ten minutes early, but already the room was packed and sweaty. The walls were bare but for a framed poster of Mount Everest with the words 'Reach Out For Your Goals' printed underneath. 'Smooth' by Carlos Santana was pumping out of the stereo. Everyone in the front six rows was wearing a white shirt. Half of them were on their feet, punching the air or giving each other high-fives. I thought I'd walked into a religious meeting. When the owner walked in it was as if Jesus had turned up as a surprise. There was an enormous roar.

His name was Jason. He looked much too young to be a millionaire car dealer, handsome and lean, with cropped hair and *Miami Vice* beard. Someone said he was an Iranian immigrant. 'How y'all doin'?' he yelled, like a game-show host. He turned down the stereo. 'I can feel a lot of love in the room today.'

There was a lot of eye-rolling in the back two rows, where the used-car salesmen were sitting. I looked along the line. We were a scruffy bunch in comparison to the zealots up front – a pack of mongrels gatecrashing Crufts Dog Show. Mickey had been up all night partying. His hair looked like a borrowed wig. Tony had spilled coffee down his jacket. Sam was one of those unlucky people who would never look presentable, even if you dressed him in a five thousand-dollar suit. Hughie was already sleeping, a dark line of drool creeping down his shirt front.

'Today I'd like to talk to you guys about psychological profiling,' Jason began. Everyone slid down their chairs a little further, though God knows why. Personally, I thought what he had to say was fascinating. It seems there are four different types of people in the car-buying world:

1. Dominant Drivers: '. . . like General Patten,' he said. 'Just give me the tank with leather seats and the sun roof – OKAY!'
2. Extroverts: 'He's flashy, an egocentric like me. The most important thing to this guy is how the car looks.'
3. The Amiable Type: 'Maybe she's the receptionist at work – the kind of person that takes three days off if the boss yells at her.'
4. The Structured Type: 'The guy who wants to know all the facts, does all the research, knows all the numbers. We've all had them, we all know them as *Propellerheads*.'

Propellerheads? The word prompted a roomful of groans and a handful of helicopter impersonations. I wrote it down in my notebook. The car business had a language all of its own and I was determined to become fluent.

Jason's theory was that a salesman had to work out quickly what kind of customer he was dealing with and then start behaving like them. 'There's no point in getting pushy with an amiable type – be amiable. And when a guy starts acting like an asshole, you start acting like an asshole too,' he said. 'We only like people like us. You got that? Okay?'

'Okay,' the new-car salesmen said in unison. The used-car salesmen, those who were still awake, sighed and looked at their watches.

Lesson over, next business. It was a holiday weekend, Cinqo de Mayo, celebrating the Mexican victory over the French at the battle of Puebla in 1862, and the good news was that the parade in San Jose had been cancelled because the organizers hadn't paid last year's police bill. Denied the chance to celebrate the biggest day in its cultural calendar properly, the city's big Mexican community would hopefully go shopping for cars instead.

'So this is our chance to make some money, guys. Okay?' Jason said, clenching his fists. The mood darkened a little. 'Come on, guys. I need you to sell some cars. I *really* need this, guys. I need you to give me some *fuckin'* passion, guys. Agreed?' He stalked about the room, trying to make eye-contact and then he clapped. 'OKAY. Let's get out there and do it.'

For the next three days I tried to be passionate. I was the Sacha Distel of car sales. I tried mirroring the customer, but some people are beyond the powers of amateur psychology, like the bearded Neanderthal who drove on to the lot, refusing all efforts to get him to park. 'Can we take your order, sir? Two Big Macs and a what?' Mickey shouted, as he edged past the office door at two miles an hour. Tommy sent me out on mission impossible.

I finally flagged him down over by the used trucks. He was wearing fingerless black leather gloves and an Ozzie Osbourne T-shirt. 'How much is this truck?'

'Why don't you get out and take a look at it, sir?' I said, sunnily.

'Just get me the price, asshole.'

He was gone by the time I had walked to the office and back to get the price.

Then there was Mark Swann, who almost but not quite bought the Lexus from me. After that, the closest I came to a sale was to an aircraft engineer who liked the fold-down back seat in a used Toyota because it meant he could take his guns on holiday – but he'd have to talk to his wife before buying. A good-looking Mexican in a black mini-skirt said she loved an old Ford we had on offer for $6,700 – but she couldn't spend that amount of money without asking her mother. Kevin, a surly car mechanic from south San Jose, said he could afford the seven-hundred-dollar payments on a BMW sports car – but he had been made bankrupt only last month. But, but, but . . . everyone had an excuse for not buying.

By closing time on Sunday, my body felt as if it had just returned from a barefoot walk across the Andes. What made things worse was that everyone else had been selling cars. Mickey had sold four, and I hadn't seen him leave his seat for three days. Tony, Sam, Jackson, Wayne – they were all wearing the dreamy glow that comes from success. Mal from B Crew had made fifteen hundred dollars from one deal after telling the customer he'd given them the wrong price and could they help him out by paying a bit more, otherwise he'd get fired. I consoled myself with the thought that I was too honest to think up scams like that.

I started locking up. We were supposed to close at 10 p.m. on weekdays, nine on Saturday and eight on Sunday, but in the real world we stayed open until the last customer had left. It was after ten o'clock. Tommy, Frankie and Sunny were on the porch, smoking and chatting. I overheard someone say forty cars had been sold since Friday.

'Forty cars?' I yelped.

The three of them laughed, then Frankie disappeared through the sliding door into the sales office. You didn't have to have a persecution complex or Superman's extrasensory hearing to figure out that someone had said something about me.

'What is it?' I said, locking the final car.

Tommy stood up tall, then walked away without saying a word. I laughed nervously. 'Come on, what is it?'

Sunny leaned on the rail and smiled like a doctor trying to soften the bad news. He threw his cigarette to the ground. 'We're were just saying you're too soft, Scotty — you ain't gonna last in this business, are you?'

5

Andy took rejection like a doctor faced with a patient who has turned down life-saving kidney treatment. 'You're off your head,' was the initial diagnosis. The long-term prognosis veered towards the apocalyptic. 'Do you know how much money this is going to cost you when my company takes off?'

'I don't know – a billion, trillion dollars?'

Trust me to mock someone whose only crime had been to be a kind and generous friend. What I should have said is, 'What about the soul, Andy? What about following the dream, Andy? What about that old chestnut, there's more to life than money?' But what was the point? This was Silicon Valley, right? I'd only been here a few weeks but I already knew there wasn't much more to life than money.

Sure, people had other interests. It was possible to get them to talk about their children, for instance, but it didn't take long for the conversation to get round to the price of Junior's college education. Compliment someone on their house and five seconds later you were guaranteed to know the square footage and how much the place was worth. Nice car. 'Yeah, I got a great deal.' How's work? 'Terrible, my stock dropped twenty-five points in five minutes.' Watch out, your hair's on fire! 'Damn! I paid $175 for that cut and blow dry.'

It was tempting to believe the locals couldn't help themselves, that they had simply been born shallow and hopelessly materialistic. However, that would have denied me the chance to indulge in some amateur sociology and suggest that the reason everyone was so obsessed with money was that there was so much of it around. What were people to think when they read in their newspaper that the head of the computer company Cisco made $120 million in a *single* year? Or that the ten best-paid Silicon Valley executives made enough in 1999 – $722.7 million – to provide shelter for eight thousand homeless Californians for the next sixteen years? Or that a receptionist at Yahoo! had just cashed in her options and bought a house for four million dollars?

Communist revolutions not being the American Way, the only alternative was to obsess about why you weren't as rich as someone who answers telephones for a living, or spend every minute of the day in front of a computer screen watching the stock market, hoping with all your heart that it would climb high enough to allow you to buy a top-of-range Mercedes rather than just the base model.

Frankly, it wasn't me who was off my head, it was everyone else. And the truth about the job was that I'd had a lucky escape. Not that Andy saw it like this when he telephoned one Friday afternoon.

Apart from telling me for the eighty-fourth time that I was a retard for turning down his job offer, he wanted to invite us to the Cattle Barons' Ball. This was the social event of the year, an occasion when the Valley's Great and Good – or, rather, the Rich and the Even Richer – turned out to show their support for the American Cancer Society. There would be line-dancing, pig races, country-and-western music, an authentic cowboy finger buffet and a fund-raising auction. All guests had to dress up as cowboys. The cheapest tickets cost a hundred dollars each.

'Do you want to go?'

Of course, I didn't want to go. But I didn't want to let him down again either. Plus, he said the tickets were his treat. 'Yes, of course we do.'

It is almost impossible to describe how much Maggie had taken to California. Her naturally sunny, optimistic, try-anything disposition was perfectly suited to the climate and to dealing with the frustrations of settling in. Where others (i.e. me) came back from the DMV office with dark thoughts about ending it all, she returned with a brand-new friend and a certificate for scoring 100 per cent in her driving test. I got sunburned, she got suntanned. I began to wonder if we'd done the right thing in leaving Scotland, she wished we'd done it years ago.

While I went off to the car lot in the morning, she worked alone at home, writing newspaper articles and filing reports for BBC radio. Because of the time difference, she finished work at noon most days and spent the afternoons visiting her latest new friends, art galleries and the shopping malls. In what she claimed was an act of investigative journalism/irony, she even signed up for classes at the neighbourhood centre with ludicrous Californian titles like 'How To Connect With Your Inner Self' and 'Raising Your Colour Comfort Consciousness'.

Part of the problem was my inner self. Call me a miserable Scottish git, but subconsciously I have long believed that life wasn't meant to be perfect. Constant sunshine and happy, healthy living might satisfy normal people like Maggie but it makes me feel uneasy, as if I'm being softened up in preparation for some terrible disaster. I walk around expecting disappointment, although for some unfathomable reason I'm always disconcerted when it arrives. Take my new career. Deep down, I didn't expect to be the best car salesman in the world after just eleven days, yet I was surprised and puzzled when I wasn't.

That's right: eleven days and I still hadn't sold my first car. I'd asked around: a sale on day one was pure luck; day four was average; after a week the boss normally spooned you an easy deal – one of his relatives or friends who was getting such a cheap deal they didn't require selling, only help with the paperwork. Anything to end the agony. Eleven days was verging on a statistical freak. I tried to pretend I wasn't counting but how could I? My abject failure was mapped out for everyone to see.

Behind the sales counter there hung what was known as the Board – a record of every day on the lot, who had sold cars and how many they'd sold in the month. Frankie filled it in every morning. Against my name there was a row of eleven dots. In the time it had taken me to accumulate this remarkable score, Mickey had sold ten cars, Ernie had sold seven, Tony five, Sam five, Hughie three, etc., etc., etc. Everybody had sold something except me. I was marooned at the bottom of the league; pointless, the Bradford City of Orchard Boulevard Pre-Owned Autos.

On *Match of the Day* I could have cited inexperience and niggling sunburn injuries but the real reason was this: I was trying my best not to talk to customers.

I hadn't worked out yet that this strategy was fatal to any successful career in car sales. But that was because I was too busy concentrating on the rejection, of which there was plenty, from the polite 'Leave us alone, we're just looking' to the puce-faced customer who grabbed me by the collar and screamed, 'I'd loved to fucking punch one of you guys. For the last time, leave me alone.' The only way to avoid the rejection – the hatred, frankly – was to hang out on the porch all day, chatting to the shoeshine guy or drinking coffee. Meanwhile, others could take care of the customers.

Nobody mentioned my lack of immediate success, except the boss, and only then in an obtuse way. 'I like you, Scotty. You don't give up, do you?' he said. This was day six, just after I'd failed yet again to persuade a customer to take a test drive, or even speak to me, and just before I became the world's first recluse salesman.

Technically, Tommy the crew boss was in charge of training me but he was always busy or eating or heading off somewhere to buy food. Even when he did make an effort it was obvious he hadn't read past page three of the worst sales training manual on the market: 'I'm sorry, all my relatives have got cars,' he said when I asked for advice on day seven. 'Just keep trawling through the customers. Someone will buy from you eventually.'

Fortunately, a few of the other salesmen took pity on me, although I had to beg for help in the end. It wasn't that they didn't feel sorry for me or didn't like me but because they feared if they came too close they might catch the same terrible disease. Another of the unwritten rules in the car business is that a salesman never brings up the subject of a colleague's slump unless he mentions it himself. Of course, some people don't live by the rules, like Sunny, who arrived on his Triumph on day ten, disappeared inside to look at the board and then came out cackling, 'Hey, Scotty, still not sold any cars yet? *Ha!*'

I'd had enough. Half an hour later I grabbed Tony as he was getting ready to go home. 'You don't know anything about cars,' he said. 'What's the difference between a 1996 Toyota Camry and a 1997 Camry?'

'One's older than the other?'

He looked at me disapprovingly. I was helpless. 'Christ, Tony, who cares?'

The next day he brought me in a copy of *The Buyer's Guide to New and Used Cars*. The 1996 Camry and the 1997 have different body shapes: the 1997 is sleeker, with a more rounded rear end. See what I mean? Who cares, right? I didn't learn much from Tony's book, mainly because I couldn't read more than a page without falling asleep.

'Don't be so friendly,' Ernie said. 'You're too friendly. If you're too friendly, it makes it easier for these people to blow you off. You gotta be pushing hard all the time. Always be closing.'

Sam: 'Form a relationship with the customer. Find something in common with them. You gotta be their friend.'

Jackson: 'Ditch the ugly green shirt. Americans don't like green shirts, trust me.' All 250 million of them?

Mickey: 'Selling cars is like fishing. Hang on, there's a customer, gotta go . . .'

Hughie was the most helpful. As befitted an ex-masseur who spent half his working day meditating in an empty sales booth, there was a calm, other-worldliness about Hughie. The solution wasn't to be found in my wardrobe or business cards or even on the end of a fishing rod, he said. The secret to selling cars was within myself. 'What I want you to do for me is this.' He lowered his voice to a conspiratorial whisper. 'I want you to spend every minute of the day saying to yourself, "I will sell a car, I will sell a car." Just before you go to bed tonight say to yourself, "I will sell a car tomorrow. I will sell a car tomorrow."'

Normally, I don't go in for spiritual mumbo-jumbo but these were desperate times. I decided to have an early night, the better to be ready for the coming onslaught of sales predicted by my new guru, provided I followed his instructions. I switched off the reading light at 11 p.m. and, ignoring the tittering, convulsive female lying beside me under the covers, began to repeat in a low, expectant voice, 'I will sell a car tomorrow, I will sell a car tomorrow, I will sell a car tomorrow . . .'

'. . . I will sell a car today, I will sell a car today.'

I did sell a car today. In fact, I almost sold the most expensive car in The Orchard's history – a blue and white Dodge Viper, with a 450-horsepower, ten-cylinder engine, six-speed manual gearbox and top speed of 192.6 m.p.h. 'Zero to sixty in 4.1 seconds. The fastest production sports car in the United States . . .' I was standing at the front of the lot, reading aloud from Tony's book after having retrieved it from the bucket. '. . . three thousand miles on the clock and it's on sale today for seventy-five thousand dollars. But because I like your smile, Kay, I'm going to give you a one-hundred-dollar discount.'

I was never this cheesy with customers but it was late in the day, I was tired and, as Maggie had predicted the night before, Hughie's homemade chicken soup for the salesman's soul had proved a flop. Frankly, I was past caring. I was in post-modern, ironic salesman mode. *Because I like your smile?* At least it made Kay and her boyfriend Steve laugh.

She was a beautiful, fortysomething businesswoman with a figure hand-sculpted by angels. He looked like the guitar player from REO Speedwagon; sun-bleached curly hair, shirt buttons open to reveal a hairy chest, cream jacket with the sleeves pushed up to the elbow. She was carrying a bouquet of white lilies picked fresh from the Garden of Eden. He was wearing a gold chain that was thicker than the iron one we used to lock up the lot at night.

Normally, a couple like this wouldn't have been seen within fifty miles of Orchard Boulevard Pre-Owned Autos but they had been driving home from lunch when they spotted the Viper. It had been sitting on the narrow strip of grass at the front of the lot for a week. It was a rare car and had quickly become a beacon for every juvenile speed freak and penniless sports-car fanatic in northern California. All of them wanted to take it for a test drive and all of them had been told to go home and start saving their pennies.

The salesmen all wanted the sale – and the five-thousand-dollar commission – but they didn't want to sift through the countless time-wasters in search of a real customer. This was why no one bothered with Kay and Steve when they wandered on to the lot. No one except me. I didn't know any better.

'You want to take it for a test drive?'

Kay shook her head. 'No, thanks,' she said, coyly.

Steve pushed her playfully in the back. 'Go on. You've always wanted one.' He turned to me, saying, 'She's wanted a sports car like this since she passed her driving test.'

She has? 'You have?' I was cool, surprisingly so. 'Well, now's your chance to see how it drives.'

She looked at him. He nodded enthusiastically. She hesitated for a second, though it felt like an hour. 'Oh, why not?'

Out of the corner of my eye I could see stirrings of interest among the salesmen on the porch. They watched me walking to the office to get the keys. 'This is it, Scotty – the *big one*,' Mickey jeered.

'Leave the boy alone,' Hughie hissed.

Tommy flashed me a not-again look. 'Why are you bothering with these people? They're not going to buy this car.'

'No, no, these folks can afford this car. You should see the size of his gold chain. Give me the keys, would you?' They were in a desk drawer.

'Yeah, right. Are those the keys?' He grabbed them from me. 'Let me talk to them.'

Tommy thought he had more chance of selling this car than I did. With my record, I couldn't blame him. But there was something about this couple . . . I didn't think they would respond well to a fifty-year-old closer with tropical armpits and dusty shoes telling them they were about to get 'the deal of a lifetime'. They were snobs, Silicon Valley aristocrats. They looked down on me as well – I was a used-car salesman, after all – but I think they liked my bumbling amateurism. I appealed to their sense of benevolent superiority.

'You like the car?' Tommy nodded, his hands on his hips. He didn't bother waiting for a reply. 'Great. Well, we've got a rule with the Viper. The salesman has to go on the test drive.'

I could feel sweat rolling down my back. Kay hesitated, less than thrilled at the prospect of sharing a confined space with an overheating, overly familiar Scotsman she'd only met three minutes before. Thankfully, Steve was becoming more enthusiastic by the second. 'Come on, honey,' he said, holding open the driver's door. 'In you go.'

We climbed in. I could feel my wet shirt sticking to the black leather seat. 'Do you know how to work the air-conditioning on this thing?' she said.

Silly question. Of course I didn't.

As we edged out into the traffic, Tommy and Steve were deep in conversation. The gist of it was that Kay was celebrating her forty-first birthday, she was the chief financial officer for a computer company, she made a million dollars a year, she could afford the car. She was a fun girl, Steve loved her a lot.

We turned right on to the freeway. Kay rammed the car into gear. 'Right, let's see what it can do,' she said, with a Jack Nicholson smirk.

There's a scene at the end of every episode of *Star Trek* when Captain Kirk says, 'Take her to warp speed ten . . .' and the Starship Enterprise disappears to the top of the screen in a blur. That's exactly how it felt as we accelerated away.

'Noooooooooooooooooooooooooooooooo . . .'

We were heading towards the tailgate of a white pick-up truck at 120 m.p.h. But just when I thought I was about to enter the afterworld with the word Toyota imprinted on my forehead, she braked and flicked the steering-wheel. I opened my eyes. The pick-up was gone. I grabbed my chest, which was hot and heaving.

'This is nice,' she said, relaxing into her seat. She started telling me about herself. The engine throb was so loud I couldn't make out anything she said, except five words I didn't want to hear: 'I'm a part-time racing driver.'

She drove for another ten miles on the freeway, passing the other cars as if they were being towed. 'You want to go for a drive up to the hills?'

'You're kidding, you suicidal maniac. Take me home this second,' I said, except it came out as, 'If you like. You're the one who's buying the car.'

We veered off the freeway at five yards' notice, turned left past a shopping mall and started climbing up through parched, gentle hillside. The road was smooth and straight. My heartbeat slowed to a gallop. The speed-limit signs said forty-five but we were doing seventy as the car eased into a right-hand bend.

'Look, there's water on the road,' I said, just as Kay stamped on the brake pedal.

Too late. The back wheels gave way and we started to slide. I was about to die but for some reason I felt strangely calm, as if I had a front-row seat for the last act of someone else's life. 'God, look at those people in that car spinning round down there,' I said to myself. 'Wouldn't it be sad if a huge truck appeared over that hill just up the road and ran right over them and their heads exploded like overripe melons dropped from the thirty-fourth floor of the Empire State Building . . .'

The car stopped with a judder and stalled. I opened my eyes. We had performed a perfect 180-degree turn. I looked at Kay. She brushed the hair off her face, as if she was in a shampoo advert. 'Well, that was fun.' She turned the ignition key and the engine roared into life again. 'We'd better head back.'

We drove in silence for fifteen minutes until I remembered what Sam had said: 'Form a relationship with the customer. Find something you have in common with them.' Perfect! We'd almost died together. 'You meant to do that, didn't you?' I said.

She started giggling. 'You don't say?' I could tell she liked me well enough to write a big cheque.

Tommy was waiting with Steve when we turned into the lot. They looked expectant. Kay got out of the car. She brushed away the creases on her Donna Karan sapphire suit, adjusted her hair again.

Tommy spoke first. There was a nervous crackle in his voice. 'You like the car?'

Then Steve. 'Did you enjoy the drive, honey?'

I was scared to say anything with Tommy around in case it was interpreted later as a sackable offence.

Kay ran her fingers slowly across the roof of the car, like a half-naked model lying on a tigerskin rug. I closed my eyes and tried to imagine how shocked the other salesmen would be if the moon turned out to be made of chocolate cheesecake or, even more astoundingly, I sold a seventy-five-thousand-dollar car.

'I loved it.' She tilted her head in contemplation.

'Let's go to the office and we'll do a deal,' Tommy said eagerly. There was something not quite right about this approach, as if she was a nun and he was the doorman at a twelve-booth porn shop trying to persuade her to come inside and have look. 'We've got a big sale on today.' He pointed at the Godzilla sitting on the office roof. 'I could maybe get a thousand-dollar discount for you.'

They both looked at him as if he'd just suggested a threesome: synchronized snobbery. I knew then that we had lost the sale. These were not the kind of people who responded to a giant Godzilla or quibbled over a thousand dollars. They probably wouldn't have bent over to pick up a thousand-dollar bill if it had been stuck to their shoe with chewing-gum. He'd mortally wounded their inflated sense of self.

'How about I take fifteen hundred off?'

'How about it if we go away and talk about it, then come back in an hour?'

'Two thousand?'

'Give us an hour,' Kay said, more firmly this time.

Tommy sighed the sigh of defeat. He knew she had just revealed herself as the salesman's worst nightmare: She was a be-back – as in 'I'll be back in an hour/a day/a week/a month/a decade.' The time frame didn't matter, the sincerity of the promise was incidental. In fact the more sincere the promise the more definitive the outcome: a be-back never, *ever* came back. They would go home and compile a list of reasons why they shouldn't buy the car. Or, like Kay and Steve were about to do, they would go to the coffee shop and have the following conversation:

'What do you think?'

'I don't know, what d'you think?'

'The Scottish guy was a bit weird – he hardly said a word.'

'Right. And that other guy – did you notice his jacket? *Ugh*.'

By the time their *caffe lattes* were ready, the Dodge Viper would have been filed away in the drawer marked 'Passing Fancy'. The test drive would be just a story Kay would use to amuse her motor-racing friends next weekend.

Tommy and I watched them leave the lot, like heartbroken parents on the dockside as our beloved children left on an immigrants' boat to the New World. When they were safely over the horizon, he turned to me and said, 'Fucking time-wasters.'

I didn't have the guts to tell him that they might have bought the car if only he'd trusted my finely honed amateurism, or polished his shoes. Nor did I tell him about my near-death experience on the test drive. There was no point. All he would have done was shout at me for almost wrecking his precious car. Instead, I just stood on the porch and stared into space, wondering what on earth I was doing trying to sell a $75,000 car when I could be doing something commensurate to my talent, like selling wash-pegs door-to-door. I felt suicidal. I felt so depressed, in fact, that I went off and made a deal with the very next person I spoke to.

Why hadn't I thought of it before? Don't try to sell them the car, let them ask to buy it.

Her name was Claire. I was contemplating which would be the most painful way to end it all when she walked up to the porch and said, 'I'd like to take that car home tonight.' She pointed to a little white Dodge that had lain neglected at least since I'd started working on the lot, though probably longer. I'd only seen it driven once, by Jackson, who'd disappeared off to the coffee shop in a haze of poisonous grey smoke. It sounded like a First World War biplane heading for a messy end in the Channel.

'*That* car?'

'Yup.'

'The white one?'

'That's right.'

'Are you sure?'

'Well, if you don't want –'

'Let's go.'

She took the test drive at a steady 50 m.p.h., appearing not to notice that a Metallica concert was taking place where the engine should be. She loved the sound of the radio. Her boyfriend Pete liked the legroom. Sitting in the back, I eavesdropped as they planned days out to the beach and long romantic drives to the wine country. They looked so happy that I didn't have the heart to tell them they might be making the biggest mistake of their young lives.

'It's our first car,' she said, filling out a cheque for five thousand dollars. 'It's exactly what I've been looking for.'

'I'm happy for you,' I said, and believe me I was happy for her. But I was much, much happier for myself.

6

Duran Duran was miming its brand-new single on breakfast TV –
a deadly combination. Put together a group of jaded British pop
stars and any of the hairdressers' dummies who front early-morning
American television and you were guaranteed a cultural experience
to turn the milk in your cornflakes sour.

'Great song. You guys look just like you did twenty years ago,'
the host declared when, thankfully, the music stopped.

It's hard to capture how much of a lie this was. Simon Le Bon
looked every day of his 104 years. 'Thank you so much, Dave,' he
said wearily.

Under normal circumstances I would have heaved the television
out of the window but not this morning, because this was the
morning after the evening I'd sold a car. Nothing in the world –
not even the brand-new Duran Duran single – could make me feel
sour. Was Prozac better than this? I don't think so. In future years
manic depressives will go to the doctor, who will tell them, 'Take
a week off work and go sell a 1993 Dodge.'

I leaped out of bed, I sang in the shower, I hit a bucket of balls
at the golf range, all of them straight at the flag. I drove the ten
miles to work, though given half a chance I would have skipped all
the way. I was due to start at two o'clock but I got there an hour
early.

When I arrived Tommy and Mickey were on the porch looking
out across a deserted lot. 'Hi there, Scotty, how you doin'?' Tommy
said miserably.

'Fantastic.'

'You couldn't move that out of the driveway there and park it
against the wall, could you?'

'Sure, no problem.'

I grabbed the car keys and parked the car, straight in, perfect, as suave as James Bond. I jogged back and joined the two of them on the porch.

'How's tricks? Any sales so far?'

Tommy sighed. 'Oh, man, no sales. Just a lot of hassle today.' He stood up straight, then tucked in his shirt. 'Oh, by the way, that deal you did yesterday, it unwound.' He walked to the other end of the porch.

'Unwound. Oh, right. Fine.'

It took a few seconds for the words to register. Unwound? I'd never heard that before. What did that mean? If I'd been paying attention, the look on Tommy's face would have saved me the bother of asking.

'Unwound? What's that?'

Mickey had huge hands, with fingers like bananas. He wrapped them round my neck and started shaking me, playfully. 'You got your first unwind, boy. Tell him, Tommy, I said tell him.'

His head bowed, Tommy looked like a policeman who'd just turned up at the front door with bad news. 'Yeah, the little car you sold yesterday to that girl, it packed in when she was driving it home. Man, it was ugly. Up on Highway 17. Apparently, it just blew up when she was in the outside lane. It was pissing down at the time. She almost got run down by a truck when she ran over to the verge.'

I'd driven along Highway 17. When it rained, the road turned into a bobsleigh run for cars, a narrow, winding, slippery death trap. I'd read in the newspaper only that week that it had just been declared the most dangerous highway in California. Locally, it was known as Blood Alley.

'She had to get it towed in here this morning. Very pissed, believe me. Then Sunny started shouting at her, told her she couldn't get her money back. That got her *very*, *very* pissed off. She wanted to call the cops, said she was going to report us to the consumer people. Said she was going to report you to the DMV, get your sales licence taken away.'

Mickey laughed. 'What she's complaining about? She should be grateful she's still alive.'

Tommy handed me the voucher all salesmen got when they made a deal. It listed the customer's name and address, the car's details and the amount of commission due. 'It's $173, but don't worry about that, you won't be getting any money now.'

I looked at Tommy closely, trying to figure out from his body language if this was some elaborate hoax. If so, I was witnessing an Oscar-winning performance. 'You're joking, aren't you?'

'I tried to persuade her we could get the car fixed –'

'Yeah, right,' Mickey interrupted. 'The car blew up, almost got her killed on America's most dangerous road. She's really gonna want to keep it for ever, isn't she?'

This, judging by the blood vessels popping in his forehead and the jeers from a couple of salesmen on B Crew who'd appeared out of the office, was the most hilarious sentence ever spoken in the history of the English language. Looking back, I suppose it was mildly amusing but for some reason I got it into my head that I was Joe Pesci in *Goodfella's* and Mickey had just mixed me the wrong drink.

'What's so funny? I amuse you? I make you laugh?'

Unfortunately, I don't do menacing anger very convincingly. Even if I did I don't suppose Mickey would have taken me at all seriously. He stopped laughing just long enough to pile on the insults. 'No, no. All I'm just saying is just that you're such a crap salesman that even when you sell a car it doesn't stay sold for more than a day.'

In another world, this would have been seen as unforgivable cruelty. On a car lot, it was classed as everyday banter. It was assumed that if you weren't able to take it, you would find another job. I decided I would take it, though not flat on my back, beaten and humiliated in front of everyone else. 'Oh, is that right? Well, you won't be saying that when I'm Salesman of the Month at this place.'

Apparently, it was me who was cracking the jokes now. 'Who, you?' Mickey said, mock-serious.

'That's right, me.'

'And when will that be, 2010?'

'The end of the year.' *The end of the year?* Where did I pull that from? On current form I would be lucky to sell one car by the end of the year.

'That's six months or so.' Mickey offered me his hand. 'How much would you like to bet?'

I've never been much of a gambler. 'A month's salary.'

'Whose salary? I sell twenty cars a month and you sell none. I'll make ten grand this month, so far you've made nothing.'

Christ, he was nimble. No wonder he was always winning the sales contests. 'Okay. How about a thousand dollars?'

'A thousand bucks?'

'Right.'

'Right.'

'Right.'

Frankie finally lost his patience after marking dot number sixteen against my name. He switched on the intercom as he said, 'Right, Scotty, it's time for a proper sales lesson. Park a car out in front of the office. All sales professionals to the front of the lot, please.'

A communal groan drifted back on the cool breeze of the air-conditioning. It was hot outside, up towards the nineties. Most of the salesmen were lounging around in the sales booths, drinking ice-cold Coke and phoning their friends. The last thing they wanted was advice on how to become better at their job, especially as it required them to fry in the sun for half an hour. 'Why don't you give Scotty a private lesson?' a muffled voice – Mickey's, I think – shouted.

Frankie went back on the intercom: 'Mickey, Hughie, Sam – the guys who think they know it all, you're excused.'

To be fair, the lesson wasn't just for my benefit. Frankie was fed up with salesmen trailing into the office every five minutes to ask how much we were selling such-and-such a vehicle for. It would have helped to have the prices on the windscreens but most of the cars didn't, for the following reasons: (1) Nobody could be bothered. (2) It was a good way of keeping customers on the lot. It made them curious. If someone wanted to know the price, they had to talk to a salesman. Then they were trapped. (3) If there wasn't a price on the car, the salesman could make one up, depending on how expensively dressed the customer was or how ill-informed they seemed to be.

'Okay, when people are pinning you on the price, jacking you all over the lot, asking how much is this, how much is that, what's the best way to overcome the issue?'

Four of us were standing around an old Honda, varying shades of interest etched on our faces. Jackson had been at the recording studio all night making a demo with his 'Crew' and was barely awake. On a good day, when Wayne Leiter wasn't hung-over or wearing the trippy smile of the truly devoted dope smoker, he had the attention span of a four-year-old forced to watch an Ingmar Bergman movie. This was not one of his good days: he was looking past Frankie to the BMW dealership across the street, where a hostess in a short skirt was standing outside smoking. I had my pen and notebook ready. But any pretensions I had to being class swot were brushed aside by Tony, whose hand shot up as soon as Frankie asked the question.

'Don't worry about the price, sir, we'll get you the best price,' he said, beaming.

'Good boy, Tony.' Frankie started walking round the car. He looked solemn, like a maths professor pacing a lecture hall. 'What if the customer jumps up and down when you eventually do tell him the price?'

I never knew what to say when someone complained about the asking price. Agree with them that it was too high and you were admitting a conspiracy to rip them off and they would leave in a huff. Disagree with them and it felt like you were insulting their intelligence and they would leave in a huff. Usually, I just smiled or stuttered or tried a combination of both.

It turned out the secret was to deflect the customer's attention.

'Tell him, "Okay, sir, don't worry, I wasn't expecting you to pay that price. Let's find a car that you like first. What kind of vehicle are you after? Manual or automatic?" What we don't want is you running all over the place like a dog. I've been watching you, Lawrence, and that's what you've been doing. Okay?'

He was right. I was always chasing around trying to find out prices for customers, buying them Cokes and blowing up balloons for their kids. I thought salesmen were supposed to ingratiate themselves with customers. I was wrong.

'You've got to have some dignity. Don't let these mutts push you around,' Frankie said. He grabbed my notebook and wrote in capital letters, SELF-RESPECT and BE STRONG.

'Okay, now the "walk around".' He opened the driver's door, reached down and popped the engine hood. 'You've got to hit the car with power, with energy. I would say you've got four minutes exactly to get the customer juiced on the vehicle. So what am I going to talk about? Tony?'

'Crumple zones.'

'Correct.'

Jackson pinched Tony's leg for being a know-all, as Frankie delivered a two-minute lecture on the wonders of crumple zones, which, contrary to all reasonable expectation, was enthralling.

It was easy to see why he'd been such a star when he'd been working the line. He wasn't physically imposing – he was the same age as me, smaller, walked like Charlie Chaplin and wore a pair of brown leather slip-ons that would have had him thrown out of the Mormons for being square – but he had the stage presence of a Broadway musical. It may have been his blue, unblinking eyes, or his voice, which aimed to be friendly and sincere but came out as knowing ('Isn't this ridiculous? We've only just met and I'm pretending to be your best friend') and weirdly charismatic. Perhaps it was just that I'd never seen someone sell a car the way it was supposed to be done and I was wrapped up in my own wonderment. Whatever it was, it worked. Frankie could sell, even I could work that out. The crappy old Honda he was showing us had 120,000 miles on the clock and was scandalously overpriced but I would have bought it from him there and then.

He walked to the back of the car. 'Have any of you ever

considered climbing into the trunk and jumping up and down just to show how much space there is in there?'

I would now.

The next phase of the sale was all-important. As Frankie so delicately put it: 'Without a test drive, you've got dick. Got that?'

There then followed a treatise on how to persuade a customer to take a test drive. He was speaking so passionately, so quickly, that I couldn't get everything down but here are just a few of the highlights. Never make the mistake of actually asking the customer if they want a test drive, just get the keys, open the door and act like you're trying to escape after robbing a bank. Tell them: '*Get in.*' Don't talk too much when you're out on the road. In fact, don't talk unless the customer talks to you. If there's an unhealthy noise coming from the engine turn the radio up loud and start admiring the stereo system. Remember: this is the time to build a personal relationship. The car business is a people business. If the customer doesn't like you, they won't buy from you.

'Okay, you're back from the test drive, the guy says to you, "Has this car been in an accident?" What d'you tell him, Jackson?'

Jackson, still half asleep, shrugged. 'I'd tell him no.'

For the first time Frankie's enthusiasm flickered into exasperation. 'Christ, Jackson, that's stupid. How do we know if the fucking car has been in an accident? We don't know what might have happened to this heap of crap five years ago. See, guys, that's the difference between being a salesman and being a liar. Don't ever lie, it's bad karma. What you tell them is this – write this down in your notebook, Lawrence.'

He spoke slowly, just in case it wasn't clear enough already that he thought I was a complete idiot. '*I don't know if this car has been in an accident, sir, but if it has they sure put it back together real nice.*'

'Awesome,' Tony said, scarcely able to contain himself at the thought of actually saying something so ridiculous in a public place. Even Jackson managed a dopey smile. I thought it sounded like something from the *Bob Hope Joke Book* (which is to say, about as funny and charming as a terminal illness).

Wayne was just appalled: 'You've got to be kidding, man. No way am I saying that to a customer.'

This was a terrible mistake, not just because Wayne had sold only two cars for the month and therefore shouldn't have been attracting attention to himself, but also because Frankie considered himself to be the Seamus Heaney of used cars. He was proud of his lines. 'Hey, I've been saying that for twenty years, Mr Leiter, and it ain't done me any harm,' he barked, his mood suddenly turning sour. 'How many cars have you sold this month anyway?' As if he didn't know.

All of the salesmen liked Frankie. They respected his reputation as a great car salesman, they appreciated that as a boss he didn't try to fiddle their commission – an occupational hazard in some dealerships. But they were all scared of him too. One minute he was everybody's best friend, standing on the desk and declaring himself the captain of a pirate ship, the next he was running around on the porch like a headmaster breaking up a gang of smoking teenagers, pointing at two short-haired women over by the used trucks and hissing, 'Hey, who's got the lesbians? That's a car deal.'

He hated customers wandering around the lot unattended, especially lesbians (in Frankie's world, a lesbian was any woman who wore shorts, no makeup and had cropped hair), Vietnamese people and anybody who was fat. Two decades in the business had taught him that these were people who could be persuaded to spend money and not haggle over a price. 'Show me a fat Vietnamese lesbian and I'll show you a car deal,' he always said.

Actually, he didn't. But the point was he was a man of strong will, fixed opinions and mercurial temperament. You could tease him but only if he was in the right mood, or if you'd sold twenty cars in a week. One car in sixteen days barely qualified you to breathe in his presence.

'Now that Mr Leiter has given us the benefit of his experience . . .' he shot Wayne a look that hovered somewhere between contempt and you're fired '. . . next thing is the sales booth. Once you get a customer in the booth anything can happen, so do everything you can to get them in there. If they ask you a question about the car just say, "Come on inside and I'll get that information for you, sir." Turn around and walk away. Never look back. They will follow, trust me.'

I was always getting stuck at this stage. As soon as I asked someone to follow me to the sales booth, they suddenly realized they hadn't eaten since last Thursday, or remembered that their twelve-year-old son was in hospital with a broken leg and ran away. This part of the lesson in particular was for my benefit so I paid special attention.

'So if they ask, "Hey, Scotty, are you a homosexual?" what do you say?'

'I could be if you bought the car, Big Boy,' Tony said, *sotto voce*.

Frankie chose to ignore this. 'Just tell them, come inside, sir, and I'll find that out for you. "Did you have sex with a donkey last night, Scotty?" No problem, sir, let's go inside and I'll get that information for you. "Are you having an affair with my wife?" Inside, sir, let's find out. Why do we want them in the booth, guys?'

Just then there was loud metallic crunch from behind us. Everyone spun round. An ancient gold Cadillac was facing across the boulevard, perpendicular to the pavement. The driver's door was bent inwards, the front wheels pointing in opposite directions. Fragments of a motorcycle were scattered all over the road. Someone screamed. The motorcyclist was trying to get back on his feet, his grey-pink T-shirt was already darkened by blood. The bottom third of his helmet was swinging around his chest, as if on a hinge.

'Fucking hell!' Jackson yelled. He ran out to the street and started waving down traffic. Tony went to phone an ambulance. Wayne dashed into the office to get the first-aid kit. Being one of Mother Nature's more squeamish offspring, I remained rooted to the spot. Frankie stood beside me, watching the ensuing panic with an Olympian scowl, as if it had been staged to disrupt his sales lesson.

'I'm trying to teach these people how to sell cars and all they want to do is run around trying to save some guy's life,' he said, as the ambulance arrived. I didn't feel brave enough to point out this might be a little heartless in the circumstances, what with some poor motorcyclist just having had his jaw rearranged by a rusty wing mirror. Instead, I shrugged sympathetically at the terrible injustice of it all.

Eventually, he gave up.

'Lesson over.' Defeated, he walked back towards the office, stopping momentarily to deliver a matter-of-fact but chilling update on my prospects of remaining in the car business much longer: 'And can you please try to sell a car over the next few days, Scotty. Otherwise it might be best if, well, you know . . .'

That did it. I only needed one day, and this time the car – a shiny silver BMW – didn't blow up or unwind or any of that nasty stuff. So let me say now, thank you, Terry Purchase of Burlingame, California. You saved my career as a car salesman from a premature end. I'll never forget you. And I'm sorry that you paid four thousand dollars more for your car than you should have.

I was sitting in a car listening to the radio when I saw him wandering across the far end of the lot. He was wearing a dirty red baseball cap and a pair of brown overalls. There were other salesmen around but nobody was interested. It was getting near the end of our shift and he was looking at expensive cars. To the experienced eye, he didn't look like he could afford a twenty-thousand-dollar car.

I jumped out of my seat and raced over to say hello. He nodded cautiously, laid his hand on the roof of the 1994 BMW he'd been looking at for a couple of minutes. 'Has this one been in an accident?'

I cleared my throat. 'I don't know, sir, but if it has they sure put it back together real nice.'

The sales lesson worked! From every last corny line, to the confident but firm instruction 'Get in, let's go', to the carefully choreographed silence as we drove down the boulevard. When we got back I even jumped up and down in the trunk to show Terry how much space there was for his suitcases. In the circumstances, he had every right to suspect I was a smarmy sociopath who might well attack him with a wheel jack if he decided not to buy the car. But all he did was laugh. He seemed to like me, or at least he liked this version of me.

I was amazed. So this was how it was done! This was how you sold a car – with no inhibitions or self-consciousness. Forget the daft idea that the rules of ordinary life applied in any way to a car salesman. Sure, some of my best friends had serious jobs as doctors and journalists and art directors and potential computer millionaires but, secretly, they would have given up everything to be under the Californian sun, bouncing up and down in a car boot. Wouldn't they?

When Terry laughed it felt as if he'd let me out of prison. 'Do you think you could get my credit approved for a loan to buy this car?' he said.

'Come on inside and I'll get that information for you.' I spun round and walked towards the office, not daring to look back. Just as Frankie had promised, he followed me inside.

Fifteen minutes later it was over. Tommy closed the deal. Terry didn't even ask for a discount. Frankie finished off the paperwork, then held it up and pointed at the space where he'd filled in the salesman's commission. 'There you are, Scotty, you had eight hundred and sixty-seven reasons for coming into work today.' He shook my hand. 'Good job.'

'Eight hundred and sixty-seven dollars commission for selling one car. Can you believe that?'

Andy wove his car through the Saturday-night traffic. 'Wow,' he said, absentmindedly. We were heading to the Cattle Barons' Ball and we were late. 'And how many cars did you sell in the entire month?'

'Two, if you don't count the one that blew up.' A couple of days after I'd sold the BMW a young Mexican couple bought a battered old Buick for three thousand dollars less than the asking price. I made thirty-three dollars commission. 'Pretty good for my first month as a car salesman, eh?'

'Oh, fantastic.' Andy snorted. 'You'll be the richest man in the room tonight.'

The ball was taking place in an aircraft hangar at Moffat Military Airbase, just north of San Jose. We arrived at the gate, showed our tickets to the guard and were directed past the Double Gold Baron parking, the Gold Baron parking, the Silver Baron and the Land Baron parking, and on to a tarmac wilderness that didn't have a label but I assumed was the cowpoke parking. From there we were bussed back to the venue – pariahs revealed to the monied masses in all our $100-a-ticket miserliness.

That was bad enough but I was already feeling out of my depth, not least because of my outfit. Only in Silicon Valley could Western Outfitters ask for, and find some mug to pay, seven hundred dollars for a frilly red shirt with white trim. I wasn't going to blow a month's commission dressing up as Doc Holliday's secret gay lover and went for the economy option instead. I borrowed a pair of suede boots and a bootlace tie from Andy and splashed out eleven dollars on an imitation Stetson at a thrift store in Los Gatos.

'You look great,' Maggie said, as we were leaving the apartment but she couldn't fool me. I knew I looked like Hoss Cartwright on his way to a Calvin Klein party.

We walked through the door and all my fears were realized. The place reeked of wealth, from the rhinestone-studded outfits to the tennis-in-Barbados sheen that people get from having a few million in the bank. As always in the Valley, money had negated the usual genetic rules. There was a disproportionate number of couples consisting of tall, beautiful women and short, bald, moustachioed men. Likewise, there were elegant older women with partners young enough to be their nephews. Everyone seemed to know everyone else, except us.

Fortunately, aircraft hangars aren't exactly intimate and we disappeared into the crowd. Andy and his wife, Jane, went off to meet some business contacts, leaving Maggie and me to wander round the various stalls. We watched the pig racing for a while, then had a look at the silent auction. I bid five cents for a signed photograph of George W. Bush dressed as a ranch-hand. The tinny echo of the country-and-western band playing at the far end of the hangar drifted around in the rafters, lending the event a deathly atmosphere, as if we were floating around in the *Hindenburg* waiting for it to explode.

Ever the ingrate, I wanted to go home after an hour but Andy insisted we stay for the live auction. 'It'll blow your mind,' he said. He was right, although not in the way he'd meant it.

We took our seats at the end of the auction area reserved for cheapskates, next to the restroom. The first item on offer was a handbag designed by someone called Judith Leiber, which sold for $4,750. This sounds like a fortune but it wasn't really when you consider the lucky buyer also got a first-edition copy of Judith's torrid account of her life as furnisher of accessories to the rich and daft, *The Artful Handbag*. A Doris Day lookalike at the table in front of us paid $3,500 for a signed Michael Jordan basketball shirt. That was as cheap as the evening got.

The rest of the action took place near the front of the auction area, in the Double Gold Baron seats. This made it difficult to follow what was happening so we kept our eyes on the auctioneer. When the bidding got really frantic he would run between tables, baiting the underbidder in a way calculated to inflict maximum embarrassment.

'Forty thousand dollars. You can't beat that, sir?' he sneered at someone who'd had the temerity to offer a mere thirty-five thousand to have his dinner cooked by Gustave, the temperamental chef at San Francisco's premier French restaurant.

When the hammer came down at the end of every sale, Andy leaned over and gave a brief synopsis of the winning bidder's business history and financial status: 'Tom Smith, founded Phonehome.com – sold the company last year for five billion,' and so on.

I watched the scene with a growing sense of discovery. So this was what it was like to be a billionaire – stuck in a draughty aircraft hangar on a Saturday night, dressed as a cowboy, being bullied into paying forty thousand dollars for a meal that any rational person wouldn't have paid a hundred for. The more I thought about it, the more my eleven-dollar Stetson seemed like a badge of honour.

In all, $540,000 was raised from the sale of thirteen items. The highlight was the sale of a day out at a ranch recently featured in a local antiques magazine. In one corner, there was a distinguished-looking man in a red checked shirt, in the other a younger man with unkempt hair and a stick-on Pancho Gonzalez moustache. The bidding escalated in five thousand jumps to a hundred thousand dollars. This was greeted by a huge roar and an arbitrary decision by the auctioneer to raise the increments to ten thousand dollars.

Egged on by the others at his table, Pancho leaped up and held ten fingers in the air. He did it again and again but there was a cool persistence about the older man, like Gary Cooper. Pancho took an age to bid $210,000. It was obvious he was out of his depth. Eventually he sat down, humiliated.

'*Two hundred and twenty thousand dollars,*' yelled the auctioneer. The room erupted. 'Telecommunications guy, multi-millionaire,' Andy whispered, before jumping out of his seat to cheer. 'Come on, give him a clap.'

'What for?' I said. 'He's only showing off.'

He shook his head, clearly disgusted. 'The guy has just coughed up a quarter of a million for charity and all you can do is sit there sneering. Why are you so negative all the time?'

I shrugged. He was right in a way, I suppose. It was a pretty generous donation. Mind you, if someone was so desperate to support the American Cancer Society they could always have written a cheque and stuck it in the post. But what would be the point of that? The neighbours would never have known, would they?

7

We only had two customers all night, a 'drive-by shooter' everyone ignored and a friend of Wayne Leiter's who bought a shabby old truck with (a highly dubious) forty-one thousand miles on the clock. Ordinarily, the tougher salesmen like Mickey and Sam would have been angry at missing the only deal of the night but they let it pass. It was Wayne's friend. It was also his first sale of the month – on the twenty-fourth! He needed it. No wonder he didn't relax until the truck pulled out on to the boulevard, trailing wisps of black fumes that would have worried a more alert buyer.

'Well done, Wayne,' I said.

'Thanks.' He lit a cigarette.

Tony slapped him on the back. 'How much d'you make?'

Wayne blew a long, satisfied jet of smoke, like Rasputin after a night in the sack with the Tsar's wife. 'Eight hundred bucks.'

'Eight hundred bucks.'

This was terrible. Just about the only perk of being a salesman was that your friends and relatives were able to buy cars cheaper than anyone else. The rule was the dealership didn't take any profit, while the salesman got the minimum hundred dollars' commission. If Wayne had made eight hundred, then the profit on the sale was at least four thousand. He'd just persuaded his friend to sign the worst deal of his life.

Tony said, 'He was supposed to be your friend, Wayne, how could you do that to him?'

There was an embarrassed silence while the accused scrambled for something to say in mitigation. 'I ain't here to make friends,' he said, sniggering. 'I'm here to make money.'

I thought he'd stolen the line from Donald Trump's autobiography, although he insisted it came from the heart. Whatever the case, his remarks started a debate about who had behaved the most despicably in the pursuit of a car deal. (Mickey won with a complicated story about selling a customer back his own car for five thousand dollars two weeks after the man had traded it in for three thousand.)

Bored with car talk and bereft of customers, Tommy announced a contest to find out who was fastest on their feet. The winner got to go home early, the last-placed runner had to buy coffee for everyone. The rules were changed quickly when it became clear that I was the only man on the lot who had done any physical exercise in the last five years. We had a fastest fat salesman run-off instead: Mickey against Tony. Call me immature but there is something inherently funny about watching two 250-pound salesmen with high blood pressure and tight trousers trying to run the length of a car lot. I can't remember laughing so much for years.

Tony won by a pot belly, though Mickey feigned a pulled muscle and Tony went for the coffee anyway. While he was gone, Jackson persuaded Tommy to tell us some of his war stories. It turned out he'd been in Vietnam, as a member of a specialist Marine unit that had had the job of flushing the Vietcong soldiers out of underground bunkers. Once grenades and smoke bombs were thrown in, it was Tommy's job to climb down and strangle anyone left alive. He'd been wounded three times. Much as I would have liked to, it didn't seem like the right time to denounce the Vietnam War. When he had been called up by the draft board, Tommy was twenty-one years old and petrified. It was possible to disagree with the cause but there was no arguing with his courage.

Nights like this were the best thing about working at the lot, apart from selling a car, of course. But that was a rare treat, like a gourmet meal. The fun and games, the camaraderie, the realization that the more I found out about my new colleagues the more I liked them – these were staples of a salesman's life and I couldn't get enough of them.

It might have been because I wasn't one, but it was obvious to me that car salesmen were not so much criminal but criminally misunderstood. There had been a survey in the newspaper a few weeks before in which the public was asked what it thought was 'the sleaziest way to make a living'. Seven of the ten sleaziest occupations involved selling. Two of the other categories were drug-dealing and television evangelism (both forms of selling, when you think about it). Overall, selling cars was deemed the sleaziest job of all. Prison guards were in tenth place. I couldn't believe that. I'd met a few prison guards and as far as I could judge the only difference between them and neo-Nazis was that they wore white shirts to work rather than brown. Okay, so Wayne had ripped off an old friend for a few hundred dollars. He shouldn't have done it, but I've been involved in the music business, I've worked in a building full of ambitious journalists – trust me, car salesmen don't have the monopoly on unscrupulous behaviour.

Listening to Tommy's war remembrances got me thinking. If only the dealership made our nameplates big enough to carry some biographical information – Tommy (War Hero), Mickey (University Law Graduate), Jackson (Budding Rap Artist), Lawrence (Bass Player in Mildly Successful Mid-1980s Pop Band), Frankie (Loving Father to Two Sons), Tony (High School Heart-throb), Sam (Master Chef) – selling cars might have been a little bit easier. It would have made us appear more human. Instead, customers looked at us and what did they see? Cardboard cut-outs. Money-grabbing con men in cheap, dusty shoes. They were entirely wrong. Almost.

For once in his life, Mickey said it best as we locked up that night: 'We're just blue-collar guys trying to make a living.'

There was a handwritten notice on the office door threatening a three-hundred-dollar fine for any salesman who didn't turn up for a specially convened meeting. Sam phoned in sick, Hughie just didn't show up and Joe from B Crew was sent home for wearing a black turtleneck to work instead of a collar and tie ('Who do you think you are, Julio fucking Inglesias?' Sunny, his closer, said). This left thirteen of us gathered under the tent at the back of the lot waiting restlessly for Frankie to arrive. To pass the time, Tommy showed everyone his war wounds.

One strange thing I'd discovered over the last few weeks was that no one trusts a used-car salesman less than another used-car salesman.

'What war?' said a sceptical voice from the row in front.

Juan hadn't been around the night before when we were revisiting Saigon. Naturally, he didn't believe a word. That was when Tommy started pulling up his shirt to show us his wounds. Frankie arrived before he got the chance to show off the shrapnel slash across his left buttock.

'Okay, guys,' he said, clapping his hands to get everyone's attention. He was trying his best to look serious. 'This dealership is starting to roll like a big fucking snowball. We're doin' great but there are a few mistakes creeping in, and these mistakes have cost us twenty thousand dollars' profit in the last two weeks.'

The biggest problem was that too many salesmen were making outlandish promises to customers in order to close their deal. 'The car is the wrong colour? Will you buy it if I get it painted the colour you want for free?' and so on. I overheard this kind of generosity being offered in the sales booth every day of the week. CD changer? New wheels? Go-faster stripes? Sure, sure, sure. Come in on Tuesday and I'll get it done for you. Sign here, please.

'Of course, Tuesday is always that salesman's day off,' Frankie continued. 'So what happens is my talented closers Sunny and Tommy are running around like idiots trying to stamp on fifty rattlesnakes. It's gotta stop, gentlemen.'

He had a host of other complaints. Cars were going missing, customers were being ignored when they walked on to the lot, paperwork was ending up in the wastepaper basket when it should have been put in filing cabinets. In a normal business, management consultants would have been called in long ago but at The Orchard it didn't seem to matter. Organizational chaos was merely background noise, like the traffic whizzing past on the boulevard. Frankie made speeches like this every once in a while, calling for a more businesslike approach from his salesmen, but no one took much notice. I think secretly he preferred a touch of anarchy about the place.

When he finished, there was a muted round of applause and a premature sigh of relief that the lecture was over. 'Before you go, gentlemen, I want you all to meet Gil, who will be running this weekend's sales promotion.'

It was well past breakfast time. Everyone groaned. 'Don't worry, I'll be quick,' Gil said, handing each of us a leaflet declaring we were having a Prices Crisis.

I read it with a growing sense of wonderment. Apparently, we were eliminating red tape. Our primary banks had asked us to assist them in liquidating a huge quantity of used cars. Another dealership had gone bust and we'd just taken delivery of 250 vehicles from southern California that morning. All the salesmen had been told to slash prices by 30 per cent.

I had a quick glance across the lot – it looked exactly the same as it had the night before, except for the empty space where the truck Wayne had sold to his friend used to be. The delivery of 250 'liquidated' vehicles was a fantasy, just like the rest of the promotion. 'We've posted the leaflet through thirty thousand doors across the Valley . . .' To look at Gil, he didn't seem capable of deception on such a grand scale. He was young, bright, athletic, good-looking and well dressed. '. . . and this place is going to be rockin', so you guys can expect to make a lot of money this weekend.'

The solitary non-fiction element of the Prices Crisis event was a 'secret number' delivered with every leaflet that could win a customer one of two prizes: twenty-thousand dollars in cash or a commemorative US Mint dollar coin. Yet even this was taking a baseball bat to the truth. 'Don't worry about losing the twenty-thousand-dollar prize money,' Gil said, grinning. He held up one of the dollar coins. 'I've been doing this for five years and this is the most anybody has ever won.'

After the meeting I took a car I'd sold the previous week to be repaired at a garage down the street. There was a lot of excited laughter in the air when I came back. Jackson had just announced it was his birthday. 'We're going to a strip-club. Coming?' Tony said, when I asked what was going on.

Let the record show that I've long believed strip-clubs are a crime against humanity in general and womanhood in particular but there was no way I was going to miss a work's night out. I was trying to fit in, not get a reputation as Orchard's very own Germaine Greer. Besides, I was curious, and when I phoned Maggie to ask if she would ever forgive me for looking at other women who were naked she insisted God showed mercy to all sinners, provided they bought their girlfriend a new Kate Spade handbag at the first available opportunity.

We all met in the bar across the street from the lot after closing time, drank beer and played a few games of pool. I'm sure I could imagine more awkward social occasions – Christmas at Sandringham with the Royal Family springs to mind – but I'm just as certain none of them would have left me so bemused and disappointed. It was if, suddenly, we didn't know each other. We spent hours together on the lot, endlessly talking the most inconsequential drivel, and yet out here in the real world I couldn't have a conversation that didn't feel like I was an actor struggling to remember my lines.

I retreated to a corner of the bar, silently nursing a beer and a growing uneasiness. California was my home now and the salesmen in the room were the closest thing I had to friends. It was a depressing thought. I tried hard to understand what was wrong, and and then I looked across at Jorge Fernandez, one of the salesmen on B Crew, and it all became clear. He was a forty-nine-year-old El Salvadorian *émigré*, a farmer before the civil war broke out. He gave up his land and went off to fight. He hardly spoke any English and had a well-deserved reputation for stealing deals from his colleagues. His nickname was The Kink. Would I get an invite to Jorge's fiftieth birthday party? No. Would I want one? No.

One of my favourite films is *Tin Men*, which is about a group of aluminium-cladding salesmen in Baltimore in the 1960s. More than anything, it's a film about friendship. The salesmen spend all their free time together, they try to help when one of their number can't make any sales, they care when one of the gang has a heart-attack.

It's a great movie but, standing at the bar watching Jorge not talking to Wayne who wasn't talking to Jackson who wasn't talking to Tony and me, I could see it was nowhere near the truth.

The truth was we weren't friends at all. What we had was a facsimile of friendship. Salesmen were good at that: it was part of the job to fake friendship with customers. But take us all away from our natural habitat and we started acting like strangers with each other. The fact is, we were rivals. If a customer didn't buy a car from Salesman A, then it meant Salesman B had a chance of making the sale. That was why Mickey wouldn't give Tony and me any tips on how to become good salesmen – not because he was disobliging and mean-spirited (though I was beginning to think he was) but because it might cost him money if he helped us. It also explained why I always felt a tinge of regret whenever Tony and Jackson sold a car, though I always made a point of telling them, 'Good job, well done.'

Was I really capable of being so smarmy and two-faced? I took a sip of my beer, gave Jorge a high-five as he sank the eight ball and decided that I was. It's a brutalizing business, selling. I was going to have to watch out that I didn't end up hating myself.

The strip-club was a twenty-minute drive away, along wide, deserted roads that led to an industrial estate. I wasn't expecting the London Palladium but from the outside it looked like a bus-station toilet. The walls were high, with tiny slotted windows and a crown of barbed wire on the roof. The only give-away was a small, blinking red sign above the door. It was late but the queue snaked all the way down the street and round a distant corner. I wasn't surprised.

Silicon Valley has a sex problem – or, rather, it has a woman problem: there just aren't enough. For every female working in the computer industry there are five males. What makes matters worse is that most of the men are – there is no kinder way to put it – work-obsessed nerds. No single woman in her right mind wants to date someone with the personality of a fridge. Likewise, most of the men in the Valley don't want to date women whom they think are gold-diggers. 'I've never seen such misunderstanding between the sexes,' one Valley dating-agency owner told the *New York Times*. 'It's brutal.'

The upshot of this misunderstanding was a sex industry the likes of which I'd never seen before. It was all around, from the legion of hookers who did their business in the shopping mall car park not far from the car lot, to the personal ads in our local newspaper, which were straight from the *Sodom and Gomorrah Gazette*. I read these avidly, purely for the purposes of research, you understand. My favourite one of all time read, 'Want to give me nine inches? Call me ASAP.' Where were the romantic possibilities in that? There were pages and pages of this stuff every week.

It is, of course, a terrible old cliché to point out that strip-clubs are seedy, desperate dives. Far more fashionable to argue, as I did when I got home and Maggie insisted on calling me a dirty old man, that nowadays they cater for the professional gentleman and empower women in ways that Emily Pankhurst could only have dreamed about. Maybe this is true elsewhere, though I seriously doubt it, but it certainly wasn't true of the place we went to. Even standing in the queue was depressing. There were no raucous stag parties or under-age schoolboys nervously awaiting their first glimpse of a naked woman, just a lot of lonely men in button-down shirts and chinos quietly waiting their turn to get in. It was like the buffet line at a Boy Scouts' reunion.

By the time we got to the ticket window I would have paid everything I had to go home. Instead I had to pay everything I had to go inside, and only then on the most stringent conditions: no yelling, no touching (yourself or anyone else), no fraternizing with the staff, no dancing and, incredibly, no alcohol. 'You can only get alcohol at topless clubs. This is an all-naked club,' the barman said solemnly, as if the rules had been inscribed on marble tablets.

The entire experience was designed to provide the maximum profit for the owners and the minimum pleasure for everyone else. The entrance fee was thirty-five dollars; a 'private dance' cost a hundred. A glass of non-alcoholic beer, which tasted as if it had just been drawn from the club's septic tank, cost ten dollars. I will concede this, however: the dancers were both gorgeous and outstandingly agile. The prized seats in the house were around the circular stage, where customers placed dollar bills along a wooden rail. Every ten minutes a bikini-clad girl would emerge, make a few perfunctory steps while removing her outfit, then sweep up the dollars with a part of her anatomy not specifically designed for lifting.

Impressive though this dexterity was, it still didn't amount to a great night out and it wasn't long before we all got bored. All of the older, married salesmen, for whom the naked female form no longer held any mystery, left after ten minutes. Determined to extract full value for our thirty-five dollars, the rest of us stayed for another hour. As it turned out, I'm glad we did – otherwise I would have missed the night's big excitement.

It started with an argument in the restroom between Wayne Leiter and Jackson and ended up on the street outside the club with Wayne running off into the night and the rest of us surrounding Jackson, desperate to find out what had happened.

'He's a cop! He's a cop!' he yelled excitedly.

Tony tried to calm him down. 'Who's a cop?'

'Wayne Leiter.'

'What are you talking about?'

'Wayne Leiter. He's an undercover cop. I know where he's stationed, I know his police number, I know what case he's working on. Trust me, man, he's a goddamn cop.'

'Are you smoking crack?' Juan interrupted, laughing.

He had a point. Wayne was the least likely cop imaginable. He was unfit, unreliable and untrustworthy. Not only that, his daily intake of marijuana was enough to keep King Kong docile for a month. Of course, disreputable behaviour didn't exclude him from being a California police officer – after all, the LAPD existed solely for the purpose of throwing innocent blacks in prison – but Wayne barely had enough energy to drag himself out of bed every day, never mind construct and sustain an elaborate disguise as a used-car salesman over a period of weeks.

I explained all of this to Jackson but he refused to budge. 'I'm

85

telling you, man, he's a cop. Why do you think he was never bothered about selling cars?'

Come to think of it, Wayne did spend most of the time at work on the phone to his girlfriend or eating. It was as if he didn't want to make any money. He never showed any interest in talking to customers, unless it was to tell them we didn't have what they wanted. And if we did have what they wanted to buy, he always went and found another salesman to finish the deal. Very odd. As Tony then pointed out, to general hilarity, no one sold fewer cars than Wayne except me, and I had an excuse: I was a crap salesman.

Luckily, our crew was on the late shift after the night out. It was the first day of the Prices Crisis sale. Like everyone else, I expected the lot to be teeming with customers, but when I got there just after two o'clock it was deserted. I found Gil sitting under the canopy to the side of the office behind an empty table. He was wearing aviator shades and a scowl worthy of Hillary Clinton opening a birthday card from Monica Lewinsky. A mini-van was parked beside him with the windows open. The radio was tuned to a college station playing 'Heaven Knows I'm Miserable Now' by the Smiths.

'How's the Prices Crisis?'

'In crisis,' he said, flatly. 'It's the weather, man. Too hot.'

He'd had two customers in five hours, both of whom had travelled from the other end of the Valley under the delusion that they had a chance of winning twenty thousand dollars. The unexpected visit to a car lot hadn't fuelled a hitherto latent desire to buy a new car – which was the purpose of the entire charade, of course – and they had left immediately, muttering wholly justified remarks about the worthlessness of a dollar coin in modern America and the unctuousness of Gil's sales patter.

Just as I was about to say it served Gil right for being such a shameless con man, a slim, bleached-blonde woman approached the table. 'Is this where I pick up my prize?' she asked, waving an envelope.

'Sure, madam, sit down,' he said eagerly. He took her envelope and began opening it tremulously, like an Egyptologist unwrapping the bandages from a mummy.

I left him to break the bad news and went to the porch, where I found Tommy rubbing a generous layer of sun-cream on his face. The forecast was for 100 degrees. It was an umbrella day, a day to avoid sitting in a black car with black leather seats.

'Better put some of this stuff on, Scotty, otherwise you'll fry.' He handed me the tube.

'Where is everybody?' I asked.

He shrugged. 'I've just had Wayne Leiter on the phone. He ain't coming in. Says he's sick.'

Gradually, the rest of the crew drifted in. Mickey, Tony, Hughie, Sam, Juan. Jackson was last to arrive, twenty minutes late. He parked his car at the back of the lot and ran up the wheelchair ramp breathlessly. 'Where's Wayne Leiter? Is he here?' he yelled at no one in particular, not waiting for an answer. 'Bet ya he doesn't turn up today.'

Tommy, who preferred to spend his evenings at home with his Irish girlfriend and a bottle of Cabernet, hadn't been at the strip-club and was bemused. 'Where have you been, Jackson?' he moaned, before taking the chance to have a more general gripe about the rest of our crew. He got a two-thousand-dollar bonus if we sold seventy-five cars a month between us. With a week to go, we'd only sold forty. 'We're getting killed by B Crew. It's embarrassing.'

Maybe so, but it wasn't a surprise. Sunny ran the other crew like a Gestapo unit. He was always issuing orders or barking mean-spirited homilies about the glory of winning at all costs. He hated his salesmen taking days off and always pressured them into working late. Every sale was celebrated as another step towards a crushing military victory.

Tommy didn't say as much, but these juvenile antics clearly irritated the hell out of him. As someone who'd fought in a real war he obviously didn't see the point in fighting in Sunny's pretend war, which was why we were all eternally grateful he was our crew boss and not Sunny. It was also why no one paid attention to him when he occasionally got angry. We knew he was too laid back to be annoyed for more than five minutes.

'He's not here, is he?' Jackson said, the instant Tommy finished his pep talk.

'Who?'

'Wayne.'

'No, he ain't here. He called in sick. Again.'

'Told you. Told you. He's a cop.' Jackson slammed his fist on the porch rail. 'I *knew* it!'

Tommy told him not to be so ridiculous. But how was he to know that none of us would ever see Wayne again after the night at the strip-club? How could any of us have known? If we had, no one would have rolled their eyes when Jackson told us he'd over-heard Wayne on the phone at the strip-club describing himself as 'Officer Johnson' and asking to be put through to the detectives' room. Nor would anyone have laughed when he told us Wayne was spying on Ryan, a salesman at the dealership next door who happened to be one of Jackson's best friends. How were we to know that two months later Ryan would be carted off to San Quentin for two years after being caught driving the getaway car in a bank robbery?

Instead, everyone treated Jackson's elaborate conspiracy theory as a gigantic joke. 'Fuck me, if Wayne Leiter's an undercover cop I'm in big trouble,' Mickey McDonald sneered on behalf of us all. 'I only smoked dope with the guy about forty-three times.'

8

They don't give out certificates confirming that you've made the transition from Greenpea to proper salesman. Who knew how or when it happened? I asked around. Ernie reckoned you had to sell fifteen cars a month for three months in a row. Mickey insisted you had to be in the business two years before fully understanding how it worked, although he was such a natural-born salesman it had only taken him six months. Tommy shrugged and said, 'You just *know*.'

Whatever it took to complete the journey, three sales I made over the following few weeks gave me hope that one day – maybe not in this decade but possibly before cars are replaced by telepathic body transporters – I might just make it.

Michael Biggar: proud purchaser of a 1996 Toyota

Frankie had high hopes for the Sunnyvale Credit Union Used-car Sale. It was being held in the parking lot of a bank in one of the Valley's many middle-class enclaves and had a captive audience of 'pre-approved customers'. A bank clerk could have provided a long and tedious explanation of what this meant but all we needed to know was that, in an uncertain world, this was as close as a salesman ever got to guaranteed money.

Four of us were press-ganged into driving the cars from the lot to the Credit Union the night before the sale. 'Everyone who comes to the sale has enough money to buy a car and is ready to drive one away, *right now*,' Frankie said, in an effort to placate us. 'You can't fail, boys.'

'Even Scotty?' Mickey said.

Frankie took the question too seriously for comfort. 'Even Scotty.'

We'd just finished lining up the cars and were waiting for a minibus to take us back to the lot. 'TEN DEALERS, 200 CARS' declared a red and white banner strung across the entrance. It was a storybook summer's evening, pinky warm and still. Kids were having fun in the playground next door while their parents wandered through the lines of cars, taking notes as they went.

Sam and I watched a middle-aged couple fuss around the Volkswagen stall. 'Can you smell the juice?' he said.

I nodded. (After a bewildering start, when I often felt like Alan Bennett guest-starring on MTV, I was beginning to get the hang of the car salesman's vocabulary: 'juice' was profit. A person who looked ready to buy was 'juicy'. A person who looked both ready to buy and rich enough not to argue too much over the price was called a 'grape'.)

'Grapes?' I said.

He rubbed his hands together, greedily. 'Oh, boy, we're gonna make some money tomorrow.'

He was right. The sale was due to start at 7.30 a.m. We arrived fifteen minutes early and customers were already milling around. A black-haired man in a leather jacket and Levi's was leaning against a red Mustang convertible. 'Would it be possible to make an appointment to test drive this car?' he said, before I could introduce myself. He had a German accent, which explained his ignorance of how the used-car business worked in the United States: he didn't have to beg me for a test drive, I was supposed to beg him to take one.

I was looking for the keys to the Mustang when I felt someone tap me on the back. 'I was wondering if you could help me with this car . . .'

I now had two customers. A salesman like Mickey would have welcomed the chance to show the world how good he was. He would have thrown the customers the keys and told them to take the cars for a ride, sat them down afterwards, made them feel as if his only purpose on earth was to serve them alone, and finally he would have pocketed the commission on two sales. I felt the first stirrings of panic. Two customers in a single day, never mind simultaneously, was more than I could handle. Customer number two was Michelin Man enormous. Without being too unkind, I wasn't certain we had a car with wide enough doors to accommodate him. 'Sure, could you wait a moment?' I said, urgently. 'I've just got to speak to a colleague.'

This is where I have a confession to make on behalf of America's car salesmen. There is a rule about customers – an unwritten rule: unwritten because if it was ever committed to paper every lawyer in the country would spend their entire career successfully suing car dealerships for ageism, racism, sexism, fattism and any other kind of -ism you care to mention. The rule is this: certain types of customers are more likely to buy a car than others; invest your time in these people; ignore the others.

As Frankie had so helpfully explained in the past, lesbians and Vietnamese were, of course, gold dust. So, too, were couples with young children (they agonize less about buying, especially when their children start crying), Japanese customers (a spendthrift race, apparently) and, especially, fat people (the fatter they are the less stamina they have to shop around for the best prices). Customers to be ignored: single women (they can't make a decision without the help of a man, poor dears), anyone from the Indian sub-continent and China (too good at negotiating, hence no profit to be made), and Europeans (misers – all 350 million of them).

I'm not condoning this behaviour, merely saying that it exists and that it has nothing to do with prejudice and everything to do with making money. Mind you, if I saw an Indian family or a single woman wandering around the lot I always tried to sell them a car. So far, I had a 100 per cent failure rate but at least I stayed true to my beliefs: every customer should be treated equally. Until now.

Jackson was sitting in the front seat of a BMW, checking his hair in the mirror. I had ten seconds to decide. 'Come on, I've got two customers here,' I whispered, handing him the keys to the Mustang. 'You have the European. I'll take the fat guy.'

Michael, the fat guy, had a thousand questions. Could I get him a warranty for the engine? New tyres? What about an owner's manual? What about the driver's seat? Would it move back far enough to accommodate a backside the size of a three-berth bean-bag? Even though I say so myself, I handled him with a verve hitherto missing from my selling career. I think this was because we were away from the lot and I felt more relaxed. There weren't so many bored salesmen hanging around the porch with nothing better to do than give running critiques on my performance or, even worse, try to steal the deal from me.

Four of us, three salesmen and Frankie, were crammed into the bank's tiny canteen along with crews from all the other dealerships. For some reason we were doing better than everyone else. Mickey had made a couple of deals in the first hour, and Jackson sold the Mustang just as Michael and I shook hands on a '96 Toyota.

I felt like the proud father of newborn baby. It was the first time I'd ever taken a deal from start to finish without help from a closer. Jackson and I exchanged a series of elaborate high-fives as Frankie finished the paperwork.

'Stop that,' he hissed. 'Never high-five in front of the customers – they'll think we've made too much money out of them.'

Chastened, Jackson and I went outside for some coffee. 'How much commission did you make on the fat guy?' he said, lighting a cigarette.

'One hundred and eighty dollars,'

He nodded. 'Not bad.'

'What about the German I gave you? Bet you didn't make much money out of him. You know what Europeans are like.'

He blew a jet of smoke, then started laughing. 'On the contrary, my fine Scottish friend, I just made five hundred bucks.'

Chin-Lin Yen: proud purchaser of a 1999 Honda

Chin-Lin had been at the lot three weeks earlier, when a salesman on B Crew promised him he could buy a black Honda coupé for five thousand dollars less than we were asking. This was what was known in the trade as a low-ball. The purpose was to punish the customer for wasting the salesman's time. It was cruel, it was unnecessarily vindictive, and it always worked. Armed with this fantasy offer, Chin-Lin had spent three weeks wandering around other car dealerships trying to get an even better price when he could have been spending quality time with his family or attempting something with a more realistic chance of success, like arranging a candlelight dinner with Cameron Diaz.

He wanted to know if we would still sell the Honda for fifteen thousand dollars.

'Fifteen thousand?' Al Davison, Frankie's managerial sidekick, sighed when I handed him the offer. At that price, we were making a tiny profit. He looked at the name. 'Chinese?'

I nodded. 'I think so.'

'Okay, I'm going to sell this guy the car for fifteen thousand but this is how you are going to do it. I have worked with Chinese people, I know their culture. If you go back in there right now and shake his hand, he will think that he hasn't negotiated hard enough and will walk out. This is what I want you to do. Tell him you need to know the name of the other salesman. Tell him that this other salesman will be sacked for offering him such a low price. However, tell him we are an honourable dealership, that we like to stand by our promises and what you are going to do is call the owner of the dealership and ask him if he will sanction the deal. Then come back in here and wait for ten minutes.'

'Someone's going to get sacked?' I said, puzzled.

'Don't be so stupid. Nobody's getting sacked. Just get in there and tell him that somebody is.'

I know what this sounds like: he was asking me to lie, right? Before I became a car salesman, I would have said so. Now I wasn't so sure. The line between truth and lies didn't seem as well defined as it used to. It's hard to explain why, though Gable Shaw came close when he said, 'We don't lie in the car business, we negotiate.'

Gable was our Internet manager, a bald, lugubrious man who looked like he'd just stepped out of a John Updike novel. He'd been in the car business for twenty years, a career he'd sustained alongside a strong religious faith. Rumour had it that he'd once been a TV evangelist on a cable access channel. He'd started working at the lot a few weeks before I did. We'd become friends. The old-school salesmen, like Tommy and Ernie, didn't like him, or at least they didn't like the *idea* of him, because he attracted the wrong sort of customer – younger, earnest types who carried folders stuffed full of computer printouts and were way too well-informed to make much money from.

If you logged on to Gable's website you got the following message: 'When you visit our showroom please ask for me and I will apprise you of our special Internet prices.'

A practising agnostic, never mind a retired TV evangelist, would have had problems with the accuracy of this statement. For a start, we didn't have a showroom, and, for another thing, we didn't have 'special' prices for Internet customers: they got the same price as everyone else. I said as much to Gable, which was when he came up with the line about negotiation and lying.

I went back into the booth to talk to Chin-Lin Yen, armed with Al's script and feeling guilty as hell.

'Can you remember the other salesman's name?' I began.

'Joe, I think.'

'Okay. The thing is, Joe shouldn't have given you that price and he's probably going to be sacked . . .' I was word perfect, if a little flushed around the neck '. . . so if you can give me ten minutes, I'll call the boss and try to persuade him to clear the deal for you.'

I smiled a smile as sincere as the second-place finisher in the Miss World contest. 'Good,' Chin-Lin said firmly. He looked like a man who had just got a great deal and for once in Orchard Boulevard Pre-Owned Autos' history the customer was 110 per cent right.

'Okay, pal. Did it work?' Al said. I nodded, partly pleased but partly ashamed. I'd never seen him so happy. He almost hugged me. 'See? I told you it would work.' He banged the desktop triumphantly. 'You listen to me, Scotty, and I'll make you a –'

'A liar and a cheat?' I was joking, which was always a risky strategy with Al.

This time he indulged me: 'No,' he said, straining hard to maintain his smile. 'I'll make you a proper salesman.'

We spent the next ten minutes discussing the relative merits of the two Japanese take-aways within walking distance of the lot, until Al whispered, 'Go shake his hand.'

Anyone with a taste for the dramatic cliché, or who – like me – is racked with Catholic guilt, might have said that selling the car to Chin-Lin Yen in such a sneaky fashion was the first step on a journey to car-salesman hell. But when I went home that night I wrote down the twenty most despicable things I'd done in my entire life. All of them were a great deal worse than blurring the line between negotiating and lying. Call this a self-deluding exercise (Maggie certainly did) or a maturing view about the way the world of commerce worked (my own preference), but I slept soundly knowing I wasn't such a sleazeball after all.

Isaac Thurston, aged seventeen: proud new owner of a 1995 Dodge Stealth (with 124,000 miles on the clock)

I showed Isaac and his father, Tom, a dark green Dodge Stealth. 'Too many miles, too much money, terrible car anyway,' Tom said, leaning inside to look at the dashboard. He slammed the door but it popped out and hung limply from its hinges, like a broken wing.

I couldn't argue. The car had done 124,000 miles – almost five times round the world. I'd learned enough over the previous few weeks to know that five times round the block for most American cars was enough to reveal some terrible design flaw, like detachable doors or spontaneously exploding tyres. The Stealth was a prime example. Here was a car that was named after the world's fastest, most destructive military bomber. It looked like the Batmobile, yet you couldn't open the doors without breaking the key in the lock.

Father and son drifted through the lot, engrossed in one of the great rituals of suburban American life. This was Isaac's first car. He was seventeen years old, still at school, and wanted a car that

95

would improve his currently negligible chances of having sex with the Britney Spears lookalike who sat next to him in class. In theory, it was his money and his choice. In practice, Dad was picking the car, and he was looking for something safe, reliable and cheap. Most of all, he was looking for the opportunity to show his son that real American fathers don't take any crap from used-car salesmen.

'Why don't you just leave us alone and we'll call you if we need help?' he said, as he flicked his hand at me, like Prince Philip brushing off an obsequious courtier.

'No problem.' I slapped on the fake smile, then started to walk away. I waited a couple of beats and turned round. 'Actually, I've just had a terrific idea.'

Actually, I hadn't. I was just trying to make sure they didn't leave the lot. This was a tip I'd picked up from Tommy in one of the rare moments he'd remembered he was also being paid to teach the Greenpeas like me how to sell cars: tell a reluctant customer you have a great idea and watch their interest flicker. Don't tell them what the great idea is, leave it hanging and walk away urgently. It didn't matter that they hated you before, you could leave them standing there for as long as you like – a minute, an hour, a week – and they would still be waiting to hear your great idea when you came back. The point was to buy some time to find another salesman. With any luck he'd sell the car and I'd get half the commission.

I walked over to the porch. 'I'll take them,' Bhagwan Naresh said, before I opened my mouth.

'That'll be the day,' Tommy snapped, barring his way to the steps. 'Stay where you are. Mickey, talk to these nice, white American folks, they look like your kind of people. Go introduce him, Scotty.'

Mickey sighed. He'd been in the bar across the street until midnight the night before, then spent a couple of hours in a Vietnamese sauna in downtown San Jose. Sheltering behind a pair of ludicrous blue-framed sunglasses he'd bought at Wal-Mart for three dollars, he had barely moved from his seat on the stereo speaker all morning.

Tommy clapped his hands. '*Mickey*. Let's go.' Mickey pulled himself to his feet, moaning, 'Scotty, you're the worst fucking car salesman I've met in twenty years in the business. Look at these people. My cat could sell them a car.'

Miraculously, the short walk from the porch transformed him from a heavy, sweating slab of discontent into a verbal ballerina. He even managed a smile as I made the introductions. 'How are you folks doing today? Great, terrific . . .' He ruffled Isaac's hair. 'Your first car, is it?'

Tom looked at me expectantly, but Mickey launched into his sales pitch before I was forced to come up with the details of my terrific idea. He put his hand on Isaac's shoulder and gently escorted him back towards the Stealth, saying, 'I think I've got just the car for you.'

'What about the miles?' Tom protested, but it was like trying to smother Hurricane Martha with a tartan travel rug.

Mickey eased him gently into the driver's seat. 'Don't worry about the miles. It's a good ol' American car, it'll run for ever.'

It was strictly against car-lot etiquette to hang around when someone else was selling but Mickey didn't seem to mind and, like the crowd at a public lynching, I couldn't bear to take myself away. I was mesmerized. Every time Tom came up with a perfectly reasonable excuse for not buying the car – 'It's a wreck' – Mickey would brush aside the objection or change the subject: 'Now would you look at this back seat? It's never been sat in. *Perfect!*' He was funny, friendly, charming and manipulative until, finally, Tom's resistance began to wane.

Nestling ever more comfortably into the cracked leather seat, he ran his hands round the steering-wheel. That was when Mickey threw him the keys and told him to come back in a couple of hours. We watched them drive away. 'That's how you do it, Scotty,' he said, weary again, before going back to the porch for a sleep.

I had to drive Isaac home in his new car to pick up his driving licence. We needed it to finish off the paperwork. Mickey refused to go because it meant getting out of his seat again. I didn't mind because it meant I would get half the commission on the sale. Tom followed us in his truck. They lived about twenty miles away, in one of the suburbs to the south of San Jose. The journey took an age because of the Saturday-afternoon shopping traffic. I passed the time quizzing Isaac about his life.

Everything I knew about American teenagers had been picked up from watching reruns of *Beverly Hills 90210* so it was a shock to discover he didn't have a secret drug problem or a multi-millionaire grandaddy who was withholding his inheritance until he left his rock band to join the family banking firm. In fact, getting his own car was the most exciting event of his young life. He had a job stacking shelves at Macy's for eight dollars an hour and had been saving for months. His parents had loaned him another thousand, but only on condition he bought a car that was reliable and wouldn't catch the eye of the traffic police.

'Mom'll go crazy when she finds out Dad let me buy this one,' he said, with a gee-shucks smile as we took a right turn into a housing estate lined with identical white bungalows. 'I hope she's not there when we get home.'

'Me too,' I muttered, under my breath.

We parked outside the house. Tom and I admired the Stealth while Isaac ran inside to find his licence. 'Is your wife at home, Mr Thurston?' I asked, as casually as I could.

He laughed, joylessly. 'No, thank God.' He nodded at the car. 'I'm going to have to explain this to her later. I don't think she's going to like it.'

I could feel the tide of uneasiness swell in my gut. Fortunately, Isaac came rushing out of the house a few seconds later waving his licence. 'You drive, it's your car after all,' I said, squeezing into the unblemished back seat.

Isaac turned the key. The engine wheezed momentarily into life then stopped. He tried again. This time the only response was the empty click of the ignition failing to engage. 'I'm sure it's not a big problem,' I guessed, leaning through the gap between the two front seats. 'Let me have a go.'

I had a go, then Isaac had another go, then his father had fifteen goes, then we all climbed out of the car. It occurred to me that this was what it must be like to rob a bank then run out into the street only to discover someone had stolen the wheels off the getaway car. I looked around anxiously for any sign of Mom. The neighbourhood was deserted but for a couple of kids playing round a basketball hoop in next door's driveway. They stopped to watch the three of us scratching our heads and poking around the engine. While Tom tried a battery charger, I asked if I could use their phone and Isaac took me to a damp, dark kitchen. I watched an army of ants marching between the back door and the breakfast bar while the phone rang out.

A thousand civilizations rose and fell before Tommy finally answered. I had to shout to make myself heard above the racket at his end. 'Listen, Tommy, the Stealth Mickey and I just sold to the dad and his son, it's broken down. I'm at the house and the thing won't start and the mother is going to turn up any minute and kill me. What'll I do?'

'I don't know, man,' he yelled back. I could hear someone calling his name. 'Listen, I've got to go, this place is rockin'.'

'But, Tommy —' The phone went dead.

I went back outside, blinking in the sunlight and whispering to myself, 'Please, God, don't let Mom be home, please, God, please, God.'

Mom was home.

'What were you doin' letting him buy this car? Don't we have enough trouble with the police already?' Her face was heart-attack red from the effort of holding down a kicking, screaming rage. 'How could you?' she said, in a low, furious hiss.

Tom was standing by the Stealth, head bowed and silent. Isaac shifted nervously from foot to foot, his hands sunk into his trouser pockets like lead weights. Eventually Mom saw me standing on their lawn. 'Did you sell him this car?' She pointed accusingly at me, then at her husband.

Technically speaking, it wasn't me who sold him the car, I wasn't a good enough salesman. It was Mickey and, honestly, if she'd been there she would have bought it too, he was so brilliant. If I'd been really bold, or looking for a swift and easy way to end my life, I would have told her the back seat was perfect, that it had never been sat in. But even I knew this wasn't the time to start speaking technically. I nodded an unspoken but deeply felt 'sorry'.

Her anger gave way to disbelief. 'The bloody thing doesn't even work.' With that she stomped off towards the house, presumably to call a divorce lawyer.

Tom and I made a couple of more attempts to start the car, pushing it down the street while Isaac turned the key, but to no avail. Exhausted, I flopped to the ground. Never had I felt so helpless and alone, which might explain why I was on the verge of tears when a beige Toyota with $9998 – Automatic! Best Price! spelled out in luminous orange and lemon letters on the windscreen screeched round the corner. It was Mickey.

'What's the problem here?' he said, getting out. As usual, he didn't wait for an answer. 'Don't worry, folks, we've got an engineer coming out, everything is going to be fine.' There was no regret in his voice. Someone else was responsible for this terrible mess, his body language said, but don't worry because I'm here to straighten everything out. Remarkably, he got away with it. If anything, Tom Thurston was more glad to see him than I was, and I was very, very glad indeed.

The breakdown truck took ten minutes to arrive. Mickey filled the time waffling on about cross-country trips that I suspected never happened in a Dodge Stealth that I was pretty certain he'd never owned. Listening to him, it suddenly occurred to me that the trick to being a great salesman was knowing how to dance your way round the obstacles. It didn't matter if you knocked over a table and smashed some glasses, as long as you acted as if it was all part of the plan, got back on your feet, brushed yourself down and started dancing again.

Driving back to the lot, I felt like a hostage being released after five years in captivity. We didn't speak until Mickey turned down the radio. 'You're an unlucky guy, ain't you?' he said.

'What do you mean?'

'Well, there was that other car that blew up a few weeks ago.

Then there's this one.' He indicated left and steered into a drive-thru McDonald's. 'Twenty years in the business and nothing like that has ever happened to me.'

'Really?'

He nodded. 'Oh, well, at least it can't get any worse for you than this.'

He was right, of course, and I was happy about that. It couldn't get any worse, which meant from now on it could only get better.

9

It was the Fourth of July, Independence Day, the day that celebrates the birth of the most powerful nation in the history of the world or, as Jason the owner put it at the weekly sales meeting, 'Guys, it's *money time*. Believe me, if you don't make a minimum of a grand in commission over the four-day holiday, you're a total loser.'

In a tribute to the British role in the momentous events of the 1770s, I had gone for option number two. I was a total loser. The big day had arrived and I was a grand short of Jason's target. It was uncanny, spooky, even. I'd kept a tally. Over the previous seventy-two hours I'd talked to the only thirty-seven people in Silicon Valley who didn't want to buy a car. I sneaked a look at the board when I arrived at work with the forlorn hope that I wasn't the only salesman who'd blanked for the holiday. Depressingly, I was. It didn't help my mood that Mickey began the morning with a detailed account of his own brilliance as a salesman. He'd sold six cars in the last three days – twice as many as I'd sold in the whole of the previous month.

'How many cars did you sell last month, Scotty?' he said.

'Eight,' I lied.

As pathetic as taking an entire month to sell three cars may sound, I actually considered it an achievement. For one thing, it meant I was no longer the worst salesman at Orchard: Hughie and Juan had sold just two cars each over the same period. Despite the statistical evidence to the contrary I was sure I was becoming a half-decent salesman. I wasn't scared to talk to customers any more, and I knew enough about cars now to bluff my way past most technical questions they threw at me. Most importantly, I had found a 'personality' with which to dazzle and charm them. Tony was the jolly fat guy, Sam was Honest Joe, the weary old pro who gave it to you straight, Ernie was the streetwise huckster. I was the bumbling but charming British *ingénue*: Hugh Grant meets Norman Wisdom. People liked me. They admired the accent and were disarmed by the non-existent sales technique. They just weren't ready to buy cars from me yet.

Not that Mickey cared about any of this. 'That ain't going to win you Salesman of the Month, is it? How much is our bet again? A thousand dollars, right? You just want to give the cash to me now?' he said, pulling a piece of paper from his back pocket and waving it in my face. 'Twenty cars I sold last month. Thirteen thousand, seven hundred and eighty-one dollars and sixty-five cents. Biggest cheque I've ever made in the car business.'

Another thing I'd learned over the last couple of months was to ignore Mickey when he was in this kind of mood. It took too much energy to slap him down. Besides, B Crew was due to start in a couple of hours. The porch would be crawling with salesmen and my best chance of getting a sale would be gone. I concentrated hard on the traffic as it sped past on the boulevard, determined to get to the next customer before Mickey did. Fat chance.

'Hey, Scotty, Al wants to see you in the sales office. He's waving at you,' Mickey said, easing himself off the stereo speaker.

I turned round, breaking my concentration for a nanosecond, to look through the plate-glass windows. The sales office was empty.

'Hup, there's one.' He skipped gaily down the steps. 'That's where you're going wrong, Scotty. You gotta keep your eyes on the lot for the customers.'

I would never have told Mickey this, not least because it would have made him more unbearable than he already was, but I would have stuck a dagger in my thigh to be half as good a salesman as he was. I simply couldn't conceive of selling twenty cars a month, in the same way I couldn't imagine running a four-minute mile. The average car salesman in the US sold 8.3 cars a month, but that figure included new car salesmen. New cars were easier to sell. They didn't blow up on the way home from the lot or have scratches on the paintwork or suspicious mileage. Selling used cars required a lot more guile, especially when you couldn't dazzle the customers with fancy showroom furniture or paper in the customer toilets.

So how did Mickey do it? Not by reading the textbooks, that's for sure. Tom Hopkins, the great sales guru, would have told him sales was all about personal relationships. Maybe this was true for ordinary salesmen, but Mickey spoke to fewer customers than any of us. His business cards were collector's items. His idea of after-sales care was to hide in the restroom when someone came back to complain about the car he'd sold them the day before. I wasn't even sure he liked people, yet they were drawn to him, despite the fake sincerity, the split in the crotch of his trousers and the less than conscientious service.

Yet Frankie said he was the most naturally talented salesman he'd ever known. 'Watch him and you'll learn everything there is to know about selling cars,' he told me, and I did, every day, until I finally worked out that he was John McEnroe minus the tennis racket: he had charisma, perfect timing and a first-class honours degree in unsportsmanlike behaviour. He was undeniably brilliant. I wanted to be as good as he was, but as I watched him sell an eight-thousand-dollar Chevy to a young couple who were rightfully my customers it occurred to me that there had to be a better way to win than his way.

As it turned out, the day wasn't entirely wasted. Later that morning I stumbled across a Greek couple who wanted to pay cash for a 1997 Honda as long they could find a salesman who wasn't slick, devious or any of the terrible things they believed used-car salesmen to be. I told them it was their good fortune they had found me and not Mickey. The commission was $216 but it wasn't the money that mattered. At last there was a '1' against my name on the board and not a dot. When everyone sat around drinking coffee the next day and dissecting the holiday sale, I would be able to finish my litany of complaints about Mickey's deviousness on an upbeat theme: 'Well, at least I got one out.'

I left work at 3.45 p.m., fifteen minutes early, a relieved and happy man. Then I remembered that Maggie had made big plans for our first fourth of July in the United States. We were going to the Independence Day music festival in downtown Los Gatos and then to a Fourth of July party at Andy's house. Frankly, I would rather have bathed in a vat of rancid sheep dip than sit in the baking heat listening to the San Jose Symphony Orchestra play a selection of America's (the country not the band, which was a minor consolation) greatest hits. I wanted to stay at home and watch *The Simpsons* followed by a basketball double-header on ESPN sports channel but, as Maggie pointed out, this was hardly the most imaginative way to spend the biggest holiday of the year.

'Come on, we're late as it is – get changed,' she said, throwing me a pair of shorts. 'And stop whining – you're supposed to be living the American Dream, remember? What's more American than the Fourth of July?'

As usual she was right, though as we walked down the hill from the flat into town it occurred to me that the American Dream was proving more elusive than I had imagined it would be. Sure, our lives had changed. The weather was warmer and we did things we'd never have done had we stayed in Scotland, like drive across the desert to Dallas, take out a daily subscription to the *New York Times* and sit behind home plate at a San Francisco Giants game. But when I thought about it, these were holiday excursions rather than bold steps into a brave new world.

When I toured the States with the Bluebells it was as if I'd landed on another planet. This time round I felt I hadn't wandered too far from the end of my street in Glasgow. Since 1983 the world had shrunk. Nowadays even Scotland had fifty TV channels, Chicken McNuggets, shopping malls and bowling alleys. In fact, the only staples of American life that hadn't made it across the Atlantic in the last seventeen years were the death penalty, a ubiquitous twit called Carson Daly, who appeared to host every show on American TV, and the Los Gatos Independence Day music festival. Frankly, I wasn't too keen on any of them.

No wonder I loved working at Orchard Boulevard Pre-Owned Autos, despite Mickey's best efforts to make my life miserable. It was the only place I was going to find whatever it was I had come to California to look for.

However, I will say one thing: America knows how to commemorate a revolution. If Britain had had the good sense to boot out the monarchy a few centuries back, I guarantee the annual public holiday would have been marked with a march down Whitehall by a few nutters bearing 'Bring Back the Queen' placards and an hour-long episode of *Coronation Street*. Not so the Fourth of July, at least not in Los Gatos.

I confess I'd grown heartily sick of the town and all its Walt Disney perfection but there was no denying it was better appointed than the Gorbals. It was picturesque every day of the year but a special effort had been made for this particular day. Trees, lamp-posts, everything upright had been adorned with American flags. The town square was packed with kiddies paddling around in the shallow fountain pool, while their parents shaded themselves under oak trees. Everyone was wearing at least one item coloured red, white and blue. It really was a stirring sight. A lesser man than I – one who couldn't see beyond the superficial beauty to the empty soul beyond – would have been seduced.

Naturally, the Independence Day concert was a Hollywood production, staged in the grounds of the local high school against a backdrop of a pink sky, fluttering stars-and-stripes and real live cannons. At the end of the '1812 Overture' (historical relevance was clearly not one of the event's higher priorities) the late-afternoon air filled with a series of enormous bangs. They woke me up just in time to hear the closing *The Stars and Stripes Forever* before we headed swiftly for the exit.

By the time we got to Andy's house the party was in full swing. It was a grand affair, the kind where waiters carry trays of nibbles around rather than the kind where the guests shake beer cans then spray the contents at each other. My old friend had indeed come a long way since his days as the host of Glasgow University's most debauched social gatherings.

A few guests were hanging around in the kitchen but most were outside in the floodlit garden, eating barbecued lobster and sipping champagne. Of course, a proper salesman would have seized the opportunity. I cursed myself for not bringing a pocketful of business cards, then I remembered I was a conscientious objector. I made the decision on my first day at the car lot that I wouldn't add to Silicon Valley's stockpile of unwanted cardboard. It was impossible to ask someone the time without them offering you their business card. I wanted to be different. I wanted customers to say, 'Hey, let's call that used-car salesman who didn't have any business cards.' If they didn't have a phone number where they could contact me, then that was a price I was prepared to pay.

If he'd known, Frankie would have been furious. 'Always hand out your card,' he said, at least seventeen times a day. 'I'm proud to let people know I'm in the car business.' He would have loved the party. It was his kind of audience: people with high disposable incomes who had five-car garages to fill and were too busy at work to waste time haggling over the price. He would have finished the night with at least three guaranteed car deals.

Alas, it wasn't my kind of audience, though it was great to see Andy again. He was his usual ebullient self. He'd been on the road for weeks, meeting potential investors in Sweden, Singapore and all points between. He mentioned the name of an internationally famous investor – so famous even I had heard of him – who wanted to buy part of the firm for millions. Everything was going brilliantly, even without the benefit of my valuable input. But enough about rip-roaring business success.

'How's life in the used-car trade?' he said, hugging me warmly.

Andy's bemusement at my chosen career path had evolved into a kind of avuncular concern. I was grateful that he took an interest but I wasn't ready to be anyone's wayward nephew quite yet. He asked if I would like to meet a couple of guests who owned car dealerships and who might be persuaded to employ me in a trainee management post. In what others might have viewed as an unsavoury show of disloyalty, Maggie almost had a seizure at the suggestion but I suppose she had a point.

I laughed too. 'No thanks, Andy, I made two hundred and sixteen dollars today. What do I need a management job for?'

'Oh, well, whatever,' he said, grabbing my arm before I could escape. 'But come and meet everyone anyway.'

He introduced us to a group from his office, whom I'd recognized when we arrived and had hoped to avoid for the entire evening, then on through a parade of extremely pleasant but, to my mind at least, sadly single-minded people. Needless to say, they all worked in one branch or another of the computer industry. I won't bore you by recounting every conversation I found myself trapped in as the night dragged on, but I feel beholden to pass on a small sample of what passes for sizzling party conversation in Silicon Valley:

Me: 'So what do you do?'

Simon (whom I'd met at the punch bowl): 'I'm an Internet consultant.'

'Oh, really? What does that mean in English?'

'Starting up companies, finding venture financing, buying up URLs, that kind of thing.'

I had no idea what he was talking about. 'How interesting. Anything I might have heard of?'

'Not really.'

Short, awkward silence.

'I was working on something called Baked Potato.com.'

'You're kidding.'

'No, I'm not actually. We wanted to revolutionize the home-delivery baked-potato market, hot baked potatoes to every household in the Bay area within ten minutes of the order coming in.'

'What happened?'

'Well, you know, the whole business-to-consumer thing collapsed. We couldn't get enough venture capital. We had a few problems with the name as well.'

'Really.'

'Yeah, someone already had Bakedpotato.com. That meant we had to go with Bakedpotatoe.com – you know, with an "e" at the end of potato.'

'Potato with "e" at the end, you mean like –'

'Yeah, yeah, sure, like Dan Quayle.'

'So what's happened to the company.'

'We've still got the name. You want to buy it?'

'How much?'

'Seventy-five bucks.'

I'd like to report that this kind of surreal detour into the barren outer reaches of Valley capitalism was confined to small gatherings like Andy's party but it happened all the time. From the day I arrived, it seemed as if everyone I met was an entrepreneur or a DIY stockbroker or a potential Internet millionaire, even when it said plumber or car salesman on their business card. No doubt they all believed this unremitting, money-driven optimism was exactly what the American Dream – at least the Wall Street, Gordon Gekko version of the American Dream – was all about. But where was the quality control? Where was the *reality*?

Hardly a week passed without a customer who could hardly afford to buy a seven-thousand-dollar car trying to recruit me for the Internet company they were going to launch very soon. Some of the ideas were farcical. Did the world really need a company that sold personalized obituaries over the Internet? Even if it did, which was doubtful, would such a company really need me as its director of marketing? It wasn't just me. Mickey, Tony and Juan had similar offers. Jackson actually took someone up on one but came back to work a day later when it turned out that the world's next great pioneers of the Third Paradigm hadn't actually done anything as pioneering as renting an office or buying a computer.

Naturally, he was a laughing stock for a couple of days but he did all of us a favour by letting us know that working life elsewhere in the Valley wasn't as lucrative as we imagined it was. Sometimes being a used-car salesman felt like the worst job in the world, especially when your wages were adjusted upwards to ensure you were paid the minimum wage. But when Jackson asked for his job back it hinted that it might be a job worth having after all.

Mind you, it didn't stop the Orchard Boulevard Pre-Owned Autos Shareholders Club – Mickey, Frankie, Bhagwan and Jorge – dreaming of an easier life. Every morning they gathered round the computer screen to check how their stocks and shares were doing on the NASDAQ index. Earlier in the summer, Wall Street had decided the Internet wasn't such a great invention after all, which meant the air was usually filled with anguished cries as they logged on to discover they'd lost yet another chunk of money.

It was hard to break through the uncharmed circle and discover exactly how disastrously they were doing. Like any gambler, they only wanted to tell you what they had won but, in an unguarded moment, Mickey admitted he'd bought twenty thousand dollars' worth of shares in one company just before the market peaked. They were now worth about a tenth of that. Even worse, he'd persuaded Frankie to sink ten thousand into the same outfit.

Still, they had got off lightly compared to Bhagwan. A week – and, I might add, two car sales – after the fourth of July holiday I came back after a day off work to discover he'd resigned. He was odd at the best of times but recently his behaviour had been even more eccentric. On the days when he bothered to turn up for work, he spent most of his shift in the sales booth reading either the *Wall Street Journal* or the Bible. Apart from Mickey and Frankie, he hardly spoke to anyone except to say, 'Everything is beautiful.'

As it turned out, everything was far from beautiful. 'He's lost everything he had on the stock market,' Frankie explained, when I asked what happened. 'One hundred and fifty thousand dollars.'

I was stunned. Bhagwan drove an ancient Volkswagen. He owned one pair of black Dockers and one white work shirt, which he washed and ironed every night and wore the next day. He was always borrowing a dollar for the Coke machine. He sold a lot of cars but never seemed to have any money. Now I knew why.

'What's he going to do?' I asked.

Frankie shook his head in disbelief. 'Day trading. He wants to be a stockbroker or something. Can you believe that? The guy's lost a hundred and fifty thou' playing the markets and now he wants to take it up as a full-time job.'

Day trading was the latest craze sweeping the country. People would hire a desk and computer screen at high-street trading shops and spend their days gambling on incremental movements in the stock market until they either lost all their money or – as had happened in the case of a one-time chemist from Atlanta called Mark Barton – they went home, killed their wife and stuffed her in the closet. What a desperate way to make a living. It was Silicon Valley in microcosm, combining as it did pure capitalism, pure greed and pure madness in equal measure.

No doubt about it, you had to be off your head to become a day trader. As Frankie said before disappearing back into the office, Bhagwan was highly qualified for the job.

10

There was a lot of schoolboyish jostling as Tony, Juan and I piled into the back of a Toyota mini-van. We were heading to a sales training conference in Freemont, a sprawling mess of shopping malls, commuter housing and industrial estates on the East Bay. Once there, we were going to be crammed into an airless room in a hotel basement, forced to drink stewed coffee and listen to a 'power sales consultant' tell us why we didn't sell as many cars as we should.

Believe it or not, I was looking forward to the experience. As Greenpeas, we all were. It was a rite of passage. We knew you weren't a proper salesman until you'd spent the day at a third-rate hotel with a nametag pinned to your lapel, getting yelled at for being useless.

Jackson volunteered to drive and screeched the mini-van out on to the boulevard before anyone could wrestle the ignition key from his grasp. I was petrified. Getting around Silicon Valley by car was traumatic enough without being chauffeured by a twenty-one-year-old who approached life as if it was a Sony PlayStation game. Nor did it ease my nervousness when Juan produced a joint the size of a cucumber – 'Just to make us forget about traffic jams, guys.'

I spent the journey cowering in the back seat with my hands over my eyes, thus missing the moment when Tony bared his expansive backside to Highway 880 and all who drove on her. Judging by the hysterical-laughter from our now stoned driver, California hadn't seen anything as funny since Lenny Bruce appeared live at the North Beach in San Francisco.

Luckily, the hotel was right next to the motorway and easy to find. It was exactly as I had imagined it would be: a square breeze-block tower with dark, vomit-patterned carpets and a cocktail pianist bearing a grudge against Burt Bacharach. The lobby stank of stale banquet food. The staff were all young, presumably under-paid and easily the most demoralized people I'd seen since moving to California. It probably didn't help their mood that the place had been crawling with car salesmen for the last hour, all of whom had been trying to sell them a car.

The concierge directed us to the basement and the Regent Suite. Frankie threw the four of us a filthy look as we burst breathlessly through the door. We were half an hour late. Fortunately, the guest speaker was late too and the session hadn't started. About fifty people, salesmen from car dealerships across the Bay Area, were sitting behind trestle tables, wearing DIY nametags and the silent, simmering expressions of men confined in a windowless cell against their better judgement.

We sat near the front, by the coffee machine, where a young, terrified-looking Mexican waiter was trying to fend off six piranhas.

'Hey, buddy, what kind of car do you drive?' I overheard someone say, in a tone he would normally have used to confront his wife's secret lover.

The poor waiter was only trying to deliver a plate of chocolate brownies. 'A Toyota,' he replied, nervously.

'How would you like to drive a pre-owned certified used Honda?'

Were salesmen allowed to poke potential customers in the chest? I had no idea.

'No, thanks –'

'What do you mean, *no thanks*?'

'But – but –' The waiter stumbled backwards towards the exit. He would have been stripped of his life savings if the conference chairman hadn't called everyone to order.

After a few half-hearted remarks about how much potential we all had as salesmen, and a pitch for his $150, eighteen-cassette boxed set entitled '*Sales Tips for the New Millennium and Other Crap You Don't Need to Know*', he introduced the main speaker. A small, neat man wearing a jungle green safari suit and wire-rimmed spectacles stood up and smiled. 'It's a war out there guys,' the chairman went on, 'and Joe here is going to provide more bullets for you to use out there in the firing line. It should only take a couple of hours.'

A groan of despair went up from the row behind us, where Hughie and Sam were sitting. After a combined total of twenty years in the business they were in no mood to listen to any more advice on how to sell cars. Within minutes both of them had drifted off to sleep. I expected to join them in short order, but as Joe began his pitch I found myself enthralled.

He'd been selling cars for thirty-five years. In the early 1970s, he was the top Volkswagen salesman in the United States. He'd made a hundred thousand dollars a year when a hundred thousand was a lot of money and not what Gwyneth Paltrow spent on a dress for the Oscars. The most cars he'd sold in a single month was forty-four – at a time when, by his own admission, he had been the most obnoxious drunk in New York. It was easy to see why he was so good.

There was a hypnotic rhythm to his delivery, which was quick but utterly clear and assured. He was self-deprecating, funny and, most impressive of all, he appeared honest.

'If you ask the general public what they thought of us car salesmen what d'you think they would say?' he said, ten minutes into his speech.

'Liars?' Tommy volunteered, breaking the uncooperative silence

'Crooks,' someone else said, which got everyone in the room into the spirit.

'Cheats . . . gangsters . . . sleazeballs . . . bloodsuckers . . . Mafiosi . . . vipers –'

'And are they right?' Joe interrupted, not waiting for a reply. 'Of course they are. I was all of those things. I lied to everyone. When I started out I was the biggest fucking liar in the world. But not any more. These days, gentlemen, you don't have to lie to sell cars.'

'We don't?' sighed the back row.

'No, guys, get real. The car manufacturers are looking to get rid of us. They want to sell all their cars on the Internet. We can't let them do that, guys. We gotta get serious – *we can't play games any more.*'

I took copious notes. Don't lie, stay busy, and tell the customers a story. If they ask for a discount, tell them to go to hell but make sure they enjoy the trip. Practise your technique on your girlfriend. He even provided us with a few off-the-peg stories. 'The average person in this country will buy twenty-two cars in their lifetime,' I explained to Maggie when I got home. 'If I can save you two thousand dollars every time you buy a car, that means I'll save you forty-four thousand dollars. If you invest that money over the fifty-six years it'll make you half a million dollars, darling. Would you buy from me now?' She looked at her watch, unimpressed. 'God, is that the time? I must go and dry my hair.' I wouldn't have minded but her hair wasn't even wet.

Joe took a break after an hour for coffee and biscuits. When the meeting resumed Hughie, Sam and Jorge had disappeared. Jorge claimed he had to meet a customer at the lot. The other two didn't even bother making up a feeble excuse.

Tommy was furious. 'The company paid a hundred and fifty dollars each for those guys to come to this meeting,' he complained to Mickey as we filed out into the car park after the session was over. He asked around if anyone knew where they'd gone. Met with silence, he shook his head and said, 'Right, that's it. They're gone.'

This wasn't like Tommy at all. He never got so angry, and he certainly never sacked anyone. That was Sunny's game – he'd fired a salesman called Chris earlier in the week when he turned up without his nametag. Then there were Ron and Pete, both gone within a month of being hired for the cardinal offence of irritating Sunny. If he liked you (and for some unknown reason he liked me) you were fine. If not, you fell victim to the kind of management skills they don't teach at the Harvard Business School. Technically Bhagwan resigned, but we all knew Sunny hated him and had been looking for an excuse to get him out. 'Fuck me, you still here, then?' he used to say, when Bhagwan showed up for work.

It's a strange thing to say about someone who once made a career

115

out of wrestling Vietcong soldiers to death, but Tommy was too gentle, too humane, to treat people so badly.

'He'll never fire two people at the same time,' Juan said, as we drove home from the conference. Strictly speaking, he was right. Tommy didn't fire two people at the same time. He fired three, the third being Juan.

It happened right after the Friday-morning sales meeting. Juan turned up late and, as always happened with latecomers, was greeted with a low, accusatory '*ooooooooooooh*' from the front two rows. Normally he would have been told to stand at the back of the room for the rest of the meeting, but Jason the owner was in the middle of a diatribe about fresh graffiti in the restrooms at his new-car dealership accusing one of his pet salesmen – heaven forbid! – of being a crook. In the angry spirit of the moment, he told Juan to get out.

This was supposed to be a punishment but, in fact, it was a reward. As Juan said loudly as he was leaving, 'Who wants to listen to this crap for another hour anyway?'

We all knew something was up when Tommy and Frankie went into a huddle with Jason after the meeting. They turned up at the lot ten minutes later looking like a pair of undertaker's assistants. I was in the back office blowing up balloons and would have missed all the action if Tony hadn't been good enough to alert me. We rushed round to the porch just in time to hear Tommy say, 'Your attitude stinks.'

'Hey, chill, man, relax,' Juan replied, rather proving the point.

Somehow Tommy managed to refrain from throwing a punch. 'Okay, that's it, you're out. Get your stuff and go.'

Juan shrugged, then smiled slyly at Tony and me. 'Oh, no, my career is over. What'm I going to do with the rest of my life?'

Even for an eighteen-year-old punk, this was spectacular insolence. Mind you, it wasn't as if he liked the job, or needed it. He hardly sold any cars. At most, he was making two hundred and fifty dollars a week. Starbucks paid more than that. It was more than likely he would walk down the street that afternoon and get a job at another dealership. Orchard had a reputation for turning out great salesmen. It would take a few weeks for Juan's new boss to discover he'd employed Eminem's cheekier younger brother.

High-fives and heartfelt promises to keep in touch were exchanged before he finally left. For a second I imagined I caught a tinge of regret in his expression but then he rolled down his car window and shouted, 'Hey, Tommy, any chance of a job reference?' before heading off down the boulevard with Dr Dre blaring on the car stereo.

By contrast, Hughie's sacking was a subdued affair. He was invited into one of the sales booths and came out ten minutes later, carrying a couple of dirty white shirts in one hand and his lunch-box in the other. 'See you, guys,' he said miserably. 'I'm gone.'

I watched him drive away. He must have been pushing sixty. He didn't have the appetite for selling cars any more but he liked coming to work for the camaraderie and to give us all massages. God only knew what he was going to do now. Occasionally, he'd talked about setting up as a property developer but it was hard to imagine him building eighty-storey skyscrapers in San Francisco when he struggled to sell two cars a month. And that was before Tommy told me Hughie hadn't actually sold any cars for a month.

What he'd done was *pretend* he'd made two sales then hidden the cars in a car park at the back of the lot. That way he got paid commission, the 'sales' were registered on the board and he didn't get into trouble for sitting around doing nothing. When the month was over he drove the cars back on to the lot, claiming that the customers to whom he'd sold them couldn't get a bank loan and had returned them.

As an attempt at deception, it was in the same class as the pictures of bombers on the moon in the supermarket tabloids. But the pitifulness of the act only added to the melancholy of the story. How desperate must he have been? I was sure I couldn't feel sorrier for anyone than I did for Hughie at that moment. Then I remembered Sam and it occurred to me that I could.

Friday was his day off. This meant he was the last person within a fifty-mile radius to know he was leaving. When he turned up for work the next morning, wearing a new shirt and matching tie, his cheerful 'Good morning, fellas' was greeted with a bout of mortified shoe-gazing, except from Sunny, of course.

'Tommy wants to see you in the office,' he said, with a blood-thirsty grin. The heartless bastard.

Sam disappeared inside, still grinning. An awful silence descended, as if we were waiting for a gun, not Sam, to be fired. When he reappeared, he looked on the verge of tears. I wanted to hug him. He really loved his job, and he was good at it. He had been Salesman of the Month earlier in the year. But that was before a Santa Clara County judge gave him three hundred hours' community service for driving under the influence. It was his eighth offence. According to Sam, this was the greatest legal travesty since John Grisham discovered the urge to write novels, but they all say that, don't they?

Whatever the truth, it meant he could only come to work three days a week. He'd sold just five cars in a month, which was fine for a Greenpea but unacceptable for a 25 per cent salesman. It didn't help either that in his frustration he'd forgotten the first rule of good salesmanship: 'Get the fuck out of here and don't waste my time like that again,' he had been overheard telling a customer the day before. Rule number one: don't swear in the sales booth – but if you do, make sure Frankie isn't listening. Sam had become a liability. Disappearing in the middle of the sales conference was a convenient excuse to kick him out.

Nobody said a word as he wandered off to the far end of the porch and lit a cigarette. I couldn't stand it any longer so I went to join him. When I had first started on the lot, Sam had been the kindest of all the older salesmen. He was always giving me advice – 'Don't take any crap from the customers' and so on. He'd even closed a couple of deals for me and refused to accept half the commission, even though he was entitled to it. We'd talked a thousand times about going out for a meal after work but never got round to it. We never would now. Nor did I expect to see the fifty dollars he had borrowed six weeks ago and promised to give back the following day.

'You doing okay?' I asked.

'Not really, Lawrence, I'm not working here any longer.' He pulled on his cigarette. 'I didn't even know it was coming.'

'Yeah ... it's unbelievable ... Sunny has just told me ...' I was frantically searching for something else to say that wasn't a downright lie.

Fortunately, a few of the other salesmen joined us and the awkwardness passed. Mickey went inside and called a friend at another dealership to ask if any jobs were going that might suit a part-time salesman with a psychotic hatred of the general public.

Gradually, the atmosphere brightened. It was a Saturday after all, the busiest day of the week. Money was about to be made. Tony and Jackson went off to talk to customers, leaving Mal, the former college football player, and me with Sam, who clearly didn't want to go. He walked down the wheelchair ramp three times and came back.

'Hey, Mal, we gotta go to a baseball game sometime soon,' he said, hesitating a final time.

Mal had a pair of season tickets for the San Francisco Giants. 'No problem, that'll be great.' He tore a page out of his notebook and wrote down a telephone number. 'Call me here any time and we'll fix it up. Give me your number too.'

This act of kindness seemed to comfort Sam. He was almost smiling as he waved goodbye.

Watching him leave, I confess I started laughing. He had a nervous tic that caused one of his arms or legs to shoot out randomly, as if he was wired up to a faulty car battery. A stranger might have mistaken him for a madman as he twitched and jerked his way down the boulevard, his Max Wall hair fluttering in the breeze. Even those who knew him well had their suspicions.

'Fuck me, I gave that nutcase my home number,' Mal said, when Sam was finally out of sight. 'I'd better remember to call the phone company and get it changed.'

'You're all heart, Mal,' I said, grabbing the piece of paper with Sam's number out of his hand before he threw it into the bucket.

★

Tommy put an advert in the Employment Opportunities column of the local newspaper under the misleading headline 'Earn $13,000 a month'. He got a handful of calls. Two new salesmen, Kim and Lun-Ho, started a week later. Neither of them was in danger of making thirteen thousand dollars a year. I'm ashamed to admit this made me deliriously happy. By a process of elimination, I was becoming one of the more senior salesmen on the lot.

Lun-Ho had bags of enthusiasm but he'd lost his sales licence in 1994 for unspecified criminal behaviour. His impressive sales CV was a work of fiction. One lie was forgivable, but then he claimed the reason he could not bring in his sales licence was that his wife had accidentally melted it in the tumble-dryer. Frankie, who claimed Socratic insight on every pathetic excuse ever uttered on a car lot, fired him on the spot. In a profession with a million rules, the need for a salesman's licence to be on public display at the dealership was the only one that really counted. The DMV would have closed the dealership if Lun-Ho had sold a car to one of its undercover inspectors.

Kim had a licence, though there was no prospect of him selling a car to a DMV inspector. All he wanted to do was play solitaire on the office computer. Frankie would have fired him too, had he not announced one morning that he'd persuaded his friend Hoang to come and work at Orchard.

This turned out to be real coup. Hoang had been Kim's closer at the Dodge store in the East Bay. Within an hour of starting work, he had sold a flashy sports jeep to an English couple who were looking for a four-door family saloon. The following afternoon he persuaded a shifty Filipino chef to trade in his sleek black Corvette for a scruffy Ford Mustang. The profit on this second deal was twelve thousand. That was more profit for the dealership than I usually made in a month.

In his first week, Hoang made five thousand dollars' commission and won a three-day sales contest worth another thousand. He was a star, sharp and utterly relentless, with a real sense of theatre. A car deal wasn't really a car deal until he'd chased the customers down the street, dragged them back into the sales booth by the shirtsleeve and squeezed another five hundred dollars out of them.

I liked him a lot, although the feeling wasn't universal. Sunny was suspicious of anyone who boasted about spending eighty-five dollars on a haircut. Mal didn't think much of the lowered suspension on the metallic blue Lexus he drove to work every day. Ernie said he was 'too pretty'. (Admittedly, Hoang looked like a Vietnamese Keanu Reeves but that was hardly a reason to dislike him.) Mickey was just as petty but more insidious. 'What d'you make of this new guy?' he asked Tony and me, the day after the Corvette deal.

'Seems okay to me,' Tony said. 'He can sell cars, that's for sure.'

'Think so? If you ask me, I think he looks like he's one of these "Here today gone to Maui" types. I wonder why he left the last place he worked at? Bet he was up to something and got caught.'

The real reason Mickey didn't like Hoang was that he'd made three thousand dollars' commission on the Corvette. This was the biggest single deal in the history of the lot – an Orchard Boulevard Pre-Owned Autos All-Comers' Record! Mickey would have liked the three thousand, of course, but for all his obsession with money, I think he was more upset about the record. He held the old record – selling a Mercedes convertible for a ten-thousand-dollar profit. 'I don't think anyone'll beat twelve thousand for a long time,' he said when he heard the news, like Pete Sampras telling a packed press conference it wasn't about the prize money any more, it was Grand Slam titles that mattered.

Naturally, all this talk of records didn't concern the likes of Tony and me. Hoang wasn't a threat to us. In fact, we both went out of our way to make him feel welcome, knowing how much his successes annoyed Mickey. In return for our friendliness, he occasionally gave us customers that, by right, were his. That's how I met Andrea Catforth.

Hoang saw her first, walking on to the lot trailing a gaggle of teenagers behind her. Until then it had been a frustrating Saturday afternoon. I'd sold nothing. Even worse, I'd lost a quarter of my bodyweight pushing a '93 Mazda the last quarter-mile to the lot after running out of petrol on a test drive. My hair was a sticky mess, my shirt translucent with sweat.

I was sitting on the porch, dejectedly weighing up the risks of sneaking off to the golf range when Hoang tapped my leg. 'Go on, Scotty, you take her. I've got a couple of sales already today,' he whispered, as Andrea walked towards us. 'Don't mess it up now. If you get stuck come and ask me for help.'

At the time, I was grateful. For days afterwards, Hoang began every argument over whose turn it was to drive to the coffee shop with a reminder that he'd spoon-fed me the only deal I'd made in a week. If I'd known how things were going to turn out with Andrea, I would have made him get his own bloody coffee for the next six months, and mine too.

Landing a customer on the right car was one of the hardest parts of a salesman's job. Frankie had a saying: 'If you can do it in less than ten minutes, you've usually got a deal. If it takes any longer, then your name is Scotty.'

He was right. I was hopeless. We never had the car my customers wanted. Either that or they fell in love with a sports car they couldn't afford, or found the model they wanted but not in the right colour. A strong salesman would have brushed aside these excuses – 'Don't worry, madam, I'll get the car painted the same colour as your eyes' – but I always found myself nodding sympathetically or giving them directions to another dealership where the car of their dreams was waiting.

There were no such difficulties with Andrea. It was depressingly easy to land her on a car. We only had two she could afford: one was the Dodge that had blown up an hour after I'd sold it (Frankie had had the engine repaired and the floor mats vacuumed, then put another thousand dollars on the price – 'Think about it, Scotty, the car is in better condition than it was when we sold it the last time'); the other was a white ten-year-old Honda with 117,342 miles on the clock. Both had an asking price of six thousand dollars.

Andrea took an immediate liking to the Dodge. 'It looks clean.'

'No, you don't want that one,' I said, closing the door before she could sit inside.

The car was for her son Felix, who was starting college at the end of the month. He was eighteen years old and wanted a Ferrari. It was a toss-up between the two as to which looked less like a Ferrari but he chose the Dodge because Tony was showing the Honda to a couple of pensioners. No self-respecting teenager would want to be seen in anything *they* liked.

'Can we try this one?' Felix insisted, jumping into the driver's seat of the Dodge.

I shook my head. 'No, you *can't.*'

His friends piled into the back seat. One leaned over and turned up the radio to full volume. Andrea smiled. She'd driven all the way from the North Bay, around seventy miles, because her neighbour had heard the radio advert announcing there were seven thousand cars for sale at Orchard Boulevard every day of the year. This made me feel worse than I already did. Seven thousand cars and she had to pick *this* one. Excuse the Californ*ese* but the Dodge had bad karma – fifty dollars' worth of repairs and a higher price tag wasn't going to change that. Even if she got lucky and she didn't get killed on the most dangerous highway in California, what if the engine blew up again when we were out on a test drive? I'd already pushed one clapped-out wreck back to the lot today, thank you very much.

'Can we take it out, please?' she said.

'Oh, all right, then,' I said, with a defeated sigh.

Felix hadn't passed his test yet so his mother drove. We were scarcely fifty yards down the boulevard when she turned to her son and ask if he liked the car. When he nodded and smiled, she turned to me and said, 'I think we'll buy this one.'

Under normal circumstances, I would have made her reverse back on to the lot, taken her inside and filled in the paperwork, pausing only to give her a brief but heartfelt hug. This was how the car business worked in my dreams. Instead, the nagging uneasiness in my stomach suddenly snowballed into panic. 'No, don't say that. Let's keep going and we'll see how it drives,' I pleaded.

I spent the rest of the drive reciting a selection of the objections thrown at me by customers over the weeks and months: the car *doesn't* have a CD player; it *does* have spongy brakes, scratched paintwork, too many miles on the clock, and the seats sag, the engine sags, the axle sags. 'God, what was that squeaking noise – the engine, the clutch, the gear-box?'

Unfortunately, my inability to sell cars was matched by my inability not to sell cars. The harder I tried to put her off, the more determined she seemed to buy the Dodge. As we pulled back on to the lot, I was left with no other choice.

'I can't let you buy this car,' I began, forcefully.

She switched off the engine and looked at me, puzzled. 'Why not? Is it because I've got bad credit. It's not my fault, it's my husband's. He never pays any bills . . .'

'No, no, Andrea, it's not that.'

'Then why not?'

A good salesman never lies. Joe had said it in his pep talk. Frankie drummed it into us almost every day. But did a good salesman have to be forthright? If a customer didn't ask a vital, decision-changing question – 'Excuse me, did this car blow up the last time you sold it?' – did we have to volunteer the information? Was reticence any different from lying? These are interesting philosophical questions – for me perhaps but not, I suspected, for the likes of Joe and Frankie. I was about to commit a sackable offence.

I had a quick look round, then lowered my voice. 'I'm not supposed to tell you this but I sold this car a couple of months ago and it blew up an hour later.'

At last I'd got her attention. She fell silent. 'I tried to tell you earlier but it didn't seem like you wanted to know,' I explained.

'You're different from other car salesmen. You're honest,' she said eventually, her eyes wide and shiny with gratitude. 'Isn't he, Felix?'

What Joe had said was right; customers love honesty. It builds trust, it breaks down their fears, it makes them buy cars at which they had turned up their nose less than half an hour before. They didn't even ask for a discount.

Luckily, the Honda was still parked where it had been when we went out in the Dodge. Tony's pensioners had gone. We drove it round the block. Felix thought it was too old-fashioned but his mother was weary. 'Come on, honey, we don't have much choice,' she said as we walked up the stairs and into the office.

Tommy closed the deal. I didn't have the heart, not when I found out we'd be charging 20 per cent interest on the loan because of her husband's profligate ways. I felt terrible when Felix reluctantly signed a postdated cheque for a $250 down-payment. He only made $325 a fortnight cleaning tables in a restaurant. (Christ! There was a bottle of balsamic vinegar on sale at the deli in Los Gatos for $365!)

Only once, very briefly, did Andrea appear to waver in her conviction that I was a saint. It was after Tommy had gone, when we were walking over to the finance office. 'Do we get a full tank of gas? You're not going to let me leave with an empty tank, are you Lawrence?'

Frankie's rule was five gallons for every customer, with no exceptions. 'Of course, you get a full tank of gas. Everybody does,' I lied.

It cost me twenty-three dollars and fifteen cents. It was the very least I could for her. Or so I thought at the time.

11

A salesman's slump, like the universe, is one of the great unknowns. No one knows how it starts, it just exists: huge and black, scary and mysterious. One minute you've sold seven cars for the month of July and are being quietly talked about in the office as a possible future star, the next you're standing next to a silver Infiniti Q45 saloon car with grey leather trim listening to the customer who was there at the start of the downward spiral (a.k.a. the World's Most Stupid Man).

'Tell me, Lance –'

'Lawrence.'

'Yes, Lawrence. Tell me, how much is this car?'

'Twenty-seven thousand dollars.'

'No, no, I want your best price.'

'Twenty-seven thousand dollars.'

'And there is my car over there. I paid twenty thousand for it. You will give me twenty thousand, yes?'

'How long have you had the car?'

'Three years.'

'Well, to be perfectly honest, sir, I'd say after three years your car is now worth about ten thousand dollars.'

'So, let's get this right. You will give me ten thousand dollars for my car and you want twenty-seven thousand for this car?'

'That's right, sir.'

'So who will pay the seventeen-thousand-dollar difference?'

'You will.'

'You want *me* to pay it?'

'That's generally the way it works, sir.'

'Come on.' The World's Most Stupid Man waggled his finger at the World's Most Unfortunate Wife. 'Let's go.'

★

Sam lived in San Mateo, not far from the world headquarters of Larry Ellison's Oracle Corporation. It was a moneyed town, similar in size to Los Gatos but more cramped and not as pretty. Downtown had all the usual Silicon Valley haunts: yuppie clothing stores, pretentious Italian restaurants, $100-a-throw hairdressers and overpriced delis selling ostrich-meat salami. Fifteen hundred dollars a month didn't rent much of an apartment in a place like this but even so there must have been a terrible mistake – a misplaced decimal point, perhaps – when Sam signed his lease.

'I thought you weren't coming,' he said flatly, as we got out of the lift at the second floor and walked down a grey, windowless corridor. The stench of cats' urine and stale rubbish settled poisonously in my nostrils.

I'd seen Sam earlier that week. He turned up at the lot, ostensibly to pick up a pair of shoes he'd left behind and to ask Mal why the phone number he had given him had been disconnected. But, really, he was checking to see if there had been a change of mind and he could have his job back.

It was worth a try. Frankie wasn't exactly Mother Teresa but he had a genuine affection for old warriors like Sam, and would probably have given him a second chance. But it had been Tommy's decision and he was implacable – even when Mickey suggested Sam was a little crazy and that he should give the poor guy another chance before he turned up at the lot with an AK-47 and killed us all. 'No way. He craps everybody out with his negative attitude,' he said, as if he'd just been asked to take a swig from a carton of three-week-old milk.

Sam hadn't found another job yet, and had spent the time working off his community-service sentence, picking up litter for the Santa Clara probation service. That paid three dollars a day, enough to buy a *latte* and a ginger snap from Starbucks. God only knew how he was surviving. I thought a visit would cheer him up, let him know that at least he'd made one friend during his time at The Orchard, though I'd be lying if I said my trip to Burlingame was entirely a social excursion.

I was curious. I'd been working on the lot for four months and knew little of consequence about Sam, or any of the others for that matter. And vice versa. Mickey didn't know my surname. Neither did Frankie or even Tony, who was the nearest I had to a friend in the car business. Tommy thought it might be Scott: 'Scotty Scott the Scotsman from Scotland, right?'

Sure, we spent a lot of time on the porch in idle conversation but just because someone was talking didn't necessarily mean that anyone was listening. Salesmen were too busy looking out for customers walking in off the street to pay close attention to each other. Mundane information like surnames didn't register, only the startling news. Hence, all I had in my head was the greatest-hits versions of my colleagues' lives. I knew, of course, that Tommy had been in Vietnam, that Hoang was something of a celebrity on the Vietnamese karaoke circuit in San Jose, that Jackson had spent time in jail for GBH, that Sam was once a trained chef specializing in demi-glazing and sauces. But did any of them have children? Were they married? Did anyone collect stamps for a hobby?

I didn't know. Well, no longer. The next time Maggie asked me, 'Where does Sam live?' I would be able to look her in the eye and say, with all confidence, 'Fuck me, he lives in the world's grottiest flat.'

I'm not a snob, honestly. I've lived in condemned buildings with holes in the roof and water running down the walls. On one unforgettable occasion I even shared a bed with a rat. I bow to no one when it comes to creating domestic squalor. But none of this prepared me for Sam's apartment. I would say it was a pig sty but pigs might take offence.

The only furniture he had was a two-seater sofa, a nine-inch TV set and a bed that folded out of the wall. Unfortunately, there didn't appear to be any space for it to fold out on to. Rubbish was piled everywhere: newspapers, clothes, the detritus of twenty-year-old sporting enthusiasms – a wooden-framed tennis racket, rusting skis, a scattering of baseball gloves. The tiny galley kitchen was cut off from the rest of the room by a pile of black plastic bags stuffed with small dead animals, judging by the stench. Looking around the room, it occurred to me that if this was the kind of life that fifteen years in the used-car business had given Sam he should have been celebrating an escape rather than moping over the loss of a job. However hard I tried, I couldn't hide my queasiness.

'Yeah, it's not much of a place I know,' he said, looking slightly embarrassed. 'I meant to tidy up for you coming but, you know, with losing the job and all, I didn't feel like it. Come on, let's go out.'

We walked into town and had a beer at an Irish bar, then went for a coffee at Starbucks. It was a Friday night. The place was overflowing with a young, post-cinema, pre-club crowd. We sat by the window admiring their Californian tans and perfect teeth. We had been out for a couple of hours. Despite my best efforts to keep the conversation going, the truth was that we had nothing much to say other than swapping stories about the car business. As I didn't have many, Sam did most of the talking.

Disturbingly, he'd started off as a salesman the same way I had: by going to buy a car and being swept along in the excitement of the moment by a golden-tongued salesman. He had been vulnerable at the time, having just lost his life savings in a failed restaurant business and his girlfriend to a guy down the street who looked like Kirk Douglas. He'd hoped a new career would change his luck and it did for a while.

'When I first started, I loved the job,' he said, glassy-eyed.

Christ, so did I!

'I really enjoyed talking to the public, getting to know them and selling them a car. Sometimes you had to deal with the rudest or most stupid people but that only made it better when you managed to sell them a car.'

Gulp. That's exactly how I felt!

'Yeah, it's hard to describe the feeling you get when you do your first deal. It's better than . . .'

'Sex?' I said, fearing he might agree.

'That's right.'

He flashed his first smile of the night, as warm and fond as a father's, and I'm ashamed to admit I had a terrible premonition. What if the next fifteen years of my life were a pointless exercise, that I would end up the way of most used-car salesmen? What if Sam and I were the same person and I was heir to his world-breaking collection of yellowing newspapers, would one day live the heart-breaking life of a bag-person but pay fifteen hundred dollars a month in rent for the privilege?

Fortunately, the coincidences ended abruptly as he went on with his story.

'That first month I sold twelve cars, the month after that eighteen, and twenty the month after that.' I quickly transformed a sigh of relief into a gasp of admiration 'I was making better money than I ever had, maybe about seventy thousand a year. But I fell in with a bad crowd, drinking, partying, taking drugs all the time. There's a lot of sleazy people in this business, and you gotta stay away from them or you'll end up like me, lonely and broke.'

Harsh indeed, but he wasn't looking for sympathy and I didn't offer any. It was the truth, after all.

'I'm clean now, but the car business is different these days. It's harder. People are more stressed out, they know far too much for their own good. When they go to spend money on a car they don't want someone telling them what to do, especially salesmen. The problem is, they think we're making a million dollars from them. If only they knew the truth.'

On that mournful note, he drained the dregs of his coffee and stood up. He had a job interview in the morning and he was sure there was a clean shirt somewhere in the apartment, if only he could find it and then a steam iron. 'What's the job?' I asked, as we walked down the street towards my car.

'As a salesman in another dealership on the boulevard.'

'You're kidding? After all the car business has done to you?'

'Oh, the business didn't take anything away from me, it was my own stupidity, or karma or whatever you want to call it. Maybe I wasn't meant to have a lot of stuff – that's the way it is for some people. Maybe this job I'm seeing about tomorrow will be the best one I've had and I'll make enough money to buy my own car dealership. Maybe I'll find myself a nice woman to settle down with.'

'And maybe I'll be Salesman of the Month,' I almost said.

There was no point in arguing. I would have had more success persuading a junkie that messing around with needles might just possibly be bad for his health. Sam was sharp, if a touch eccentric, and eminently employable. It was probably too late for him to join the Backstreet Boys but he was living in Silicon Valley, the richest corner of the richest state in the richest country in the world – there had to be an alternative career out there for him somewhere. But he didn't want one: he was hopelessly addicted to life as a used-car salesman.

I supposed I should have been uplifted – the triumph of the indefatigable human spirit, the battle against the odds, etc. etc. – but in fact I was depressed and fearful on his behalf. What would become of him? Just like Hughie's plan to become the twenty-first-century Donald Trump, Sam's hopes of making a success of his own dealership were destined never to be fulfilled. Why was I so certain? Think about it: would you spend your hard-earned money on a used Cadillac from a place called Sam's Used Cars?

Maybe Tommy was right and Sam had a unique talent for crapping out people. Over-exposure to abject failure or hopeless optimism – and Sam could write learned textbooks on both – had a deadly effect on a salesman's fragile self-belief. The constant diet of rejection was hard enough to handle without having to watch someone else suffer through even greater misery or, worse, listen to them complain about it. It made your bones ache, like a flu virus. That was why anyone who was going through a rough patch found themselves frozen out, especially by the older, experienced salesmen. That's why Sam was abandoned by everyone but me.

So was he to blame for my slump?

The prosecution evidence was strong. I wasn't the same person after my night out in Burlingame. Before, I'd bounded into work every day like Bambi in spring-heeled boots. Afterwards, I crawled there, weighed down by listlessness and self-pity. Pre-Sam, I liked, or at least pretended to like, every customer I spoke to. Post-Sam, they all seemed to have brains the size of a walnut – the World's Most Stupid Man being a prime example. I began to think I'd never sell a car again. I went from being the seventh-best salesman on the lot to the worst, behind Tony, behind Jackson, behind – I'm embarrassed to say – Kim, who was belatedly spurred into action when Frankie pulled the hard drive from the office computer, denying him his beloved solitaire.

I wouldn't have felt so bad about any of this but I'd never tried harder in my life to be good at something. I loved being a car salesman. I had the right 'personality'. I liked the people I worked with and the customers seemed to like me – until I asked them if they wanted to buy the car, when they ran away. All things being equal, I should have been able to sell more cars than a sixty-one-year-old computer geek with the work ethic of a minor British royal. Besides, six thousand miles had been a long way to travel to make a fool of myself. Any fable that began with its 'hero' turning down a perfectly good job with stellar prospects to become a car salesman, then failing to sell any cars, deserved to end with the final line: 'Told you so.' Maggie was way too loyal ever to use such a phrase, but there were plenty of others who wouldn't have been so reticent. I was determined not to give them the chance.

As was traditional, none of the other salesmen mentioned my obvious and embarrassing failure. But I could sense a growing ostracism. I was left out of the coffee runs. Conversations halted suddenly whenever I appeared, as if I'd just walked in on an argument over who was to have the honour of telling me my flies had been open since the morning. Only Ernie from B Crew made any effort to encourage me. He'd seen salesmen suffering like this a thousand times before. I was merely having a run of bad luck. 'Don't worry about it. You've just got to keep walking through the raindrops until you get wet,' he said, mysteriously.

I took this internal exile manfully, at least for the first week. I worked extra hours. I revived Hughie's old 'I will sell a car today' mantra, adapting it slightly for the more desperate circumstances of the moment: 'I will sell a car today, please, God Almighty, I'm begging you, I promise to go to church every Sunday until Armageddon.' I even ordered some business cards.

At the Friday sales meeting, Jason the owner suggested we all keep a record of every encounter we had with customers, successful or otherwise, 'That way you'll know what you're doing right and where you're going wrong.' It seemed like a great idea at the time but when I read over my first day's notes . . .

Dave: very friendly, terrific relationship established, member of San Jose Municipal Golf Club, six-handicap, best score 67, played Pebble Beach last year, shot 82 in strong wind, missed birdie putts on sixth and 17th holes, had to leave for dental appointment, forgot to ask if he wanted to buy a car.

Ian Whittell: just arrived from New York, computer encryption specialist, will be millionaire in six months, currently broke, needed $3,000 car, showed him 1988 Taurus, not driving 'that piece of shit', showed him a 1986 Mazda, not driving 'that piece of shit', showed him 1983 Ford truck with furry seat covers and gun rack in cabin: 'Do I look like a guest on *The Jerry Springer Show?*' Gave up.

Miguel and family: wanted Mitsubishi Montero, took test drive, very impressed, willing to pay cash, accidentally slammed door on his finger, skin broken, blood everywhere, threatened to sue dealership.

. . . it felt more like self-flagellation than self-analysis.

For twenty-three days I walked in the wilderness.

Jesus did forty, but at least he suffered alone. I had to endure my humiliation in front of Mickey and Sunny. I couldn't be absolutely certain, but as the weeks passed I swear other dealerships were bussing salesmen over to our lot just so that they could watch me flounder. I was a living, breathing cautionary tale – *How Not to Master the Art of Selling* by Lawrence Donegan. Maggie eventually tired of asking me, 'How did it go?' when I got home at night and skipped straight to 'Never mind, there's always tomorrow,' before handing me a cold beer.

It didn't help either that the dealership was having a record month: 215 cars sold in twenty-three days. Eight salesmen had sold over ten cars, three of those had fifteen on the board.

A new recruit to B Crew, Gerry, was leading the Salesman of

the Month competition with twenty-three sales. This last statistic was all the more galling because Gerry, a fast-talking Irishman, was easily the crudest, most obnoxious salesman any of us had ever seen in action. His technique consisted of poking people in the chest and telling them in a loud, insistent voice, 'You're buying a car from me today, okay? Get your cheque book out.' Hoang described it as 'punking the customer'. How we all laughed. Ha bloody ha. Yet customers were queuing up to buy from Gerry, like fey third-formers waiting for an audience with the school bully. I spent night after night sitting on the porch watching and listening as he browbeat people into submission. Inevitably, amazement gave way to resentment, which then boiled up into irrational hatred. Of course it wasn't Sam's fault I was in a slump, it was Gerry's.

Mickey, in a unprecedented outbreak of concern for a struggling colleague, finally made me see sense. 'You can't blame anyone but yourself,' he said. Salesmen almost always talked themselves into a slump. He used to do it to himself all the time − when he was young and stupid, of course. Was I still trying to sell cars to Indian customers? Had I at any time believed a customer when they told me they couldn't buy a car right now because they were hungry and needed to eat but they'd be back in an hour with their cheque book? Did I ever step aside when another salesman said the young couple with the screaming child who'd just walked on to the lot were his next-door neighbours and they'd made an appointment with him to buy a car? Check, check and check again. I nodded.

'Exactly. Your problem is that you're a weak suck,' he said. 'Only one person's going to change that.'

Just then Frankie wandered out on to the porch for some fresh air. 'He's right, Scotty. You gotta get stronger. And remember, stick to fat Americans. That's where the juice is.'

Finally the torture ended when Tommy called me aside early one morning and told me that his brother would be coming in at noon to buy a car. He was my customer, he said, as long as I promised to pretend I was interested in his endless stories about his surfing trophies and war medals. It was a well-known fact in the car trade that closers only spooned customers to their very worst salesmen. I should have been deeply offended but there was no point in denying the truth. He walked away before I could kiss him.

Terry Browne's official title at the dealership was finance director. 'Bad Credit? No Problem!' declared two kitchen-table-sized billboards at the front of the lot. It was his job to fulfil the promise, which he did with a combination of rattlesnake charm and ballbreaking interest rates. Even the worst bankrupt could get a car loan from Terry, but at 22 per cent with penalty fees for late payment. Any objections and he quickly reminded the unfortunate buyer that they were in no position to negotiate. A tall, wiry New Yorker with pockmarked grey skin, he carried himself with military stiffness, tie loosened, trousers hitched closer to the chest than the waist. His manner was as abrupt as a head–on car crash.

Like everyone else on the lot who was looking for a quiet, non–confrontational life, I did my best to stay out of Terry's way. Fortunately, he wasn't around much. He spent half of the week in Reno, gambling his six–figure salary at the blackjack tables, and the other half schmoozing bankers over breakfast, lunch and dinner. At weekends he sat behind the sales desk with Frankie and Al, flicking through customers' credit reports like a detective sifting through the remnants of a suspicious warehouse fire.

'Fuck me, this guy don't pay nobody. Where d'you get him? In the gutter?' was as expansive as Terry got in conversation with a junior salesman like me. If he said any more it was only to deliver an insult or bad news, which was why I felt suddenly unwell when I heard him shout out my name. At the time I was still basking in the five–watt glow of my first sale for almost four weeks, certain at last that the only way left to go was up.

'Hey, you, Scotty,' he barked, waving me towards him. 'Come here a minute. I need you to go out with the Repo Man.'

I looked at him blankly, not sure what he was talking about.

'The Repo Man. You gotta pick up a car. *Comprende?*'

Eventually, I registered what he was saying. 'Why me?'

'You sold the fucking thing. That's why.' He shook his head, amazed that anyone so stupid would actually be allowed anywhere near a car lot without adult supervision. 'The guy'll be here in ten minutes. Go with him, pick up the car and bring it back here. I need it back today to keep the bank happy.'

Bad news. The Repo Man wasn't as muscular or threatening or tattooed as I imagined or hoped he would be. I found him sitting in the cab of his red Ford truck, studying the pages of a motorcycling magazine. The radio was tuned to a classical-music station.

'Dick?'

He looked up, smiled and stretched out his hand through the open window. 'Lawrence, right?'

Long-haired and clean-shaven, he exuded a quiet, priestly calm, like Jesus without a beard. At least he had an Alsatian dog, though it, too, was far from the snarling, flesh-ripping monster that any self-respecting debt collector should have owned. Tiger – *Tiger?* – barely stirred in the back seat of the cab as Dick turned on the engine and we wove through a maze of newly delivered cars towards the exit.

Good news. We were repossessing a 1993 Dodge I'd sold two months earlier to a customer called Chuck. I was still at the stage where I could remember every person who'd bought a car from me as clearly as if they were old girlfriends. Chuck was a mouse of a man. He was a bus driver, originally from Alabama, with short, spindly legs and a lustrous Elvis haircut that smothered his sun-wrinkled face like an oversized coat.

It had been an easy sale. He'd spotted the Dodge parked out front on the lawn when he'd been going past in the number thirty-two to downtown San Jose and had come in for a closer look after finishing work. He took the car for a test drive but only as far as two sets of traffic lights, never letting the needle rise above 30 m.p.h. 'It's not that I don't love the car, I do,' he said quietly, when we got back to the lot and I tried to coax him into a sales booth. 'I just can't buy it today. I need my wife with me.'

Naturally, I never expected to see him again but when I came back from McDonald's the following afternoon he was sitting under the tent with Sam, filling in a credit application. His wife was beside him. It turned out his credit rating was beyond resuscitation – even by Terry – which meant she had to write a five-hundred-dollar cheque for the down-payment. She looked unhappy as she scratched out her signature. It bounced, along with the first two monthly payment cheques.

'Don't worry about Chuck,' I said, remembering his soft Southern drawl and impeccable manners. 'I don't think he's going to be too much trouble.'

'We'll see,' said Dick cannily, like a wise old ship's captain heading towards the eye of a storm. Somewhere near the soles of my shoes I felt a tiny whirl of unease. I spent the rest of the journey trying to prise him out of his natural reticence while he did his best to keep me at bay with enigmatic shrugs and three-word answers.

Chuck lived on the west side of San Jose, about fifteen minutes from the lot – just enough time to squeeze out a few facts from Dick: repossessing cars wasn't his full-time job, he was a car mechanic, but the money in debt collection was good and it didn't take up much of his spare time. Nor was it dangerous work. Most bad debtors were relieved to get rid of the car and gave it up without an argument. Only once, when he'd gone to pick up a Cadillac in one of the rougher parts of Oakland, did someone brandish a shotgun at him. That was when it was time to call the police.

'I've been doing it for six months and I ain't been shot at yet,' he said solemnly. I half expected him to pull a black cloak across his face and laugh demonically. He did the next best thing: he reached out to touch the crucifix hanging from the rear-view mirror then muttered, 'Praise be to God.'

A Technicolor vision of Chuck barricaded inside his car, dynamite strapped to his body and a Kalashnikov trained on my crotch, flashed across my mind, until I caught the faintest grin on Dick's lips. 'You're taking the piss, aren't you?'

He started laughing. 'Of course I am, man. Don't worry, it's going to be all right. This is a nice neighbourhood, there shouldn't be any trouble. What we do is this: I've got a master key for the car. When we get there we put the dog in the car – they always get a fright when they see an Alsatian sitting in the back seat – then we knock on the door and tell them what we're doing. You drive it back to the lot, and that's it.'

Looking back, I almost wish Chuck had been lurking in the back seat of the car with a machete, or even an indignant expression on his face. For once, I would have had a story to impress the other salesmen. ('Shut up, Lawrence, we'll wait for the mini-series,' was the usual response whenever I tried to grab their attention with the details of my endeavours.) But it was as Dick had predicted, desperately tame.

The house was on a crescent of small but well-kept bungalows. It was a balmy late afternoon and most of the front doors were thrown open to the heat. Only number fourteen – our target – appeared deserted. The car was parked in the driveway. I stayed in the truck while Dick sneaked alongside, opened the driver's door and slipped his dog inside. There was a momentary flutter of excitement when a curtain stirred, then a window opened. It was Chuck's wife.

'What do you think you're doin'?' she said, in a slightly raised voice. Dick explained the bounced cheque and missing payments. She shrugged, as if it was none of her concern, and disappeared back inside.

It turned out she had never wanted the car in the first place. 'She actually said thanks,' Dick beamed, throwing me the keys.

An odd thing happened when I got back to the lot. There was a line of bored salesmen leaning on the porch railing, like spectators at a race track waiting for the two forty-five handicap to start. It was the hiatus between office closing hours and the little surge of customers that always arrived once they'd finished their evening meal.

'Look at this chump, selling cars to guys who can't afford them, getting me into trouble with the bank,' a voice from behind said, as I climbed the stairs and took my place on the rail. Terry had been watching me from the office. 'Hey, chump, you got the keys?'

I guessed this was what passed for light-hearted banter in the world of finance directors but I wasn't in the mood. It had dawned on me on the drive back that I now had the grand total of zero sales for the month — Tommy's brother's car minus Chuck's. There were only five days left to get on the board. Frankie had told me not to worry about being fired — 'I like your attitude, Scotty. I've never seen a guy take so many kickings and come back for more' — but even so the thought of blanking an entire month was depressing beyond belief. The last thing I needed was for Terry to humiliate me in front of the other salesmen. Besides, I hadn't taken the dud cheque from Chuck's wife, Sam had.

'I'm only trying to do my job, Terry,' I said, suddenly finding my indignation rising. 'And while you're at it, stop calling me a chump.'

I left out the 'or else' because there was no 'or else', though I was hoping he might have thought there was. He didn't.

'Listen, pal, I'll call you anything I fucking want. *Chump.*'

'Come on, guys, back off,' Tony said, laying his hand on Terry's shoulder. Suddenly, everyone looked interested, as if the horse race had just rounded the final bend.

'Hey, buddy, you know how long I've been working here at this lot?' He had a cigarette in his mouth. It waggled at me as he spoke, like an angrily pointed finger.

Frankly, I didn't give a shit how long he'd been working at the lot. 'Frankly, I don't give a shit how long —'

'Fourteen years, that's how long. And you know how many salesmen I've seen come and go in the fourteen years? Thousands. Ten a fuckin' penny, the lot of them.'

He walked away, lit his cigarette, then hitched up his trousers. For a moment I thought the argument was over but he turned round again. 'If you don't like anything I say, you know what you can do, pal. You can pick up your licence and hit the fucking pavement.'

I looked at Terry. He was smirking, playing to the crowd. If I'd been thinking straight I would just have ignored him but it had been a rotten day, a rotten month. Suddenly, it seemed like the best idea in the world so I did what he suggested. I hit the fucking pavement.

12

I took my seat at the San Jose arena too late for the communal hug but just in time for the incantations. Far below me, on an Amazonian stage set of potted plants and fake plastic trees, a man in a dark blue suit wandered around looking like Tarzan's tax accountant. 'Repeat after me,' he boomed. 'At last, at last, the past is past, we've broken free and won, and now it's time to love ourselves and really have some fun.'

I'd come across Anthony Robbins before. He'd once revived the career of a friend of mine, a professional golfer called Ross Drummond, who had bought a tape of his called *Awaken the Giant Within* at a motorway service station for a couple of pounds. I didn't stop laughing for two days. What giant? No offence, but here was a man who hadn't won a golf tournament in nineteen years. A week later Ross beat Nick Faldo by fourteen strokes and won the biggest cheque of his life. That's what persuaded me to go to the Anthony Robbins roadshow. If a cassette tape could inspire one of the world's most under-achieving golfers to greatness (albeit fleeting), what might a close encounter with the great man himself do for one of the world's most under-achieving used-car salesmen?

The cheapest ticket cost a hundred dollars. This entitled me to the worst seat in the house, somewhere near the rafters beside a wide-eyed legal secretary called Barbara ('Isn't this the greatest thing?' she said, with a born-again smile as I sat down). I vaguely remembered reading somewhere that California's 'self-help' industry made $10 billion a year. I knew, too, that Anthony Robbins was big business. Even so, nothing had prepared me for the sight and sound – the religious fervour – of ten thousand apparently sane people on their feet with their hands in the air, reciting his greetings-card doggerel as if it had just arrived in an envelope from heaven.

The incantations over, a succession of speakers trooped on to the stage: a healthy-eating specialist, a tax counsellor, a 'goals' adviser. They were all male, middle-aged and oily. All had the same message: that every member of the audience had it in them to become millionaires in the next year but only if they purchased the boxed set of life-enhancing CDs on sale in the foyer at today's bargain price of sixty-nine dollars. Barbara dashed out and bought two sets. I sat in my seat, brooding. The 'experts' weren't telling me anything I wanted to know, they were selling me cassettes. And I had paid good money for the privilege of listening to them pitch. The roadshow ended at four o'clock. Robbins bounced back on stage, pronounced us all cured and instructed us to 'Get out there and take on the world.' Walking out into the sunshine, I felt like I'd been mugged.

I took a detour along Orchard Boulevard on the way home for nostalgia's sake, slowing down as I passed the car lot. That was when my thoughts turned to the Roll of Honour on the office wall and the name that had appeared there thirty-five consecutive times. 'The sleaziest, dirtiest, lyingest, cheatingest bastard I've ever met in my entire life,' Sunny had said, 'but the best salesman I've ever seen.' Suddenly the answer was obvious. Forget Anthony Robbins and his hundred-dollars-a-ticket New Age, existential clap-trap. If anyone could teach me how to become a great used-car salesman, it was Rob Mills – Orchard Boulevard Pre-Owned Autos Salesman of the Month, June 1993 to May 1996.

He was ancient history at Orchard, which was why none of the older salesmen had been interested in feeding my curiosity about him: it's not what you've done in the car business it's what you're gonna do and blah, blah, blah. He'd left in the autumn of '96, in disgrace. Tommy shook his head and smirked when I asked why. Sunny responded with a long stream of vitriol.

One of the salesmen from the new-car dealership had told me he was in San Quentin doing time for a $2 million tax fraud. 'Not true,' said someone else. The tax fraud was right but he'd made a plea bargain, served a reduced sentence and was paying back the money in instalments. He was out of jail now. 'He called me a year back and asked me if I'd do some sales-motivation talk for him,' Frankie said. When that came to nothing, he'd got his sales licence back and had gone to work at a used-car lot over at Cantwell Expressway, a strip of dealerships in east San Jose.

Cantwell Cars was a step up from Orchard, the kind of place that ran half-hour infomercials on cable television after midnight. Cool and calm inside, it felt more like a doctor's surgery than a car lot. Vivaldi wafted along on the air-conditioning breeze. The receptionist was dark-haired, pretty and suspicious.

'Are you a cop?'

'No, I'm a friend of his,' I said.

She hesitated then decided I looked responsible enough to be trusted with a state secret. 'He hasn't worked here for at least a year. I don't know where he is now.' Just then a salesman hurried past. 'Kenny, this guy here is looking for Rob Mills – any idea where he might find him?'

Kenny spun round. 'Who wants to know? Not another cop, is it?'

I explained again that he was a friend of mine, that I had a problem and was looking for his advice.

He looked at me as if I'd just said something immensely stupid. 'Christ, must be some problem.' He lowered his voice: 'Menlo Park Motors. You never heard it from me.'

The reception at Menlo Park was just as guarded. A couple of salesmen jumped to attention when I pulled on to the lot. The enthusiasm evaporated when I told them I wasn't buying a car, that I was trying to find Rob Mills. The younger of the two – Denis, according to his nametag – gave a dumb shrug, the other smirked. 'He's retired,' he lied.

'Come off it, I worked with him at The Orchard. Please?'

'Bad luck.'

He mentioned the name of a car dealership in Sunnyvale where the owner had apparently lost all power of cognitive thought and given Mills a job as the used-car manager, then went off to talk to a customer. I turned again to Denis, who shrugged dumbly. Clearly, this was his answer to everything in life. 'I've only been working here for a month,' he said, finally. 'I didn't know this guy you're talking about but apparently there was a lot of strange stuff going on when he was here. I heard the place almost went bankrupt because he was selling the cars too cheap.'

Selling cars too cheaply! No wonder they fired him.

First things first: it wasn't a $2 million tax fraud, it was a $248,785 tax fraud. Strictly speaking, it wasn't fraud either – it was a failure to hand over sales-tax proceeds. Second, he hadn't been selling cars on the cheap: he had been giving the customers the kind of deal that would make them his customers for ever.

'I never wanted to miss out on a deal, that was the biggest problem. I used to sell cars for a lot less than they were worth because I knew then that the customer would come back. I don't think of them as being buyers just for that one day, I look at them as part of my portfolio of buyers for life.'

I was sitting in a Mexican café across the street from the crummiest-looking car lot in the western world, listening to the life and troubled times of Rob Mills. In my head I'd pictured him as a prize-fighter, lean, compact and impatient. In fact, he was the opposite: big as a Sumo wrestler, soft-spoken, with unkempt curly fair hair hanging over his collar and sad brown eyes that seemed constantly on the verge of tears of gratitude that someone had taken the trouble to seek him out. His teeth were false but expensive-looking. He was dressed in dark grey trousers with an ironing-board sheen, pale blue shirt with a stained white collar, a loosened red tie and scuffed black leather shoes. The chunky 'Salesman of the Year' ring on his right index finger looked too golden to be real gold.

He'd been in the car business fifteen years, since he was nineteen. He started at a pot lot in a less salubrious area of San Diego and worked his way north to Silicon Valley. You name it, he'd sold it: Mercedes, wrecks, BMW, repos, Lexus, ex-rentals. The Orchard was the best place he'd ever worked. In one month at the dealership – August 1994 – he'd had his name on seventy-eight deals. Eventually, they gave him the desk manager's job. He lasted six months, long enough to make a fifty-thousand-dollar loss. 'The owner said

I was giving the fucking cars away,' he said, chuckling at the memory. 'He was right. I didn't give a shit about the price or the commission – I was just addicted to selling.'

Finally, he went into partnership with his brother and, whoops, they accidentally spent the 8 per cent sales tax they received from customers instead of sending it to the state. He spent a year in a minimum-security prison, though they let him out during the day to work. He still kept winning the Salesman of the Month competitions. And now he was reduced to this: a dusty square on the edge of a housing estate littered with a handful of ten-year-old dented cars and a garden shed dressed up as an office. It was like finding Frank Sinatra singing in a Ramada Inn cocktail bar.

'I like it here,' he said. 'I'm not the owner, I just run the place for the guy. I do my hours, go home and look after my mother. She's sick, you know. It's only going to be for a short while, until I get a few things sorted out. I still owe the tax man a hundred thousand dollars. I've promised to pay it off in instalments.'

It was tribute to his persuasive powers that the IRS had taken him at his word. I wasn't so sure. He could work across the street for a couple of centuries and not make a hundred thousand dollars. I asked him how many cars he'd sold in the last week. Contrary to Sunny's description, he wasn't a world-class liar. 'Fifteen,' he said, blushed, then quickly changed the subject. 'Anyway, what are you doing here?'

I told him I'd been working at Orchard, that I'd seen his name on the plaques on the office wall and had heard on good authority – Sunny's – that he was the best car salesman I'd could ever hope to meet.

'Sunny said that about me?'

'Kind of.' I lowered my gaze to the table. 'Anyway . . . I was hoping you could help me become a better salesman.'

'How many cars did you sell last month?'

'None.'

'No, really, how many?'

'None. Well, one – but then I had another that unwound. So . . . none, really.'

It was obviously beyond Rob's comprehension that someone could work on a car lot for an entire month and not make a single sale but then he realized I was serious and stopped laughing. 'That's not a problem,' he said, taking a deep breath.

He grabbed a milk carton that was sitting on the table next to us. 'Look at this carton, look at the beautiful design. When you go to the grocery store to buy milk it's an automatic sale, but that didn't stop the guy designing these beautiful cartons. You know why?'

I sat up straight, intrigued. What did milk cartons have to do with selling cars? I couldn't wait to find out.

'Because he had passion. He was passionate about selling milk – he wanted the customers who were buying the milk to have the best experience of their lives. You've got to be the same way.'

Frankly, I was disappointed. I was expecting an epiphany, a stunning revelation, not another monologue about passionate selling and its mythical powers. Look what had happened when I'd cast myself as the Sacha Distel of cars sales: no one had swooned or bought my records or thrown their knickers on the stage – they had gone straight to the box office and asked for a refund. Customers didn't like me when I tried to be passionate: they thought I was being creepy.

'That's because you treat their rejection as a negative,' Rob said.

'That's because rejection is a negative.'

'Don't be stupid, man. Rejection is good.' He rocked back on his seat, looking so self-assured that I didn't have the confidence to argue.

Looking back, I guess this was my epiphany. Here was someone who owed a hundred thousand dollars and had no hope of ever paying it back. He'd been exiled to used-car Siberia, his mother was ill, he'd sold his own Mercedes to pay lawyers' bills, and his ex-colleagues – at least the ones I'd talked to – thought he was a crook. All I had to complain about was not selling a car for a month and being called a chump by the finance director. So how come Rob sounded like he'd eaten Anthony Robbins for breakfast and I was the suicidal one? Why had he sold seventy-eight cars in one month and I had sold none?

He obviously knew something I didn't and perhaps this was it – Rejection Was Good! Even if he was wrong I had nothing to lose by trusting him. I could never be as good a salesman as he was but I would be happy with one-tenth of what he had. After all, one-tenth of seventy-eight deals was 7.8 cars a month. I'd settle for that.

As if he hadn't been helpful enough already, he then gave me the best selling tip I'd heard since starting out in the car business. I wrote it down and pinned it to the bathroom mirror: *When a customer says 'no', most of the time they actually mean 'yes' – they just don't know it yet. You've just got to show them that they mean 'yes'.*

'You don't have to be forceful in taking on their objections,' Rob said. 'You can sell to customers by making them feel that there doesn't have to be a sale today. Do this. I promise you it'll work. Sell them a car just like you're selling them milk. Imagine you're standing behind the counter at the grocery store and they come up with this carton of milk in their hand. "A pint of milk, sir? Great, let me just ring that up for you." Be relaxed. Let them think you couldn't give a shit whether they bought the car or not.'

This was perfect! I might not be able to sell cars but I could definitely sell milk. Passion was beyond me, but not giving a shit was right up my street.

We sat for another hour. He did most of the talking, reminiscing about his days at The Orchard. I told him about the argument with Terry and that I'd walked out. He laughed and said I wasn't to worry. In his day, a shift wasn't complete unless he'd had a fight with Terry or a customer or with Sunny – *especially* Sunny: 'I can't believe he's been saying those nice things about me.'

I felt bad. He was my newly appointed maharishi: he deserved the truth. I told him what Sunny had really said, the unexpurgated version.

For the first time since we'd met, and possibly since he was born, he stopped smiling. 'I knew it.' He looked wounded. 'People love me, people hate me. The ones who aren't positive are the ones who are jealous, the poor people who say things out of fear that they'll never be as good as me. If I'm selling seventy cars a month or whatever, I'm taking some of their income away – of course they'll hate me.'

Even I didn't believe he was a saint. 'So the stories are all made up?'

'I never lied, I never cheated – not with customers.'

As soon as the words were out he realized how ridiculous they sounded and confessed a few minor sins, like tailoring prices according to the quality of a customer's footwear (the better the leather, the more they could afford to pay for a car). It had been much worse in the old days before DMV inspectors started prowling the car lots. Back then, there were sophisticated technical scams, involving electric drills and odometers, banana skins in the gear-box, sugar in the petrol tank and five-speed gear-knobs on four-gear cars.

'Yeah, I've heard the gear-knob story.' I laughed. 'It was some guy who ended up working in Arizona – right?'

He looked at me the way Picasso might have looked at a roomful of cheap forgeries. 'Who told you that?' He sighed and shook his head, appalled that someone else was claiming the credit for his masterwork. 'No way, man, that was me. That was my scam.'

It was getting late and Rob had some paperwork to finish before going home. I paid the bill, we shook hands and when I let go he asked me if I wanted to come and work for him. I was tempted but then I looked across the street. His lot was deserted but for a dog pissing against the hubcap of maroon '91 Buick with a cracked windscreen. No matter how much he taught me I knew I'd never sell that car.

'Thanks for the offer,' I said, 'but there's only one place I really want to work.'

The plan was to go back to the lot, pretend I'd come to pick up my sales licence, then fall to my knees and beg for my job back. Frankie saved me the trouble. An argument with Terry wasn't a sacking offence, he said, it was an occupational hazard. Anyway, Sunny had fired another two guys and he was short of salesmen. A week off work was probably just what I'd needed to get my head straightened out. 'You feelin' good, Scotty? You feelin' strong? You ready for some customer love?' He opened a drawer, pulled out a disgusting green tie and threw it at me.

I nodded.

'Well, put the tie on and go out there and get them.'

It was as if I'd been gone for a minute, not a week. The weather, the mid-week torpor, the fag ends in the potted plants – nothing had changed. Tony, Jackson, Mickey and Kim were sitting round a table eating McDonald's. Hoang was out on the lot, pulling at the sleeve of an elderly Chinese customer who was trying to escape. Tommy was standing down by the radio speakers talking to Terry, who broke off the conversation as soon as he saw me.

I had hoped to avoid him for a while – at least until I was the manager of the dealership and in a position to fire him for being an objectionable big shit. My stomach tightened as he walked towards me until I noticed he was grinning. I'd never seen Terry smile before. There was a big black gap where his dental plate used to be. He looked deranged. 'Hey, pal, good to have you back,' he said, slapping me on the back. 'Sorry about that stuff the other day. But you know me – an hour later it's all forgotten.'

'It is?'

Mickey couldn't contain his disappointment at the outbreak of goodwill. 'Yeah, he really loves you – that's why he called you a fucking chump.'

'Chump?' Terry looked confused, as if a mallet had appeared out of nowhere and smacked him on the head. 'I swear, in my life I've never used that word. Chump? Did I call you a chump, Scotty?'

Once we'd established that he had indeed called me a chump and a whole lot worse but that this was perfectly reasonable because I was just a stupid European who sold cars to people who couldn't afford a bus ticket he went off to telephone his bookie, leaving me to become reacquainted with the witty, sophisticated diversions of the salesman's life that I'd missed so much.

'Fifty bucks says I can get that guy to jump up and down in the trunk of a car,' Jackson said, leaping out of his seat. A man in a pale blue anorak was walking his dog along the boulevard at the front of the lot.

'Deal.' Mickey offered his hand for a high-five. Jackson slapped it and ran down the stairs, shouting, 'Excuse me, sir, you've just dropped a ten-dollar bill. Look, here, under this truck . . .'

There weren't many chances to test drive Rob's advice. Business was awful. According to my colleagues, who discussed such matters with an expertise usually confined to editorial meetings of the *Wall Street Journal*, the greatest orgy of consumer spending in Californian history was over. Every dot com company in Silicon Valley had gone bust in the last month, interest rates were too high and the NASDAQ index was worth half what it had been at the start of the year. Worse than any of this, Al was in a rotten mood.

'If they don't like *that* price, tell them to piss off.' He threw a sheaf of paperwork back over the counter at Tony.

It was Saturday afternoon, three days after I'd come back to work, and I hadn't sold a car. The only consolation was that hardly anyone else had either. Tommy was in the middle of telling me it was the worst weekend he could remember since a Vietcong commando stabbed his backside with a rusty bayonet when a battered old Toyota sports car pulled up at the kerb and two people jumped out. One of them was carrying a folder.

'Go on, get these guys before anyone from B Crew does,' he said, pushing me off the porch.

For once in my life I sauntered rather than ran, capturing – in my own head at least – the languid cool of Frank Sinatra in 'Ocean's Eleven', because (a) that's what Rob Mills had told me to do, and (b) there was no need to rush anyway. Folders were the ultimate car-salesman repellent. No one from B Crew wanted to talk to these two people because inside that folder there were almost certainly screeds of useful information downloaded from the Internet about how to buy a used car, all of it carefully annotated and absorbed. They might as well have been waving placards that said, 'Don't waste your time – we know too much.'

Todd was carrying the folder. He was an earnest young

University of San Francisco student who'd been given money by his parents to buy a car. As I suspected, he'd done enough research to write the definitive book on the Japanese automobile industry. I could understand that, admire it, even – he didn't want to waste his folks' money. His friend Kevin, however, was a pompous twerp.

'My main field of study in genomics – I've just finished my Ph.D. – but really I'm a philosopher,' he boasted, as we wove along the row of cars.

'Oh, really?' I said, trying to strike a balance between *faux* boredom (as prescribed by Rob) and the real thing (what I was feeling). I pointed at an old Ford Thunderbird. 'How about this one? It's got a couple of bass woofers in the back that would blow Elton John's wig off.'

'Look at this!' Todd opened the door of a dark green Honda. I'd never noticed it before but at first glance it looked perfect. It was ten years old, with low mileage, springy seats and tread on the tyres. I went into the office to find out how much we were asking. Six thousand dollars.

'Good price!' By now Todd was sitting in the driver's seat with a proprietorial smile on his face. Kevin was poking around the engine. 'Can we take it for a test drive?'

This was a car deal, as long as I didn't blow it by making a stupid remark or appearing too desperate. Normally I could be relied on to do both but for once I didn't break out in a flop sweat or ask if they'd heard the one about the woman who bought a car from The Orchard whose engine had exploded as she was driving it home. Instead, I spent the entire test drive in confident silence. I didn't even flinch when Kevin, who was a bit of a rally driver as well as a world-class know-all, did a spot of two-wheel cornering in a supermarket car park.

A wonderful thing happened when we returned. A middle-aged Filipino woman ran towards the car, as if she'd just won it in a game show. The scene was so perfectly choreographed I wondered if she was an actor Tommy had hired to gee my customers along.

'You think she's going to buy it, Lawrence,' Todd said worriedly, as we watched her slide into the driver's seat.

To be honest, I was starting to panic too. She was with Ernie. If anyone could sell her the car it was him. Not even the news that she'd have to pay six thousand dollars to drive it away dampened her enthusiasm. If I'd been thinking straight I would have frogmarched Todd into the sales booth right then but my head was swimming with thoughts of Rob Mills and grocer-shop counters and a song that Frank Sinatra might have sung, 'Let me ring-a-ding-ding that carton of milk up for you right away, baby'.

'Who knows?' I shrugged, as if I had far weightier problems to think about than whether or not he was about to be gazumped on a stupid car. 'Tell you what, I'll just be over at the porch. You guys take five minutes to talk about it and let me know what you want to do.'

Tommy told me not to worry about Ernie's customer. She visited the lot at least once a fortnight but never bought anything. She just liked talking to salesmen. He provided a whispered commentary on what Todd and Kevin were doing while I extravagantly practised my golf swing. I didn't look up until I heard the sound of footsteps coming towards me.

'Keep swinging, let them come to you,' Tommy said, with a paternal smile. 'Good boy. You got us a car deal.'

I suspect even the Old Me would have sold Todd the green Honda. It was a great car. He loved it. But I don't think the Old Me would have had the confidence to go into the booth and close the deal. That guy wouldn't have had the bottle to push Al's offer across the desk and say, 'Fifty dollars discount — it's the best I can do. Take it or leave it.' In the past I wouldn't have sat in silence for ninety-five seconds — he who talks first loses! — until Todd stretched out his hand and said, 'Okay, deal.'

Nor would the Old Me have been able to keep a straight face when I told Todd I was buying him one month's car insurance out of the goodness of my heart. The truth was, he couldn't drive the car home legally without insurance coverage and Al didn't want it left on the lot overnight. If he had the chance to look again on the Internet he might have discovered he was paying two thousand dollars too much for a ten-year-old Honda and then changed his mind. 'Once he's driven it off the lot, he can't cancel his cheque,' Al had said.

'We only do it for customers we like,' I said.

'God, you guys are the best,' beamed Kevin, the great philosopher.

Rob Mills would have been proud.

13

Fiona was next. She was a soldier in Maggie's expanding army of new friends. They had met at a 'Grounding, Centring and Expanding Consciousness' class at the local recreation hall, where they discovered their mutual scepticism towards husky-voiced hippies in leotards who believed that the secret to a better life lay in breathing more deeply, as well as a shared Scottishness.

In Fiona's case the Scottishness was buried beneath three generations of fully assimilated immigrant genes. To the naked eye she was quintessentially middle-class Californian, from her healthy tan and honeyed accent to her gorgeous children and airy house in the hills above the city. This seemed to fill her with genetic remorse and she was determined to forge a spiritual connection with the Motherland. She called her son Torcuil, she could recite 'Tam O'Shanter' and once a week she went to the British Food Store in San Jose where she spent seventeen dollars on a packet of Simmers shortbread. Needless to say, she was always first in the queue for tickets to any social event that could vaguely be described as 'Scottish'.

Having long believed in the old adage 'If you loved the country so much why did you leave it in the first place?', I had made strenuous efforts since arriving in California to avoid anything and anybody that could be deemed 'expat'. Fiona fell into this category. I'd spoken to her, but only on the phone. I'd seen her, but only through the kitchen window when she came to pick up Maggie to go to their ridiculous classes. She seemed pleasant enough but I didn't want to take the risk of socializing with her in case expatriatism was contagious. Eventually, I didn't have a choice.

'Fiona's asked us to go to the Pleasanton Highland Games,' Maggie announced one afternoon when I came in from work.

'I'd rather drink weed-killer.'

'But she's bought the tickets for us. It'll be great. It's the biggest Highland games in the world.'

'Great. My one day off in the week and I get to spend it with twenty-five thousand drunks.'

'Does that mean you don't want to go?'

'How did you guess?'

'Fiona thinks you're weird – Mr Anti-social.'

'I think she's weird – Mrs Auchtermuchty. If she loves Scotland so much why doesn't she live there? There's bound to be a council flat in Partick she could rent.'

'It's not Fiona's fault her great-great-grandad was kicked out of his croft to make way for sheep.'

This domestic bickering lasted for weeks until in a moment of weakness, brought on by selling the Honda to Todd a day earlier, I caved in and went to the games. Of course I'd never admit it in public but I actually had a good time. We arrived just as the bagpiping tournament ended (always the best part, if you ask me), wandered through the endless rows of stalls selling clan regalia and then went to the main arena to watch the traditional highland games. I could have made the scorching sociological case that tossing the caber was about as relevant to modern Scotland as Mel Gibson's stupid bloody film about William Wallace but that would have been mean-spirited in the circumstances. Fiona, Brian and their children were good company, it was a glorious day, twenty-five thousand kilt-wearers were enjoying themselves and, anyway, there was something irresistible about the cosmic futility of fat, grown men in wool skirts trying to throw a tree trunk over on itself.

Afterwards, we enjoyed the more authentic Scottish experience of a punch-up during the final of the five-a-side football tournament, followed by a plate of pie and beans. We were about to head home when Brian mentioned they were thinking about buying a third car. He asked me for advice. In the past I would probably have directed him to another dealership down the street from The Orchard, where the salesmen were less pushy and the interior décor was more in keeping with his status as a company director. If I'd been feeling really bold, I might have suggested he could, but only if he wanted to, come to The Orchard and I might be able to get him a car at a good price. Not any more.

I reached into my back pocket and pulled out a freshly minted business card, saying, 'Come to the lot tomorrow and I'll earn your business.'

He hesitated. Presumably, he'd heard via Fiona, who'd picked it up from Maggie, that shopping for a car at The Orchard wasn't exactly a Rolls-Royce experience. Blushing, he made some excuse about wanting to buy a new car.

'By definition, Brian, there is no such thing as a new car,' I said, catching his evasive gaze. I placed a friendly hand on his shoulder. 'Think about it, the minute you drive that vehicle off the showroom floor it is no longer a new car, it's a used car. Do you really want to pay an extra five grand just for the pleasure of knowing that before you drove your car home it was "new"?'

Was any of this true? I suppose it was, when you think about it. In all honesty, I'd never actually thought about it before. Even if I had I would never said it to someone if there had been the remotest chance I'd ever meet them again in a social situation. It was too pushy, too salesman-y.

'Did I really tell him I was going to earn his business?' I asked Maggie, as we walked back to the car park.

She laughed. 'You sure did, and very scary it was too. Even I wanted to buy a car from you and I know how crap a salesman you are.'

I spent the journey home pondering this curious turn of events – Todd and Kevin yesterday, Fiona and Brian today – and came to the only logical conclusion: someone or something, the spirit of Rob Mills or possibly an alien with a bullying complex, had taken over my body, replaced my own wimpish personality with a more assertive model and downloaded a brand-new vocabulary into my voice-box.

When Fiona and Brian turned up at The Orchard the next morning I could sense they were only there because of Fiona's loyalty to Maggie. It was probably the first time they'd ever visited a car dealership where the toilets smelt like Calcutta. Ignoring their obvious apprehension, I quickly found them the best car on the lot, persuaded Frankie they were the best friends I had in California and were therefore entitled to a thousand-dollar discount. We finished the paperwork outside, in the fresh air. It was all over and done with in forty-five minutes.

'Good job, Scotty. Two in two days – you're on fire,' Frankie said, as they drove off in their used (but good as brand-new *and* five thousand dollars cheaper) BMW.

'I'm not finished yet,' I replied, in a clipped, moody voice that I imagined made me sound like Scotland's answer to Arnold Schwarzenegger. For once the confidence was justified. I really hadn't finished yet.

An hour later, while everyone else was sitting around drinking coffee and bitching about Gerry's latest sales pitch to female customers ('Hey, baby, you know you want it', *pause*, 'The car, that is!'), I spotted my next triumph striding through the back entrance. He was looking for a car for his son.

'How much is this one?' He pointed at a '99 Honda. 'And I don't want any lies.'

Later on, the bushy moustache, the arrogant gait and the unsurpassed rudeness all made sense when I found out that he was an off-duty California Highway patrolman, but at the time I was flabbergasted. Did he know he was talking to someone who'd sold two cars in two days? I suppressed the urge to show him my commission slips, settling instead for some mild sarcasm. 'Excuse me, sir, but we . . .' I began, in my best Bertie Wooster accent.

He opened the car door and kept talking. 'I'm fed up with car salesmen lying to me all the time. What's wrong with the lot of you? Is this car under warranty?'

'I'll have to check. If you just wait here while I go and ask someone . . .'

He kicked the tyres absent-mindedly, then stared at me as if I'd stolen his wallet. 'Don't lie to me now.'

'I'm not in the business of lying to customers, *sir*.'

'Well, you'll be the first car salesman I've ever met who isn't.'

That was when I succumbed to the feeling that I – that all car salesmen – didn't have to put up with this kind of crap. Before I could stop myself the words slipped out: 'Well, if that's how you feel you can piss off and buy a car elsewhere.'

This was pushing it, even for Arnold Schwarzenegger. Unless I hadn't been paying attention, telling customers to 'piss off' had never featured among the top sales tips suggested by Jason the owner at his weekly meetings. Of course, I'd heard Sam using this revolutionary technique but look what happened to him. Mentally, I started preparing for the disciplinary hearing but when I looked at Earl he was smiling. 'Perfect,' he said, his face flushed with admiration. 'Just the kind of salesman I like – someone with balls.'

Two cars sold before three o'clock on a Monday! This was how Superman must have felt when he leaped over tall buildings. Even Sunny was impressed. 'I'd shake you're hand, Scotty, but you're so fucking hot I'm scared I'll get third-degree burns,' he said, only half sarcastically.

I stayed past the end of my shift on the pretext of selling another car but, really, I hung around for the same reason I wouldn't want to leave the ground if Celtic beat Real Madrid 6–1 in the Champions' League final. I wanted to wallow in the moment for ever. I wanted the salesmen from B Crew to turn up for work, take a cursory glance at the board, then keel over with shock when they saw who was responsible for 100 per cent of the sales made by Orchard Boulevard Pre-Owned Autos so far that day. The one thing I wasn't hanging around for was to take a phone call from a woman called Alison, who said I'd sold her a car a few weeks before.

'Alison? Of course I remember,' I lied. I cherished my successful sales the way a philatelist cherishes a collection of stamps, taking them out of the wrapping every once in a while to admire their rarity, but however hard I tried I couldn't remember selling a car to anyone called Alison.

She sounded irritated. 'Andrea, the name is Andrea. You sold me a car for my son.'

'Andrea, of course. The white Honda, it was for your son, he was going to college. Great, fantastic . . .' Great? Fantastic? Who was I kidding? The only time a salesman heard from customers after a sale was when there was a problem with the car. 'Don't tell me, it's blown up.'

'There's nothing wrong with the car . . .'

'Oh, thank Christ,' I said, prematurely.

'. . . apart from the price you charged us.'

'What do you mean?'

She launched into a long, confused story, which started with her son not having enough money in the bank to honour the postdated cheque he'd written for the $250 down-payment and ended by veering dangerously, like a car with a faulty steering column, into a garage where she'd taken the Honda for an oil change. Apparently, the mechanic had discovered a multitude of problems while changing the oil, including, coincidentally, a faulty steering column.

'He told me the car was only worth four thousand dollars. We paid six thousand.' Somewhere in the telling of the story Andrea's tone had change from irritation to lip-trembling admonition. 'We are not rich people, Mr Donegan.'

I could have told her not to pester me with petty complaints, that her credit rating was crap and we did her a favour in actually selling her a car. But that would have been following Terry's instructions – issued when I put my hand over the phone, quickly explained the problem and asked him what I should do. I wasn't quite capable of that kind of incivility just yet, thankfully.

I scrambled around for something comforting to say, if not for her then at least for me. 'But it's a nice car, isn't it?' was the best I could manage at such short notice.

'It's okay,' she conceded, 'but two thousand dollars? That's a lot of money to a family like ours, Mr Donegan. My son is going to college and he could have done with that two thousand dollars to survive.'

If we'd been engaged in a pub brawl rather than a journey to the outer limits of pathos I would have been lying in the sawdust by now, curled up in a ball and sobbing, and Andrea would have realized it was time to stop stomping on my head with her Dr Martens. Alas, she wasn't finished with me yet.

'You seemed like such a nice person.' She sighed, though somewhere in the distance I thought I detected the tiniest hint of a sob. 'I suppose it's my own fault. I should have checked how much it was worth before I bought it. But we were desperate. Is it too late to get some of our money back?'

She was right first time. Frankie was a fundamentally decent man but the chances of him refunding two thousand dollars to a customer six weeks after they'd bought a car were too minuscule to be measured. In the circumstances, she deserved an honest answer. I settled for misplaced optimism instead. I promised to ask the boss for her money back, adding with a flourish, 'I'm not saying we'll get it all, but he's good man and we might get a thousand dollars.'

I talked to Frankie as soon as Andrea hung up. He laughed, asked me if I'd been smoking crack. When I said I hadn't, he told me I should: it might put me back in touch with reality.

There had been a time when Andrea's phone call would have inflicted terrible damage. The guilt would have grown five heads and a thousand tentacles. It would have tortured my conscience for months, inflicting stress rashes. Maggie would have wasted hours of her precious time reassuring me that I wasn't Lucifer's lanky Scottish offspring. I might even have gone to church seeking salvation. None of this happened, though I didn't sleep too well that night. But that was because of excitement.

Don't get me wrong. I felt terrible about Andrea and her son. I'd ripped them off, even though I could justifiably claim that I didn't know this at the time. I promised myself I'd right the wrong. The details could be worked out later, when I wasn't so preoccupied with the startling fact that I'd now sold three cars in two days.

I'd never come anywhere close to that before. It might have been luck but somehow I didn't think so. Consider the evidence: (1) The last place from which Fiona and Brian wanted to buy a car was The Orchard, and (2) Earl started off believing I was an inveterate liar. These weren't piddling objections, the kind you overcame by luck. Once, maybe, but not twice and not on the same day. You did it by being in control.

If you ain't leading, you ain't winning. Frankie had said that a long time ago, soon after I started as a salesman. I wrote it down in my notebook at the time, though I wasn't quite sure what it meant. Now I did. It meant bulldozing your girlfriend's friends into writing you a cheque for thirty-two thousand dollars and slapping people like Earl Steinberg back into line, yet leaving them feeling that you'd done them a favour. That's what proper salesmen did. That's why I couldn't sleep. I was waiting for the morning. I wanted to make sure I could do it again.

It wasn't just that I felt different, everybody at the lot started to treat me differently. Tommy stopped acting like he was the sympathetic primary-school teacher and I was the only one left in the class who couldn't read or write. Al started acting as if I was his friend – an unprecedented accolade for a mere salesman, according to the older hands. Tony, Ernie, Jackson, Hoang took to calling me 'the Stud'. In another line of work, this might have qualified as sexual harassment but on a car lot being called a stud really meant something. I wore the nickname like an army veteran wears a George Cross.

Even Sunny started treating me like a surrogate son. Apparently the daily insults and constant sarcasm had only ever been meant as tough love. 'I was trying to make you strong and, look, I've succeeded. I'm proud of you,' he said gruffly, as if my transformation was entirely the result of his efforts. If I had been a less forgiving person I could have told him it was too late, he could shove his paternal praise. But it wasn't too late at all. The fact is, I was proud that Sunny was proud of me. It was as if Pele had picked me to play in his five-a-side team.

I almost forgot. Why had everyone started treating me differently? Because the day after Fiona and Brian and Earl bought their cars from me, I sold another, then another the day after that, and another and another, until I'd sold eleven cars in fourteen days . . . that's why.

Gamblers only ever want to talk about the bets they've won,

never their losses. Car salesmen are the same. Spend time, any length of time, in their company and you could be forgiven for thinking every person they'd ever spoken to ended up buying a car. For the first few weeks I didn't mind my colleagues' bragging – it fuelled the dreams I had of becoming a great salesman. But as time went on and the rejections mounted I grew to hate it, not least because it reminded me of how hopeless I was.

That all changes when you're on a roll. You want to tell the world at great length, or in my case you want to tell Maggie at great length, just how brilliant you are. I knew there was nothing more tedious than listening to a salesman tell his war stories but to come home from work and say nothing would have been like A. J. P. Taylor writing *A History of the Second World War* and not mentioning the battle of Britain and D-Day. She'd suffered with me through all the defeats, now it was time to share in the victories.

To be perfectly honest, a few of the triumphs were so unremark-able – remarkable in itself, I suppose – that it was virtually impossible to turn them into winning anecdotes. Not that this stopped me, of course. Here, for instance, is the one about the red truck I sold to a plumber from Santa Clara called Tim.

Me: 'We didn't have anything he liked the first time he came to the lot. So I just took a note of his telephone number and when we got a truck a few days later I gave him a call. He came that day and bought it. I knocked five hundred dollars off the price because he seemed like such a good guy. How about that? It was for his father-in-law. He's from Spain and he's seventy.'

Maggie (loyally remaining awake): 'Incredible.'

See what I mean? Still, even she had to admit there was one war story, featuring an ageing hippie couple called Michael and Katie, that was worth retelling for a number of reasons, not least that they bought the flashiest car on the lot at fifty thousand dollars. This was easily the biggest sale I'd made, but it was the execution as much as the money that made it memorable.

They came to the lot five times in the space of a week. At first they didn't want to talk to a salesman, then I pointed out that they wouldn't be able to buy a car anywhere in the United States if they didn't! Boom, boom! Did I mention that cheesy patter had been incorporated into my sales technique? Like an art-house movie director who'd decided it was time to make Hollywood block-busters starring Bruce Willis and truckloads of dynamite, I realized there was no point in denying the general public what it wanted. People didn't go to a car lot expecting introspective dialogue and unhappy endings, they expected insincere bonhomie and crap jokes.

It helped, too, that Katie liked my Scottish accent, and that they were both impressed when I refused to sell them a thirty-five-thousand-dollar sports utility vehicle they liked, declaring with a theatrical flourish, 'I just can't do it. It's worth far less than we're asking.'

At first glance this might be construed as a purely charitable act but in fact it was tactical sacrifice. I was giving away a pawn to capture their queen. It was their first day shopping and I knew they weren't the type to make an impulse purchase. There was no point in trying to force the sale. The best I could do in the circumstances was to make them believe they were dealing with a saint.

When a salesman is on a roll, such clarity of thought comes as easily as breathing. Was I being devious? A little, perhaps. Did I care? Of course not. Michael and Katie were going to buy a car from someone and I was entitled to do everything I could within the law to make sure they bought it from me. There were worse crimes in life than pretending to be a saint.

They said they would be back later in the week. I waved them off cheerfully. This earned me a long lecture from Tommy about the futility of being nice to 'be-backs'. I paid no attention. I knew Michael and Katie weren't lying. As Rob Mills might have said, I knew they were now part of my customer portfolio.

I wasn't around for their second visit. Gerry tried to bully them into buying from him but they insisted they would only deal with the Scottish salesman with the honest face. It took another two visits, a lot of anguished marital debate and enough fake insouciance from me to last a lifetime. Finally, they settled on a beautiful, regimental green Lexus. Even then it wasn't over. Michael wanted to go home and check his bank balance one more time. I said fine. Katie sighed the sigh of someone who'd endured enough car lots and indecisive men to last a lifetime. Tommy watched them leave again, muttering dark threats involving baseball bats and kneecap readjustments.

When they came in the following day Frankie said he was sending Tommy in to close the deal: 'Fifty grand is a lot of money, Scotty. You've done well to get them this far.'

'But I've spent the last week with them. They trust me,' I pleaded, but it was a Sunday, business was unexpectedly slow and he couldn't afford to take a risk with one of the best prospects of the day.

Five minutes later, Michael and Katie walked out. 'We really, really like you, Lawrence.' Katie sniffled, looking like an extra in *Love Story*. 'We're sorry.'

At least Tommy had the decency to be embarrassed as they drove away. 'They said you were the best car salesman they had ever met. But they wanted too much for their trade-in,' he said, before disappearing back into the office to tell Frankie I'd been duped by a couple of time-wasters.

I brooded for ten minutes, kicked a couple of doors, then went to look for them. It took an hour but I found them in a Volkswagen dealership down the street. Michael was inside talking to a salesman. Katie was sitting on the kerb reading a Harry Potter book. She saw me first. 'Oh, Lawrence, it's good to see you,' she said, as if I'd just returned safely from a long and dangerous trip abroad.

We hugged each other. 'Come on back,' I said, piling on the emotional blackmail. 'You know you want to buy the car from me.'

Sunny whistled in admiration. 'God, that is fucking strong. I *like* it.'

Michael and Katie had just driven away in their new car. I was in the office explaining to a small but admiring audience how I'd just persuaded two intelligent, self-interested adults to accept two thousand dollars less than the going rate for their trade-in because

'We have a relationship, don't we?' This was the truth. We *did* have a relationship, although there might have been some confusion over what kind of relationship. They thought I was their real friend. I was just pretending to be friendly, the better to sell them a car.

'Hey, whatever works, Scotty,' Frankie said, reaching into his desk drawer for a corporate cheque book he saved for special occasions. 'I'm going to stick an extra hundred bucks on your commission because of the way you hung in there with those two – you're a real salesman now.'

Forgive me if this sounds boastful, but I've enjoyed a varied life. I've played in a rock band in front of eighty thousand people at Glastonbury, I've worked for the world's best newspaper (the *Guardian*, naturally), I've written two books. I've birdied the seventeenth hole at the Old Course and, as you probably know by now, I am blessed with the love of a beautiful and understanding (if a little sardonic) woman. But nothing, and I mean *nothing*, had ever come close to the sense of achievement and self-worth I felt as Frankie wrote me a cheque for a hundred dollars.

It wasn't the money, although it was welcome, but more what it represented. I had made it. This was where I wanted to be. This was the America I had come to find, with Sunny slapping me on the back and Frankie telling me I was a real car salesman now.

14

Frankie loved competition between his salesmen for the same reason that Titus loved to spend the occasional afternoon at the Colosseum watching lions tear the limbs off galley slaves. It provided a little welcome relief from the strains of running an empire, it kept him in touch with his subjects' appetites. Once a month it gave him the chance to show how munificent an emperor he really was. That was the day, usually the twenty-third, when he locked himself in the office to compose a bulletin announcing a new sales contest, then emerged to unveil it to the grateful masses.

Normally, I didn't pay much attention – sales competitions, like supermodels, were relevant to my world only in a theoretical, wouldn't-it-be-nice-but-oh-well-never-mind way – but this month was different: I actually had a chance of winning. I went inside and joined the throng around the noticeboard. This what had caused all the excited chatter:

> *Only the strongest horses need run in this race*
> Salesman of the month: seven days to go . . .

First place:	$5,000
Second place:	$1,000
Third place:	$500
The rest:	Losers

Frankie was standing behind his desk. 'It's the biggest prize in the history of the lot,' he said proudly. 'I've cut back on advertising in the newspaper and decided to put the money into sales contests. I want to see if the guns are gonna start running.' Just then he caught my eye. 'You think you can do it, Scotty?'

I shook my head. 'You're kidding, aren't you? I've got no chance against these guys.'

For once I was being unduly modest, as a quick glance at the board revealed. Thus far, Frankie's 'guns' had been ambling rather than running. Only 120 cars had been sold, around fifty sales down on normal. The biggest gun of all, Mickey, had just returned to work after a two-week bender in Mexico. Ernie was gone, his sales licence confiscated pending the results of a paternity test and a court hearing over lapsed child-support payments for the two-year-old daughter of a San Franciscan lap dancer. The allure of Gerry's prison-guard sales technique had begun to fade, although he was still leading the board with thirteen deals.

I had eleven sales, which made me the leading salesman on A Crew and second overall. Three others were on nine. Mickey had three, an uncharacteristically poor performance that explained the sour demeanour since he returned to work. 'Don't talk crap, Scotty,' he sneered. 'You think you can do it, don't you? You can see your name in lights, can't you? You want the Salesman of the Month plaque, don't you?'

This was the first time Mickey had spoken to me for days. He was used to being the star of A Crew and being beaten by a Greenpea was an affront to his dignity. Hence the sulk. It was pathetic, really. I should have felt sorry for him but instead, remembering his less than sympathetic response when I'd sold three cars for the month, it seemed like as good a time as any to bait him.

'No, no, honestly,' I said, with a fey smile, 'I don't think I can beat a fantastic salesman like you. I mean, how many cars have you sold this month?' I looked up at the board. 'Three! Mmmm, that's strong.'

No one ever talked like this to Mickey. In a saloon bar, the piano player would've stopped playing. 'You're a cocky bastard, you know that,' he said finally, feebly.

'And, by the way, remember the bet we had. If I win Salesman of the Month you owe me a thousand bucks,' I replied.

'Okay, gentlemen, cut it out,' Frankie said, rubbing his hands. 'I will not have my highly qualified sales professionals squabbling like a couple of fucking schoolgirls. Go outside and sell some cars. Please.'

This business of zooming up to the top of the board was exhilarating but there had been a couple of times recently when I'd felt like a weightlifter who'd taken too many steroids. This was one of those times. Afterwards, when Mickey drove to McDonald's to buy everyone breakfast except me, I decided I would apologize when the time was right – just as soon as he had apologized to me for the months of sarcasm and abuse.

But first things first. I had volunteered to drive Hoang to the courthouse in San Jose. There had been an article in the weekend newspaper saying that one in seven people who applied to become a car salesman had a criminal record. What it failed to mention was that most of them were now working with me. This was Hoang's third offence. He had been three times over the blood-alcohol limit when he'd driven into the back of delivery van at two thirty in the morning. Of course it wasn't his fault – what was the delivery van doing on the road at that time? Nevertheless, jail was a distinct possibility.

At least he had a good lawyer: a phlegmatic, middle-aged Mexican attorney called Manuel Gonzales. He came highly recommended by Freddie, a new salesman hired by Sunny the week before. 'Guaranteed! This guy can keep anyone out of prison,' he said, handing Hoang the lawyer's business card. It was obvious Freddie knew what he was talking about. He looked like a minor character in a Raymond Chandler novel, with bad skin and an ever-changing CV. One minute his last job had been as a bass player in funk band, the next he'd been the boss of his own mortgage company.

Mr Gonzales worked out of a converted garden shed a couple of blocks west of the courthouse. When we got there he was calming a hysterical middle-aged woman. There was no waiting room. We sat beside her as she recounted a sad story about a no-good boyfriend now in jail, a false moustache and a failed drugstore robbery. 'Five years minimum sentence,' the lawyer declared, which set off more hysteria.

This time it was Hoang who needed calming. When you were as good-looking and puny as he was, the mere mention of prison was enough to inspire anxiety attacks. Mr Gonzales tried to reassure him while we walked from his office to the courthouse, saying, 'Seventy per cent of the people driving on California's roads after ten p.m. on a Friday night are over the legal limit. They can't put you all in jail.'

After years of watching cop shows back home in Britain, I was absolutely thrilled at the prospect of seeing the inside of an American courtroom. That, and the fact that everyone else had said no when Hoang begged for someone to keep him company, was why I'd gone with him. I was curious. I wanted to see if real life was as exciting as *LA Law*.

It wasn't. It was just as confusing and tedious as a British courtroom. The only differences were the accents and orange jumpsuits worn by the line of murderous-looking prisoners waiting to be remanded in custody. Listening to the charge sheets being read out, Hoang's offence seemed mundane by comparison. Luckily, the judge agreed. After a languid presentation from Manuel, focusing on his client's infinite remorse and his promising career as a professional karaoke singer, he announced a sentence of seventeen days' community service to be served over six months.

Never had anyone looked so thrilled at the prospect of picking up litter from the side of the highway. 'Thanks for coming – I owe you one,' Hoang said, when we finally got back to the car.

'You sure do,' I replied, wearily. Between waiting at the lawyer's office and the court, I'd lost four hours. I could have been selling cars.

We got back to the lot just as Mickey was closing a deal on a '95 Oldsmobile for a three-thousand-dollar profit. Meanwhile, Gerry was standing on the forecourt with a sheaf of paperwork in one hand, the sleeve of a middle-aged man in the other. The customer didn't know it yet but he was about to buy a car. (I could have written the script: Gerry had stuck an extra five thousand on the price, generously knocked off five hundred dollars on the test drive, another five hundred in the booth and, in ten seconds, would drop another thousand – enough to convince this customer he was getting a bargain rather than paying three thousand more than the real asking price.) He let go of the customer's sleeve, spread his arms and feigned a tortured expression, like Jesus getting measured for the cross. 'Tell you what,' he said, 'you seem like a good guy, I'll knock a thousand bucks off.'

Will the general public never learn? I was now trailing by three car deals.

Tuesday was Gerry's day off and he didn't show up, though he called around 7 p.m. I answered the phone. 'I was thinking about coming down and selling a couple of cars.' He was in a bar, half drunk and hoarse. 'Is it busy?'

It had been the best Tuesday for months. Seven deals done so far. I'd sold a truck to a hardware storeowner and his wife. They hadn't been sure about the price but when I brought them up to date with events in *EastEnders* – it was shown on cable TV with a five-year time lag, they were addicted – I suddenly became their best friend.

'*Phil Mitchell did what with Sharon?*'

'Just sign here, please.'

That had been at four o'clock. Since then it was if somebody somewhere was running bus trips to the lot. The place was crawling with people.

'Nothing much doing, Gerry,' I said, casually. 'I wouldn't bother. Stay at the bar. Have a few more.'

As it turned out, my next deal was a spoon from Tommy: 'It's a crazy drunk guy called Howard, who lives down the street from me,' he said, then pointed at a powder blue, full-sized Dodge Dynasty from the 1980s nadir of the American automobile industry. The car's name said it all. Imagine Joan Collins driving a stock car.

Tommy gave me the thumbs-up. 'He wants to buy that one – at full pop.'

Full pop meant selling a car at the asking price. It was a perfectly legal practice but, in this particular case, about as moral as a war crime. No one had been able to sell the Dynasty at any price, not even to the steady stream of bankrupts who walked on to the lot insisting they were so desperate they would drive anything as long as it was dirt cheap and had wheels. But what I could do? The deal had already been fixed up by Tommy at a back-garden barbecue. The only hope was to take Howard for a test drive, sprinkle a few seeds of doubt discreetly and hope they would sprout into Triffids of rejection by the time we returned to the lot.

As we trundled down the boulevard at 15 m.p.h., swapping potted biographies, it was obvious I was wasting my time. He was sixty-three, divorced, a Stanford alumnus, a former company director who'd lost his fortune gambling on the stock market. Looking at his bloodhound eyes and the tremulous drinker's grip on the steering-wheel, I guessed if he sat down and wrote a book about disappointments in his life a bad deal on a three-thousand-dollar car would barely make a footnote. That probably explained why he was so sanguine as we signed off the contracts. I was mortified, though not enough to refuse his cheque.

But that's what happens when you're on a roll: you sell cars even when you don't want to. Take the following morning. I got in just after 8 a.m., determined to spend a couple of hours drinking coffee and reading the *New York Times*. I'd barely sat down next to Tony when I felt a tap on my shoulder. The sun was in my eyes when I turned round so I couldn't make out a face but the voice was Hispanic, strong and confident. 'I want to buy that truck, please,' it said. Why me? Why not Tony? Kismet, biorhythms, the planet Venus rising in Aquarius – who knows? The only certainty was that I was now officially in salesman dreamworld.

I didn't get back to my newspaper for three hours. Ruben Gascalez wanted to buy the truck, sure, but for five thousand dollars less than we were asking. Not only that, he was a masterful negotiator. I won't bore you with the torturous details, suffice to say the sale climaxed with Ruben revving up his car at the kerb and Tommy and I in the office trying to persuade Frankie to take a hundred-dollar profit on a seventeen-thousand-dollar deal.

Tommy had his own selfish reason for wanting the sale – he needed another fifteen deals before the end of the month to make his bonus – but he dressed it up as concern for his young prodigy, saying: 'Come on, do it for Scotty, he's trying to win Salesman of the Month.' In big cities, beggars sometimes carry ragged-arsed children; their eyes are always big and watery and heart-melting. I stood silently by Tommy's side trying to capture exactly that look.

Asking Frankie to settle for a hundred dollars' profit was like asking him to French-kiss Sunny. The idea made his skin crawl but, on the other hand, the truck had been lying around the lot for over a month. There was also his addiction to competition. He glanced at the board. Another sale would bring me level with Gerry. 'Okay,' he said, then reached into his drawer and pulled out a little brown cup. 'We'll throw the dice for it.'

I rolled seven, he rolled double three. Tommy punched the air and dashed out to tell Ruben that after careful consideration, and only because we were having a special sale this week, he could buy the truck at the price he wanted. I'll say it again: will the general public never learn?

Either Gerry was too meek to have an argument about me lying to him the night before – almost unimaginable – or he was too hung-over to remember anything about it. Whatever the case, he looked puzzled when he turned up for work to discover how busy we'd been on his day off. He stood in front of the sales counter for five minutes, staring at the board as if it was an unexpected tax bill, before wandering out on to the porch and taking a place next to me on the rail.

'Hey, Scotty, three cars since yesterday?' he said.

I shrugged but said nothing, quiet and strong, like Alan Ladd in *Shane*.

Even when you're busy on a car lot there is still plenty of spare time to daydream. I thought a little about how I would spend the five thousand dollars. (Top three ideas: (1) I'd bid for Roy Orbison's guitar strap on e-Bay; (2) I'd play ten rounds of golf at Pebble Beach; (3) I'd buy Stirling Albion and pick myself as centre-forward every week.) But mostly I thought about the sales contest itself.

What I'd concluded was this: basically it was a classic fight between Good and Evil. I, of course, was Good, the acceptable face of used-car salesmen, despite the occasional lapse into the kind of behaviour of which my saintly dead grandmother might have disapproved. Gerry, naturally, was Evil. Maybe I had got him wrong, maybe he served soup at a homeless shelter in his spare time, but when he was out on the asphalt selling cars he was rapacious, amoral and oily.

'*Three cars!*' he said again, in the phoney friendly voice he used all the time.

I wanted to tell him to get lost but couldn't muster the required rudeness. 'Yeah, I got lucky,' I said quietly.

'No, no, man . . . You're a selling machine.'

That's when I knew I had him worried. No one, not even my best friends, would have described me as a selling machine and managed to keep a straight face. Tony and Hoang laughed so much at the idea I thought they might need hospital treatment. It was decided unanimously: I was no longer the Stud, I was the Selling Machine. Here's just one example of the hilarious selection of jokes announced over the Tannoy system during the course of a long, sale-less day: 'Phone call for the Selling Machine. Coke Machine on line one for the Selling Machine.'

Despite the micky-taking, I knew everyone wanted me to beat Gerry. There wasn't a Gallup Poll taken but the younger salesmen wanted a Greenpea to win the contest because it gave them hope for the future. If I could be Salesman of the Month so could they. The older, more experienced salesmen preferred to be beaten by me rather than Gerry. He was more of a threat, long-term, whereas my victory could be written off as a freak.

Mickey and Sunny were the only dissidents, Mickey because he hated my guts, and didn't want to pay out on our thousand-dollar bet, Sunny because Gerry was a member of his crew and was therefore entitled to his unswerving loyalty. 'Don't get me wrong, Scotty, I think you're a great guy,' he explained, 'but I didn't want the Kooks to win the Vietnam War either, did I?'

The next two days could best be described as calm with occasional outbreaks of wild panic. Gerry had an annoying habit of giving a running commentary on every telephone sales call he made and every conversation he had with a customer. Without exception, they were 'a done deal': the woman who called about the Chrysler mini-van was coming in with her husband straight after work, the guy on the truck was going to the bank to get a draft, and so endlessly on. It was only wishful thinking – none of them ever turned up – but that didn't stop me worrying that he might get lucky.

The closest he came to a sale was with a computer-software engineer who'd just moved out from Wales and that was such a hopeless case he even had me talk to him – 'Meet Lawrence, he's our BMW specialist.' It took five seconds to work out that Huw Owen from Aberdovey was so pissed off at being dragged into a sales booth against his wishes that we were now, officially, the last place on earth from which he would buy a car. I apologized profusely and released him back into the community.

For my part, I almost sold a Suzuki X-90, a squat little car that had been lying on the lot for months. No wonder. It looked like it was built from the component parts of a sewing machine, a pram's under-carriage and a tin bath. According to Frankie, who'd bought it for four thousand dollars at a car auction and was trying to sell it for seven thousand, it was a collector's item.

We just thought he was trying to cover his embarrassment but then I took a call from a breathless woman called Gloria. She'd seen the X-90 on our Internet site. Did we still have it? Yes. Was it blue? Sure was. Would we accept an offer a couple of thousand below the asking price? 'Between you and me, Gloria, we'd accept a handful of tap washers.' Gerry would have called it a done deal and it would have been. If only she hadn't lived in Durham, North Carolina.

We were still level, on fourteen sales each.

The Friday sales meeting kicked off with 'Smells Like Teen Spirit' by Nirvana. Otherwise it was more of the usual old crap, although Jason the owner took five minutes out of his motivational talk to deliver a stern lecture to the salesmen at the new-car store about cheating in their sales contest. Such behaviour undermined the team spirit that had helped build his company into one of the best car dealerships in northern California, he said, as angry as I'd ever seen him. The salesman in question had been sacked, and so would anyone else be who tried to cheat their way to the Salesman of the Month title. He didn't go into details of how the scam operated, unfortunately, so I couldn't take notes.

When the meeting finished, Tony, Hoang and I spent an hour at McDonald's, eating breakfast and speculating on how someone would fix a sales contest. It was a complete mystery to me but Hoang, who'd been in the car business for years, said this was how it worked: Salesman X has a chance of winning the contest; he goes to Salesman Y, who has no chance of winning and says, 'If you get a customer who's about to buy a car, hand them over to me just before they're about sign the contract. That way I'll get the credit for the deal – and one more on my sales total for the month. In exchange I'll pay you all the commission from the deal, plus an extra two hundred dollars, when I collect my prize.'

'I've seen it happen a thousand times,' he said.

Tony got up to go to the toilet, leaving just the two of us silently eating our Egg McMuffins. 'What if no money changed hands? Do you think that would still be cheating?' I said eventually.

'What d'you mean?' Hoang replied.

'Let's say Salesman X had done a huge favour for Salesman Y, and in return Salesman Y said, "Don't worry about the money, just take the deal, my friend. After all, I owe you one."'

'What kind of huge favour are we talking about?'

'Let's say Salesman Y was due up in court and he was scared. Let's say everyone at work was telling him that because he was so good-looking and puny he was going to end up as a mass-murderer's girlfriend – everyone, that is, except Salesman X, who instead of laughing at Salesman Y, went with him to court to give him moral support.'

Hoang stirred his coffee, then looked up and smiled. 'I think you're right, Lawrence. I don't think you could call that cheating. I think you would just call that a friend returning a favour.'

Thank goodness we negotiated this particular moral maze before going back to work, otherwise I would have faced a terrible dilemma a couple of hours later when Hoang suddenly remembered he had a dental appointment for noon. He asked if I would mind taking care of some customers.

'This is Mr and Mrs Nguyen,' he said, showing me into a sales booth where a young Vietnamese couple was waiting. 'They've driven the Honda and they like it. Now, I've told them you're the sales manager in charge of giving our customers the very best deals.'

As it turned out, the Nguyens were already happy with the price Hoang had offered them. All that was left for me to do was get them to complete the paperwork, put the requisite five gallons of petrol in their new car and wave them goodbye. It only took me twenty minutes, and I made $214 commission – more than enough to buy Hoang the new golf bag he wanted. It was the least I could do, especially when it turned out there had been a mix-up. He'd made a mistake: his dental appointment wasn't until the *following* Friday.

CNN headline news: I was now leading the Salesman of the Month contest by one deal. I was still leading at three o'clock, when Maggie phoned to tell me an old schoolfriend of mine called John had arrived unannounced in Los Gatos. 'He's been travelling around America for a few weeks and wanted to give you a big surprise,' she said brightly, as if this was the best news in the world.

'Tell me you're kidding, please,' I replied, convinced that it was the worst news in the world. I was all for lasting friendships and big surprises but not for the next couple of days, not until the contest was over. I was hoping to work until closing time. I couldn't afford to leave the lot unguarded, otherwise Gerry might sneak ahead of me.

Maggie had never been anything less than supportive about my new career as a car salesman, especially in recent weeks. I'd become obsessed with the contest, working every hour possible, never taking a day off. Our social life had dwindled to a bottle of cold beer in front of the TV, followed by a blow-by-blow account of my working day, then bed. However, even the tolerance of a saint has its limits. 'For God's sake,' she barked, 'John is your best friend in the world. Get your arse home right now, or else.'

She was right to be angry. I'd known John since we were seven years old. We grew up on the same streets, went to school and cheated in exams together. We formed our own punk rock band – the Cosmic Pancakes – and got drunk together. I'd always thought if ever I got married he would be my best man. I drove home as soon as I could, though not before extracting a promise from Tony, Jackson and Hoang that they'd grab every customer who walked on to the lot before Gerry could get to them.

That night the three of us went out and got ridiculously I've-always-loved-you-too drunk. John had lots of news. He'd recently started a new job in politics. He had countless stories involving smarmy men in dark suits who devoted their lives to shady dealings and backstabbing colleagues. This was an incredible coincidence because so did I, though even I had to admit his stories were more likely than mine to appear on the front page of the *Sun*.

I explained to him I wouldn't be around much for the next two days because of the contest. He didn't mind. He'd decided to go to San Francisco. One night in Los Gatos was more than enough. No offence, he said, but it was hardly the world's most exciting spot.

He dropped me off at work the following day on his way north. Climbing out of the car, I noticed Gerry on the porch with the others. He looked ominously cheerful. All I wanted to do was rush into the office and find out who had sold what the previous night but John insisted I give him a guided tour of the lot. Fortunately, it wasn't the Museum of Modern Art. There was nothing to see. Three minutes later, we exchanged a speedy but heartfelt 'See you later' and promised to meet in San Francisco the following week.

'We'll have a party to celebrate your triumph,' he said, rolling down the window of his rental car.

'I don't know about that,' I said warily, not wishing to tempt fate.

I should have saved my breath.

'Eight deals? On a Friday night?'

Frankie beamed across the sales counter, like the light of a thousand suns. 'Yeah, you missed yourself, Scotty. Best Friday we've had in years. This place was *rockin'*.'

I scanned the board. Of those eight, Tony had sold one car (good!), Hoang had sold two (great!) and Gerry had sold two (oh, shit!). I was distraught but salesman's etiquette dictated that rather than fall into a monumental sulk I had to go outside and pretend to be delighted for Gerry.

There was no point in delaying the agony. The longer I stayed inside the greater chance there was of me missing yet more deals. I slapped on a rictus smile and walked back out on to the porch. 'Good job last night, guys,' I managed to say, though I don't think I'll be getting the nod for my performance when this year's Oscar nominations come round.

I tried my best to avoid Gerry's gaze but he sought mine out. 'God, we missed you last night, man. Deals were flying everywhere – you should have been here,' he said, smiling. I almost believed him too. It was worse than depressing. Not only had he now sold one more car than me, he was a far better actor as well.

Business was quiet for a Saturday, partly because it was perfect beach weather and partly because there was yet another Mexican parade being held in downtown San Jose. (I could never understand the local Mexican community. Everyone called them 'wetbacks', they lived in the city's worst housing and the only jobs they could get were digging gardens or working in restaurants. They should have been staging riots rather than parades.)

Only after sundown did we get a trickle of customers. Tony sold an old Buick, which took him to ten deals for the second successive month and qualified him as a '25 per cent commission' salesman. Officially, he was no longer a Greenpea, though he wasn't sure if his wife would be as impressed as I was. She'd been nagging him for a month to get a proper job, one with regular hours and a guaranteed pay cheque.

Gerry proclaimed his usual quota of 'done deals' as the day progressed but when the chains were pulled across the driveway at 10 p.m. he hadn't made a sale. Neither had I, though not through a lack of effort. I managed to coax three people into the sales booth only to discover their desire to buy a car was equalled only by their lack of financial standing. Al said my third customer, an unemployed guitar player called Pascal who insisted his image required a twenty-five-thousand-dollar Mercedes, actually had the worst credit rating he'd seen in twenty years in the car business. That aside, it was not a day for the automobile industry history books.

I slept fitfully that night, as if dawn was about to bring my first day at school, two decades' worth of exams, a wedding day and a visit to Julianne Moore's bedroom. I want to say now, it wasn't about the money. Five thousand dollars would have been welcome but it was hardly going to change my life. No, it was the stupid fake gold plaque that mattered. Five months ago, I had known nothing about cars and even less about selling. Now I was on the verge of becoming Salesman of the Month at Orchard Pre-Owned Autos, the toughest used-car store at what was said to be the biggest auto-mall in the world. That would have made me the best used-car salesman in the world, right?

'Don't worry about it,' Maggie said, as I was about to leave for work. She straightened my tie then kissed me lightly on the lips. 'Go get them, honey. I know you've got what it takes to do it.'

As always her faith in my abilities was touching, and for once, it was justified. I did have what it took to do it. I actually did *it*. I sold fifteen cars, more than any other salesman on the lot with the exception of Gerry. He sold fifteen cars too. It was a tie, a draw, a dead heat. Honours even. We were both Salesman of the Month. At least, that's what I thought, but how was I to know that the definition of 'car' was about to undergo radical expansion?

Before I go any further, there are three things you need to know.

First, the day started brilliantly with the arrival of Sheila and her nineteen-year-old son, Tom. It was his birthday present, they'd been looking for a car for a week and, as they so candidly put it when I offered an introductory handshake, 'We just about had enough of car salesmen.'

'Fantastic, great,' I said sympathetically. 'What's wrong with car salesmen?'

'We just don't like them,' Sheila said, with a look that suggested I wasn't exempt from her antipathy.

'I know. We're terrible, aren't we?'

It was textbook stuff: ask them open-ended questions, get them laughing, find them a car they liked, take them for a test drive, swat away every objection they could muster and close the deal. An hour later they drove away in their new car.

Gerry and I were now level.

The second thing you need to know is that there was a car park at the back of the lot, which housed California's biggest collection of twisted metal, burst upholstery and bald rubber. We called this place the Boneyard. It was where all the cars traded in by customers were parked until they were shipped out, either to scrapyards or to a garage to be tarted up for resale. Parked in the middle of the Boneyard was a 30-foot fibreglass yacht, the *Ave Maria*. It belonged to a friend of Jason the owner and had lain there under a faded green tarpaulin for months.

About an hour before we were due to close, I noticed Gerry and another man walking round the *Ave Maria*. They pulled off the tarpaulin and clambered on board. They poked around for a while, opening cupboard doors and bouncing on the cabin couches, then disembarked and went into the office. I thought they had simply gone to get cleaned up until Sunny strolled out on to the porch ten minutes later, wearing a smile as big as a split watermelon.

'Gerry's sold the *Ave Maria* for fifteen thousand dollars,' he announced, breathlessly. 'They've just put the deal up on the board.'

It took a few seconds for me to digest this information, and it still didn't make any sense. Even so, looking at Sunny's beaming face and remembering how much he wanted Gerry to win the contest, I was worried. 'What are you talking about?' I said, quietly.

'Gerry's just got another deal – Jason's friend's boat. The one that's been parked out in the Boneyard for months.'

'This is a car lot. We sell cars, not boats.'

'Yeah, but a deal's a deal.'

'Says who?'

'Says Jason.'

'Jason who?'

'Jason the owner. Numbskull.'

The curious thing about this conversation was that Sunny actually thought *I* was the one talking gibberish.

'Sunny, what are you talking about? If Gerry's sold a boat it's a boat deal, not a car deal.'

'Call it what you want, Scotty – Gerry's beat you by one.'

'Hang on a minute. Has the boat got four wheels? Can it do a three-point turn? Does it do a hundred *fucking* miles an hour on the freeway?'

Sunny held up his hands in mock surrender. 'Hey, hey, don't shout at me, shout at Frankie. He's the one who wrote it up on the board.'

Frankie was sympathetic but implacable. He'd just spoken to Jason on the phone and his word was final. This brings me to the third thing you need to know: when the Big Boss says a thirty-foot fibreglass yacht with two eight-cylinder onboard engines is a car, it's a car.

It was pointless arguing. The sale of the *Ave Maria* counted towards the Salesman of the Month contest. Gerry had won.

15

Las Vegas looked gorgeous from above, a luminous splat in the blue-black darkness. We landed at 10 p.m. and took the shuttle bus from the airport to the hotel. We were booked into a casino called New York, New York. As the name suggests, this was an ambitious attempt to cram the world's most exciting city into a single block of the Strip. Our room was in the 'Chrysler Building', a long walk past the ranks of gamblers cheerlessly feeding the slot-machine racket.

'Take me home, I'm bored,' they all seemed to be saying.

'Me too, and I've only just got here,' I replied, though no one was listening.

I'd been to Vegas twice before, during the Bluebells' all-conquering US tour and, a few years later, on holiday with Maggie. The visit with the band had been a one-hour stopover, *en route* to a concert in Los Angeles. We ventured no further than the airport. If only I'd stuck with the same itinerary second time around. Instead, Maggie and I flew in for a week's holiday. On the advice of *The Rough Guide to America* (or perhaps it was *The Guide to Rough America*?) we booked into the sleaziest, dirtiest, most dangerous hotel in the city. We guessed this much from the steel grille across the reception desk and the drug addicts in the lobby but being young and scared that a last-minute cancellation might result in physical violence we meekly handed over our cash.

We had a rotten time, too petrified to leave our room in case it was burgled or we were mugged, but too skint to upgrade to something less dangerous like, say, a maximum-security prison. In the end we cut short our stay by four days and fled south to Phoenix, Arizona – a development that prompted a stampede among the other guests for our leftover social-security breakfast coupons.

Even when we did venture outside, the charms of Las Vegas

were singularly elusive. For a start, it was too hot, over 100 degrees every day, and crowded. Then there was the thick, choking dust. The city was a building site. At least half a dozen new casinos were being built right next door to each other. I found this bewildering because there were already too many casinos, all of them offering identical attractions: the slot machines, the same as-much-as-you-can-eat (because it's the only way we can get rid of this pig swill) buffets and a cabaret night featuring an 'entertainer' I could have sworn had died years ago, like Wayne Newton or Engelbert Humperdinck. Call us tone deaf, but we had no intention of paying seventy-five dollars to listen to either.

All of which left us nothing to do except stroll from hotel to hotel, watching others trying to have a good time. Frankly, there is only so much entertainment value to be had in watching drunk, middle-aged men picking up prostitutes young enough to be their daughter's slutty best friend. Needless to say, we were the only people in the city in bed before midnight who weren't being paid or were paying someone to be there. I was glad to leave for Phoenix and happy enough to tell myself, and anyone else who would listen, that if I never visited Las Vegas again it would probably be too soon.

Hence, the less than enthusiastic response when Frankie pulled me into the office a week after the Salesman of the Month contest had finished and made me an offer.

'Close the door behind you,' he said, pushing an envelope across the desk. It was too much to hope that it contained five thousand dollars in used bills. 'There you go, Scotty, two nights in Vegas, you and your girlfriend, all expenses paid. I was supposed to go but I can't because of family stuff.' He paused, presumably to give me time to fall to my knees in gratitude. When he saw I was unmoved he added, 'It's a reward for all your great work last month.'

'You can't go to what?' I replied, sullenly.

'The National Automobile Dealers Association annual convention.'

'What's that?'

'What does it sound like?' Frankie sighed, like a father who'd had just about enough of his temperamental child. 'It's a car salesman's convention.'

I'd spent the last seven days walking around like a man in mourning. I *was* a man in mourning. Not only had I been unjustly robbed of the Salesman of the Month prize, it had quickly become clear that the spell was broken. With a week of the new month gone, I'd sold nothing. Customers were avoiding me. I was avoiding them. Where once I would cheerfully have taken on any objection – 'Stay away from me, sleazeball' – I now barely had the strength to be civil: 'Your wish is my command. Goodbye.'

It wasn't just customers who noticed the change in my attitude. 'Smile, ya big baby. It's the car business – no one cares about what happened last month,' Sunny said, his usual sympathetic self. Hoang said if I felt cheated the best thing to do was to find a job elsewhere; there wasn't a car dealer in California who wouldn't employ me. The truth was, I didn't want to leave The Orchard, and I didn't share Hoang's confidence in the market demand for my skills.

At least Frankie tried hard to make me feel loved. The Las Vegas trip was only the latest of a number of peace offerings. A few days earlier he had written me a cheque for fifteen hundred dollars – five hundred more than I was entitled to for coming second in the contest. He'd also given me a special mention during the presentations at the weekly sales meeting – 'In second place we have young Scotty, one of the most promising new salesmen we've had in years. Stand up, Scotty, take a bow.' Best of all, he graduated me to a 25 per cent commission salesman. I was no longer a Greenpea.

Two nights in Las Vegas with thousands of car salesmen for company wasn't close to my idea of a great time but then Frankie said he was fed up with me moping around the lot with a face like a burst basketball. I was crapping out the other salesmen and, more importantly, I was chasing away customers. 'If you want to work somewhere else, leave. If you want to stay, then go to Las Vegas, have a good time and come back rested and ready to take on the world.'

When he put it like that, it was hard to say no.

★

After unpacking, Maggie and I went for a walk down the Strip. What a difference a decade had made. This was not the Las Vegas I remembered. Some things hadn't changed – Wayne Newton was still live in concert – but gone were the grim gambling dens and seedy pick-up joints of memory, replaced by shopping malls featuring Prada and Chanel (a pair of bright yellow wellies – only $325!) and vast, light-filled palaces modelled on famous cities. It was now possible to have cocktails in 'New York', a gondola ride in 'Venice' and a *café au lait* in 'Paris', and just because we could we did.

We got back to the hotel around two o'clock, had one last drink at the piano bar and went for a stroll along the lines of gaming tables, trying hard to work out why they were so busy. Hadn't these people heard the casino always wins? At one roulette wheel a middle-aged man was playing on his own, randomly scattering fistfuls of hundred-dollar chips around the table. He clearly had a system – the lose-money-fast system – and managed to spend ten-thousand dollars in fifteen minutes, yet he couldn't stop smiling. At first I thought he might have a degenerative brain disease but then I realized he was just obscenely rich. He actually *wanted* to lose his money, and do it in public. Of course, the casino was more than happy to oblige. It was Las Vegas distilled to its very essence – personal stupidity and corporate greed coming together in the name of entertainment. I don't condemn it, but I just find it hard to love.

Here's another reason I find it hard to love Las Vegas: the Strip looked awful in the morning, a washed-out, grubby ghost of the place we'd walked along the night before. We only had one full day in the city, which we planned to fill with visits to the art gallery at the Bellagio Hotel and the car museum at the Imperial Palace casino across the street.

The Bellagio gallery turned out to be not much bigger than our hotel room. I'd read in a magazine that its founder, Steve Wynn, woke up one morning and decided the city's future was as a citadel of fine art. He spent $150 million on works by Picasso and Van Gogh, welcomed the world's press to the opening night and declared himself a visionary. Big mistake. When we got there the queue at the pastry shop across the hallway was longer. After forking out the twelve-dollar entrance fee we discovered there were only twenty-seven paintings on display. Not even Maggie, who has always fancied herself as womanhood's answer to Brian Sewell, could make the experience last longer than half an hour.

At least the car museum was free, but when you spend your entire working day around cars it is hard to work up the enthusiasm to look at more cars, even if they had once belonged to Mussolini or were used by the Pope during his papal visit to Britain. We quickly found ourselves back out on the street. The curse of Las Vegas had struck again. It wasn't even lunchtime and we had run out of things to do.

The longer we traded ideas on how to spend the rest of the day – an early flight home (too expensive), a helicopter tour over the Grand Canyon (too dangerous) – the more obvious it became that we were going to do the one thing I had vowed not to do when I took Frankie up on his offer.

The convention was being held in the world's ugliest building, a vast pink corrugated shed a couple of miles out of town. I confess I was curious. Having had personal experience of being in a room with a dozen car salesmen, I wanted to see what twenty-eight thousand under a single roof would be like. I half expected to find an automotive Dante's *Inferno*, full of salesmen frantically selling cars to each other, but instead found a rather sedate trade show. Still, if we wanted to buy the latest car-wash technology or get a bulk discount on giant inflatable two-headed monsters, we had come to the right place.

Maggie took one look, shook her head in despair and headed off to the 'Spouses' Area', where delegates' wives were invited to fill their handbags with cosmetics samples while their menfolk got on with the serious business of ogling the exhibition-stand hostesses or playing on golf-course simulators brought in by companies in an attempt to attract passing trade. Generally speaking, the rule was that the more desperately tedious the product, the bigger the Astroturf putting green and the more undressed the hostesses.

I wandered aimlessly through the exhibition hall for a while, collecting free stuff – shoulders bags, baseball caps, a packet of chocolate chip cookies – and marvelling at the sheer extravagance of it all. Some of the stands were as big and plush as ocean-going yachts. Yet no one appeared to be terribly interested in what was being peddled on board any of them. As far as I could tell, the talk on the putting greens was about the whereabouts of the best strip-clubs and which car manufacturer's reception had the best free bar.

Eventually I found myself upstairs, in the more businesslike atmosphere of the seminar corridor. I noticed a sign advertising a public lecture about future trends in the American automobile market. Normally I would have kept walking but I wasn't due to meet Maggie for another hour and there was nothing better to do. The room was packed but I managed to find a seat in the back row, next to a salesman called Brad from Savannah, Georgia.

After ten minutes I began to wish I hadn't bothered, not because the speaker, an economist for a car-auction company, wasn't interesting but because of what he had to say: 'First things first, American car salesmen had a good year last year,' he began, 'so give yourselves a big pat on the back. How many cars do you think you all sold in the last twelve months?'

That was easy: forty-four, not counting unwinds.

'*Fifty-nine million.*' He made a triumphal V-sign with his arms, as if he'd sold them all himself.

A gasp went round the room, quickly evolving into a loud, manly cheer. Brad offered me a congratulatory handshake. 'That's right, gentlemen, fifty-nine million cars – 17.4 million new cars, 41.7 million used cars – worth a total of $744 billion.' Suddenly, a fancy exhibition stand and a free bar at Caesar's Palace seemed like a piddling outlay.

The rest of the hour passed in an orgy of pie-charts and statistics, each more mind-boggling than the last. For instance, you probably knew that the United States is the most motorized country in the world, but did you know it has a car population of 213 million (almost one car per person)? Or that this number was growing by four million a year? This was because cars were lasting longer. Almost 40 per cent of the 213 million were over ten years old.

'And why is this good news, gentlemen?' the speaker said excitedly. Because it meant there were eighty million poor, misguided people out there driving around in ten-year-old bangers, apparently. Everybody in the room had a duty to go out there and sell them a newer model. 'It's time to make some money! Agreed?'

'AGREED!' roared Brad, and everybody else.

'Great. Any questions?'

The lights went up and the applause started to fade. There were lots of questions, but no one asked the one I wanted to hear answered: who was going to buy cars when we were all submerged under ten feet of water?

I didn't want to put a dampener on Brad's euphoria but there was a report in the morning newspaper saying that a quarter of Florida would disappear under water if global warming continued at its current rate. In parts of California, precipitation had increased by 20 per cent over the last hundred years. Further afield, Alpine ski resorts would be lost, tropical islands might disappear, there might be massive population displacement on the Indian subcontinent because of flooding – all of it largely attributable to carbon-dioxide emission from cars.

I found it a little troubling that Brad didn't appear to give the tiniest shit about any of this. Well, why would you bother about the future of the planet when you could make five hundred dollars' commission on a Ford truck? It was worse than myopia, beyond blindness. It was madness. I was about to stand up and make a speech to that effect when I remembered I was a car salesman too. Okay, forty-four cars out of fifty-nine million was hardly going to contribute much to the sinking of San Francisco but I was still a guilty man. No wonder I looked so glum when I met up with Maggie by the newspaper stand.

'What's wrong with your face?' she said, as we headed towards the exit.

There was no point in going into too much detail as she would only have said something logical like 'If you're that worried, get

187

another job.' I didn't want to get another job. I was perfectly happy with the one I had. Anyway, I was enjoying my little bout of existential angst. The car lot didn't offer many opportunities to exercise one's social conscience. 'Oh, nothing much, I'm only helping to destroy the planet with carbon dioxide, that's all,' I said nonchalantly.

The sun was beginning to slide down below the tips of reddening hills but it was still shirtsleeve warm. Casino lights shimmered in the distance, like a half-remembered dream. It was hard to believe that Las Vegas could look romantic but just then I swear it did. Maggie grabbed my hand, then kissed my cheek. 'Come on, we'll walk back to the hotel. That'll cheer you up,' she said.

'How far is it?' I replied, suspiciously.

'A couple of miles.'

We'd been on our feet all day. I was hungry and thirsty. My calves felt as if someone had smacked them with a ten-pound mallet. A two-mile walk might have finished me off. I'm ashamed to say my new-found despair over the earth's parlous state was suddenly overwhelmed by the desire for a warm bath and a cold beer. 'Nah.' I pulled Maggie to an abrupt stop. 'Let's get a taxi.'

I arrived back at work a couple of days later to find the place awash with rumours that Tommy was about to be demoted from closer to salesman. Tony filled me in on the details. A Crew had finished the previous month thirty-five deals behind B Crew. The new month was ten days old and already they'd sold fifteen cars more than we had. They were a well-drilled military unit; we were an ill-disciplined rabble. Our crew was always calling in sick; their crew worked their days off and always arrived on time. All of this was Tommy's fault, the rumours went – he was too soft to be the boss.

As a reward for B Crew's latest triumph, Sunny had arranged a big night out in downtown San Jose. He spent most of the day leaning back in his chair, detailing the evening's programme – there were strippers involved – and berating A Crew for being an embarrassment not only to his best friend Tommy but to car salesmen in general. We pretended to ignore him but secretly kept a close watch in the hope he might lean too far back in his chair, fall over and cause himself a serious injury. It never happened, alas.

Thankfully he went home to get changed. B Crew had arranged to meet at the lot, from where Sunny would drive them into town in one of the mini-vans we had for sale.

Tony and I watched them leave, our grim demeanour in stark contrast to the clean-shaven, excited faces staring back at us. They looked like a group of prisoners being driven off to freedom; we looked like the ones who'd been turned down by the parole board. The mini-van had barely gone when Tommy's voice came on the Tannoy, all tinny and irritable. 'Attention, A Crew, team meeting in the sales office right now. That means everybody, Mickey, even the know-alls, in the office right now.'

Team meetings weren't like the weekly sales meetings. They usually lasted about five minutes. Jason the owner and Frankie were never there, which meant no one even pretended to pay attention to what was being said, not even Tommy, and he was nominally in charge. This time was different. This time Frankie was sitting behind the desk wearing an undertaker's expression. Tommy was standing beside him, equally solemn. Together, they looked like a painting from Gilbert and George's dark period.

'Get some seats, this is gonna take a while,' Tommy barked at Tony, as we shuffled into the office. If we didn't know before, we knew then we were in for a scolding.

Minutes of A Crew meeting.
Present: Tommy, Frankie, Mickey, Lawrence, Jackson, Tony, Hoang. Absentees: Kim (called in sick with flu), New Guy Called Duane Who Started the Day Before Yesterday (missing, presumed resigned).

Tommy began the meeting by saying he was 'fed up with this crap, guys, you're embarrassing me, do you know that?' There was no response from crew members. He then asked if anyone knew how many times in succession B Crew had won Sales Team of the Month. Everyone present averted their gaze to the floor except Mickey, who said, 'Thirty-six?'

Tommy suggested forcefully that this was not a joking matter; the correct answer was six months.

Tony asked if it was true that Tommy was being sacked as closer. Frankie said no. However, Tommy said that while he would remain as the closer for A Crew he would also be taking on additional duties as a salesman. This would allow him to show his utterly hopeless crew members how to sell bloody cars.

Tommy then outlined a series of measures aimed at breaking B Crew's winning streak:

1. He was going to flood the lot with additional salesmen. To this end, he offered a $250 bonus to any member of A Crew who helped recruit another salesman. However, crew members would be required to refund this money if the new recruit proved to be (a) unreliable, (b) a dope head and (c) unable to sell a car even if their life depended on it. (Jackson intimated he had a hairdresser friend from Palo Alto who would definitely be interested in selling cars.)

2. He was going to eliminate poor time-keeping. Anyone arriving late for work would be sent home for the rest of the day. Lawrence pointed out that in five months of working at the lot he had only been late once. Tommy responded by telling Lawrence to shut up and just listen.

3. He was going to have regular meetings at which crew members would be required to set 'goals'. These meetings would be monthly and would start with immediate effect. There was a short interruption to the proceedings to allow Tommy to take an urgent phone call, during which Tony leaned over to Lawrence and whispered in his ear, 'Jesus Christ, Tommy's been watching too much Oprah Winfrey.'

The 'goal setting' portion of the meeting then began. Tommy

asked those present how many cars they intended to sell in the month ahead. Mickey said his attendance record would improve considerably now he was on the wagon; consequently, he hoped to sell at least twenty cars. Tommy said fine. Jackson said he was confident he could sell twenty cars too. Frankie interjected, pointing out that Jackson's combined sales for the last three months was only fourteen. Therefore, twenty sales in one month was unrealistic. Jackson revised his total downwards, to ten. Tommy revised it further, to seven.

Hoang said he intended to sell ten cars. Lawrence said he believed he could also sell ten cars. Tommy pointed out to Lawrence that the purpose of setting goals was to 'aim higher'. He − Lawrence − had sold fifteen cars the previous month and there was no reason why he couldn't sell the same number, or even more. Mickey said that pigs might fly. There was a short pause to allow the laughter to die. Lawrence repeated that his goal was ten cars.

Tony said he wouldn't be setting any goals for himself. Tommy asked why? Tony said because he was leaving. Tommy said why? Tony said his wife had been pleading with him for months to find a new job, and that this pressure had intensified after he received his most recent pay packet. Tommy said why? Tony said a number of the deals he made during the previous months had subsequently 'unwound'. The commission on these deals had been subtracted from his wages to such an extent that rather than receiving a pay cheque from the wages department, he had received a bill.

There must have been a mistake, Tommy said. He would have a word with Maria in accounts.

Tony said it was too late, he'd already found alternative employment. Tommy said he was very disappointed, and that Tony had been one of his favourite salesmen. Tony demurred. He was disappointed about his leaving too but said that this is America, a man shouldn't have to pay to come to work.

On that bombshell, the meeting was adjourned.

Nothing much, or at least nothing dramatic, happened for the next three weeks. As promised, Tommy started selling cars. But he was out of shape and out of practice. Four days, one sale and two mild asthma attacks later he went back to being a closer.

The flood of new salesmen on A Crew never materialized. Kim's flu wasn't really flu: he'd found a job at another dealership where they left him in peace to play solitaire all day. To no one's surprise Jackson's hairdresser friend decided he was more temperamentally suited to looking after California's legion of bottle blondes than trading poisonous barbs with the likes of Sunny. Tony agreed to stay on for another month until Tommy found more salesmen. It didn't make any difference. B Crew won the team award for a seventh successive month.

I forgave Gerry for the Salesman of the Month fiasco. He wasn't to blame for me not winning the contest: it was Jason the owner's fault. If I'm being honest, anyone who could sell a yacht while working on a used-car lot was entitled to be called Salesman of the Century. He deserved the five thousand dollars and the plaque. Not that they would be of much comfort to him now that he was in hospital in Los Angeles.

After my almost-triumph of September, I only managed to sell six cars in October. Frankie told me not to worry, even the best salesmen sometimes needed to slow down. We were sitting on the porch at the time, just the two of us, waiting for ten o'clock to come round, when we could lock up. All of the salesmen had rolled the dice to see who could leave early. I lost. 'Now that you've had a good rest you'll be ready to sell twenty cars next month. *Right?*'

I nodded but, really, I knew he was merely reciting some lines he'd read in a *How to Motivate Your Employees* instruction manual. We both knew I'd never sell twenty cars in a single month. Ever. I was strictly a six-cars-a-month salesman, give or take the occasional freak month. Not that I was complaining about that. Now that I was on 25 per cent commission, I could sell six cars a month and still make two thousand five hundred dollars without breaking sweat.

I would have been happy with that, but as the conversation went on it was obvious that Frankie had bigger plans for me: 'Trust me, Scotty. In a couple of years' time you'll be selling twenty cars a month, every month. You'll be making ten grand easy. D'you think you'll stick around that long?' he said.

'Of course I will,' I replied, and at the time I meant it. But Bill Baldwin and his girlfriend Serena walked into Orchard Boulevard Pre-Owned Autos one Sunday afternoon and everything changed.

16

About Gerry. It turned out he had psychiatric problems.

He disappeared for a week. He didn't phone to say he was sick or had taken a job at another dealership. The latter was highly improbable, in any case. He'd been averaging fifteen thousand dollars in commission over the last three months. Where else was he going to earn that kind of money? The only explanation was illness, or worse.

Early one morning Frankie drove to his apartment. There was no answer but he left a note asking him to get in touch. A couple of hours later Gerry appeared on the office steps. He was unshaven, sweating and had a cramped, suspicious gait, like an astronaut taking his first steps on a new planet. We were eating lunch at the time. Mal from B Crew had treated everybody to sushi. He'd just sold an old Ford mini-van for $7,500, a scandalously high price he'd got by turning the 6 upside down on the adhesive $6,000 price-tag on the windscreen, then generously offering his customers a $1,500 discount.

We were divvying out a tray of California Rolls when Gerry made a dive for the table, grabbed an armful of food and threw it in the rubbish bin, yelling, 'They're trying to poison you!'

Mal jumped up off the bench. 'Dude, what are you doin'? I paid fifty bucks for that lot.'

Tony looked desperately between the table and the rice and avocado mush now swilling around amid the coffee dregs and cigarette butts at the bottom of the rubbish bin. 'Hey, man, that was my lunch.'

Mal was a big man, a college football player gone to seed in his early thirties. If Gerry had been thinking straight he would have apologized immediately and pulled out his wallet. Instead, he stepped forward and swung a punch. I had visions of a bloody mismatch: Stone Cold Steve Austin versus Graham Norton. Luckily, Gerry did himself a favour, fast-forwarding straight to the result of any such a bout. He started crying like a baby.

We never found out who was trying to poison us. Frankie stepped in, put his arm round Gerry's shoulders and gently steered him away, like a nurse coaxing a wayward patient back into the psychiatric ward. The last time we saw him he was slumped in the passenger seat of Frankie's car, his hands splayed out on the dashboard, his torso rocking back and forth. It was an awful sight. 'Drugs,' said Mickey, as we watched them leave.

'Definitely a brain tumour,' said Sunny MD.

'What about my fifty bucks?' said Mal.

'Hey, who's got the lesbians?' said Tommy, spotting two short-haired women in khaki shorts staring at the dashboard of a '98 Chevy on sale for $11,995.

Thus, the departure of our Salesman of the Month was marked at Orchard Boulevard Pre-Owned Autos.

Maggie said we held the California All-comers Record for turning down social invitations and it was my fault. She was the sociable, upbeat member of the partnership: she had filled an address book full of new friends. I had a long and undistinguished record of being a sour-faced misery: I could count the number of non-car-selling friends I had made on the fingers of an oven glove.

She was mostly right. In my defence, I was at the car lot at least four nights a week. When I wasn't working the last thing I wanted to do was sit at a dinner table with people I hardly knew, discussing how much money I made last month or the prospects for NAS-DAQ futures, whatever they were. Nor did I appreciate being treated like a freak. Place me in any social setting and within five minutes I began to feel like the cultural ambassador for some pariah Latin American tribe, sent out to the 'civilized world' to explain the curious ways of my people and offer survival tips for anyone thinking about making the hazardous trip out to a dangerous land.

Take Hallowe'en night. Andy had invited us out to dinner along with some of his friends. I hadn't seen him for a couple of months.

I was looking forward to a boastful evening, peppered with fulsome apologies for his ever doubting I could make it as a master salesman. But it was fancy-dress day at the lot and I was an hour late getting to the restaurant. 'A cowboy's paperwork is never done,' I explained, taking the last seat, at the far end of the table, away from Andy, Maggie, three vineyards' worth of wine bottles and, as far as I could make out, any prospect of having a good time.

I wouldn't have minded so much but I swear I recognized one of my dining companions. The Clark Kent specs, the middle parting, those distressed denims, that voice – as wooden, as soporific, as annoying as a . . . an alto fucking saxophone. Christ. It was the Kenny G disciple from Andy's office. Plus other members of the fan club.

The conversation took its normal Silicon Valley course. They told me in long and tedious detail what they did for a living, how much money they made and how many stock options they hoped to accumulate in the next five years, then I told them what I did for a living and they looked at me as if I'd just announced I owned a chain of brothels.

'God, why on earth would you want to do a job like that?' KG's disciple said.

'Because it means I don't have to sit in an office with small-minded, money-obsessed, cloth-eared bores like you every day,' was what I should have replied, but instead I explained patiently – as I always did – that selling used cars was my way of discovering California, not the touristy, guidebook California, but the fascinating, complicated, fantastic, infuriating, startling place that it really was. They all looked at me blankly, as if it was *me* who was weird not *them*.

I persevered. I scrolled through my mental filing cabinet of car-lot anecdotes and pulled out Gerry's story. I left nothing out – his 'punking' sales technique, the bullying and lies, the sales contest and the boat, the sushi incident and the day after, when his friend had turned up on the lot: 'I'm taking him to a clinic in San Diego,' he told Frankie, shaking his head, 'though it didn't do him much good the last time.' It turned out Gerry had a history of psychological problems, that he led a drifter's life, staying in one place long enough to make a stash and get wasted every night. What could be more tragic, I said, than a middle-aged, middle-class man in a suit selling Toyota Tercels during the day then going home to a bedsit every night and getting out of his skull on drink and drugs?

For some unfathomable reason I thought at least the story might help them see my point – that the car lot was an allegory for an American way of life that existed outside their safe, comfortable, narrow existence. I should have known I was wasting my breath.

When I finished telling Gerry's story KG's disciple swallowed a piece of garlic bread then said, resentfully, 'You're telling me this guy made seventeen thousand dollars a month as a *car salesman?*'

Luckily, Andy came down the table and sat beside us just then or I might have tipped a plate of steaming hot spaghetti carbonara over somebody's head.

'Hey, Andy, I haven't seen you for a while. What's the news?' I said, relieved to have someone else to talk to.

'Not much,' he replied, with a half-suppressed grin that suggested this was a lie. 'Though I did get an offer the other day for the company.'

'Great.'

'Guess how much?'

'I don't know – a billion dollars?' I was, of course, making a sarcastic joke. It was Andy I was talking to, after all: my old university friend, the John Belushi fan, the one who spent so much time partying when he was supposed to be reading textbooks that he was never going to amount to very much. Didn't he know Silicon Valley was in the midst of an economic recession? No one was buying companies these days, they were closing them down and selling off the furniture for peanuts. *One billion dollars.* Ha ha ha, that'll be the day.

Here's the biggest laugh of all. The microchip Andy's company had been working on for five years was finally complete. The diagrams he'd drawn on the whiteboard, the equations, *the core processor that moves away from the communication specific design to a more*

197

general industry-based application specific design or whatever it was – they actually worked. This wasn't a stupid idea like selling pet food over the Internet, which wouldn't last beyond the end of the month: this was an invention that was going to change the world of telecommunications. Or so it seemed, judging by how much he'd been offered.

'Close,' he replied, gripping me by the shoulders and giving me a playful shake. 'One and a quarter billion dollars.'

It wasn't long after our Hallowe'en night out that I started to become disillusioned with selling used cars. I know what you're thinking: confronted with the news that I'd turned down a job with (and a minuscule share of) a company worth $1.25 billion to sell second-hand cars for $2,500 a month, I threw myself into a vortex of despair and couldn't climb out again. Right? Wrong.

Of course I did the calculations. Forty thousand shares at twenty-one dollars each came to $840,000 – significantly less than the 'one to ten million dollars' Andy had casually mentioned when I went to see him at his office all those months ago. Even so, as Maggie helpfully pointed out, I would've had to work at Orchard for precisely twenty-eight years to make that much.

At least I'd never actually had the money in my hands. Nevertheless, it required a superhuman effort not to dwell on what life would have been like if I had it. For once I envied Maggie her transcendental-meditation night classes. She handled the loss like Zen on Quaaludes. I, on the other hand, was kept awake at nights by fantasies revolving around Aston Martins, six-month Caribbean holidays and credit-card bills that didn't include the instruction 'Do not use until overdue payment is made'.

Luckily Andy came to the rescue. 'I'm not selling,' he told us in the pub a week later. 'I am going to wait five years until the company's worth ten times as much as it is now.'

'Great,' I said, though I'm ashamed to say that what was 'great' was that in Silicon Valley anything could happen in five years. With any luck, his company might be worth nothing by then. I could only hope. The alternative was too awful to contemplate, too easy to calculate without the aid of a computer: 10 x $840,000, equals the rest of my life in a padded cell.

But, trust me, any despondency I felt about being a car salesman had nothing to do with Andy's news. It didn't happen that suddenly. Rather, it crept up on me, as if one day I had a niggling head cold, then a week later I had the flu and the week after that I was on my death-bed with full-blown pneumonia.

It started with Tony leaving. He wasn't the best friend I had in the world, but he was the best friend I had in this *particular* world. He'd looked after me on my first day, taken me for a beer when I sold my first car, commiserated with me through my sale-less troughs. Mickey once said that no matter how resilient or optimistic or successful you were, the car business eventually turned you sour. Five days, five months, fifteen years; eventually you ended up hating your customers and hating yourself.

Not Tony. He wasn't capable of sourness. Whenever anything happened on the lot, his stupid, fat, goofy grin could be seen somewhere in the frame. He was my Zelig. It wasn't just me who was going to miss him. Everybody loved Tony. Even Sunny.

We made big plans for his farewell, with balloons and a speech by Tommy and an ice-cream cake, but it was a Friday and the weekly meeting ran late because Jason played a selection of new radio adverts he insisted were going to produce a flood of grateful customers. There was another meeting when we got back to the lot, this time with Tommy, who was in a foul mood because we'd been beaten again by B Crew.

By the time we had declared our goals and decorated the lot with balloons it was after one o'clock, the cake shop was sold out and Tony had a customer. 'A Christian,' according to Tommy, and therefore a certain car deal. 'They trust everybody, and they don't like to haggle.'

It must have been the designated car-buying day on the born-again calendar because ten minutes later a customer wearing a 'Team Jesus Rocks' T-shirt rode in on a polished Harley David-son. I have never seen a better-looking motorcycle, or a fitter-looking, more handsome fifty-year-old man. He had the full set of

Californian genes: sun-bleached hair, gleaming teeth, surfer's body. His blonde, twentysomething daughter, who was riding pillion, was equally stunning.

'Would you like a ride?' he said, climbing off the bike. Thank you very much for the kind offer, I thought, but I've got a girlfriend at home. 'Come on, you haven't lived until you've ridden a Harley.'

For once, Tommy's condensed guide to the car-buying habits of America's social tribes was woefully inaccurate. Not only did Mike – 'Call me Mike, Larry' – trust no one, he loved haggling even more than he loved Jesus. At least he bought the car, though not before subjecting me to a terrifying ride down the boulevard on his Harley and the inevitable attempt to recruit me as a foot-soldier in the Lord's army. It took me three hours to get rid of him, by which time Tony had gone home. I didn't even get the chance to say goodbye.

A couple of days later Jackson left too. He found out that Tony and I had been promoted to 25 per cent commission salesmen, even though he'd been working at the lot longer than we had. He stomped into the office and demanded to be paid the same rate, otherwise he was leaving. Unluckily for him, Frankie wasn't around to reason with. 'Goodbye, paaaaallll,' Al drawled, not even looking up from his *Penthouse* magazine.

That was it. I was now officially the boy standing on the burning deck. Of all the salesmen from A Crew who'd been lounging around the porch when I turned up on my first morning – Juan, Hughie, Sam, Mickey, Tony, Jackson – only Mickey remained.

Call it selective memory but The Orchard had seemed a more comradely place to be in those days. We were always helping each other out with awkward customers, having water fights or sitting around in the shade debating the great issues of the day: 'Okay, guys, who's heavier, Tony or Mickey? Quick, Scotty, run down to Macy's and buy a set of bathroom scales.' It's not a word I ever thought I'd use without smirking, but I do believe the *karma* was better back then.

Now there was only Mickey sitting on the stereo speakers, like some malevolent Buddha, bitching about the uselessness of Jason's radio adverts (the flood of grateful customers turned out to be a meagre trickle) and a handful of new salesmen who would have been better employed as extras in a stage revival of *One Flew Over the Cuckoo's Nest*.

It was hardly surprising we weren't selling as many cars as we used to. Tommy's two newest recruits were a crop-haired, mono-syllabic ex-soldier called William and a former pizza chef, Curt, who spent most of the day carving his initials on the lunch table with a kitchen knife he brought to work every day. Judging by the twitching, messianic gleam in his eyes it was only a matter of time before he carved a matching set of initials on someone's chest.

No doubt Curt had some sparkling personal qualities but, like most of our customers, I wasn't prepared to risk being mortally wounded in a valiant attempt to discover what they were. Instead, I came into work every day, said a quick hello to Tommy and went off and sat in one of the cars at the front of the lot. Theoretically, I was watching for customers but in reality I was dozing or listening to the radio.

I grew to enjoy these bouts of solitude. I even formed an addiction to rabid radio talk-show hosts. My favourite was Rush Limbugh, who seemed to me to be a cross between Jimmy Young and Genghis Khan. According to Rush, everything that was wrong with America was Bill Clinton's fault, and everything could be put right by cutting off his testicles with a rusty kitchen knife. I confess I found this kind of rubbish refreshingly opinionated, even if the opinions were poisonous.

Another reason I liked to listen to these shows was this: when you're a used-car salesman you are always looking for even the tiniest reassurance that just because most of the people you meet in your working life hate you doesn't necessarily mean you're a terrible person. The fact that the phrase 'You're absolutely right about that, Rush' was never likely to cross my lips led me to believe that I might be a sane, likeable member of the human race. That was why it came as such a shock when I realized I was a terrible person after all.

If I'm honest the signs had been there for a while, in phoney smiles and the countless petty deceptions I used in the sales booth. Then there were the deals I'd done that didn't exactly qualify as bargains of the year, like the ten-year-old Honda I'd sold to Andrea Catforth. For a while I convinced myself it wasn't my fault that on a housing estate in the East Bay a mother was struggling to send her son to college all because I'd sold her a four-thousand-dollar car for six thousand. Who was I kidding? What had Andrea said tearfully? 'We are a poor family, Mr Donegan. Two thousand dollars is a lot of money to us.' What had I replied? 'I promise I'll get you a refund.'

I'd conveniently forgotten my promise, just as I conveniently rationalized all the other niggling incidents that might once have caused me a sleepless night or two. No air-conditioning, sir? 'Well, it's not my fault you didn't ask if the car had air-conditioning before you bought it.' An oil leak? 'That must have happened after you bought the car, madam.' You've decided you don't like the car after all? 'Sorry, it's too late – under California law there is no cooling-off period. Once a customer has purchased the vehicle . . .' When the excuses ran out, I consoled myself with the fact that I'd never actually done anything illegal. Some epitaph: *Here lies Lawrence Donegan, used-car salesman – he never broke the law (strictly speaking).*

I know what the old Me, the pre-salesman Me, would have said about that. He would have pointed out that just because the state of California says it's not illegal to sell four-thousand-dollar cars for six thousand doesn't mean it's okay to do it. And while he was in such a censorious mood, he would have asked what the law had to say about being an accessory to daylight robbery. When I saw Mal turn the 6 upside down on the sticker price of a car, was it right for me to laugh my head off and admire his initiative? Of course not. I should have warned the poor customer he was being pick-pocketed, then carried out a citizen's arrest. But I didn't. Not just because Mal weighed about 250 pounds and would have flattened me for costing him a thousand dollars in commission, but also because it didn't occur to me at the time that he had done anything wrong.

As I was saying, the signs were already there. However, it wasn't until another of Frankie's sales competitions reached its climax that it was obvious I couldn't ignore them any longer.

It was a three-day contest this time, from Friday morning to Sunday night. 'Stop sucking the tailpipe, guys . . . Too many of my stars have gone for the big puke . . . time to strap it on, folks . . . dial into the dream, guys . . . because here comes the giant spark,' he had ranted at the sales meeting. Tommy translated for William, Curt and a couple of other new recruits who were sitting in the back row wondering what on earth the boss was talking about: business was bad, people had got lazy, the weekend was a perfect time to sell some cars, and first prize was two thousand dollars.

This was huge bonus money for three days' work.

It produced sales, but at the expense of transforming the lot into a snakepit, like *Wall Street* with cheaper suits. There were squabbles between salesmen over customers, between salesmen and Frankie, whose desire to drum up business understandably fell short of giving cars away for nothing, and between salesmen and customers who had the audacity not to buy a car. When there was no one left on our lot to argue with, Mal went to the BMW dealership across the street and got into a fight with the salesmen over there when he tried to poach customers.

Mickey won the contest, though I ran him close. To do this I made three deals, each of them reprehensible in one way or another.

The first was to a computer programmer called Ben, who'd just broken off his engagement. The car was part of a personal makeover. 'I'm looking for something that'll catch the eye of the ladies,' he said – without a trace of irony, I noted incredulously.

'Isn't your sparkling personality enough?' I replied. When he missed the sarcasm I decided he was dumb enough not to notice if I added an extra thousand dollars to the asking price. I'd never 'packed' a price before but the contest was based on how much profit you made, not on the number of cars you sold. A thousand dollars might have made the difference between first and second place. Even if it wasn't, and it wasn't, it meant I made an extra $250 commission. Ben deserved it anyway, the sexist pig.

There was no excuse for the second deal. The car was one of the worst on the lot. The paintwork was flaked and faded, as if allergic to the sun. The engine sounded like a road drill wrapped in loft insulation. The woman who bought it was a public-school librarian, with the personal timidity and limited budget that this implied. It had obviously taken her weeks to work up the courage to visit a car lot. She could scarcely look at me when I spoke, never mind disbelieve anything I said. When I told her I had another customer who was interested in the car (omitting to mention that this had been six weeks ago) she became fleetingly decisive. 'Okay, I'll buy it,' she said, looking to me for reassurance.

'A wise choice,' I replied, too venal to tell her she was making a terrible mistake.

By any standard other than the statute book, this was criminal conduct. But just when you thought the hero of this story couldn't stoop any lower than mugging middle-aged female librarians, Tommy spotted a couple wandering on the lot. I was leaning over the porch rail at the time, chatting to a school-age car enthusiast who claimed his parents were going to buy him the cobalt blue sports car that was parked on the lawn.

'Hey, Scotty, get these people. That's a car deal,' Tommy hissed.

I was mid-sentence. 'Give me a minute,' I hissed back.

'*Now.*' Tommy quickly scribbled my name on a business card, handed it to my customer and told him to come back when his balls dropped or his parents gave him a bank draft for thirty-two thousand dollars, whichever came first. Meanwhile, I was half-way across the lot, trying to head off someone from B Crew as he sprinted towards them. Luckily, I got within shouting distance first.

'Hey there, folks, how are we doing today?'

They must have heard me – hell, Maggie must have heard me and she was in San Francisco doing a story for the BBC – but they didn't look up. I tried again. 'Great hat.'

Bill – Bill Baldwin – was wearing a logo-less black baseball cap, the brim pulled down to shield his eyes. His girlfriend – Serena – was wearing the grimace of a woman who wished she never had to speak to a car salesman again.

I pretended not to notice that I was being ignored. 'Great. Hey, are you folks looking for anything in particular?'

'Truck,' Serena snapped. At least that's what I think she said.

'A truck? We've got hundreds of trucks.'

We had five trucks, four that were either too big or too small and one that was perfect – though way too expensive, judging by Serena's Ferrari-sized shriek when I mentioned the price. But then Bill sat in the cab and started playing with the steering-wheel and Serena caught the distant, dreamy look on his face.

I turned the ignition key, my smile as broad as a father leading his only daughter down the aisle. 'Go on, take her for a test drive, I think you'll find she handles like a dream,' said the spider to the fly.

It took an hour but gradually they relaxed and began to speak in sentences of more than one word. They'd moved to California three weeks earlier from the Virgin Islands. Serena was a legal secretary, Bill was a carpenter. There wasn't enough work for him back home. He'd read in the newspaper that California's housing boom was turning tradesmen into kings. They knew no one in San Jose, and were struggling to pick their way through the bureaucratic spaghetti. I could tell they wanted nothing more than to be back in their island idyll.

'But we want to make enough money to build our own house, to start a family,' Bill said, nervously.

'The California Dream?' I said.

'Yeah,' he muttered quietly. 'I suppose so.'

I leaned over and shook his hand. 'Me too.'

The truck cost $16,500 dollars, three times more than they had planned to spend. 'There goes our life savings,' Serena said, signing a cheque for the two-thousand-dollar down-payment. The rest would be paid off in instalments – $359 for the next seventy-two months. (Frankie always used 'months' in contracts rather than 'years' because, he said, it made the payment schedule sound like a long holiday rather than a prison sentence.)

I had never been more certain that I'd talked someone into doing something they would regret, though it was a shock when the regretting began thirty seconds after Bill began to read the small print of the contract he'd just signed.

It was the standard document, longer than a roll of wallpaper though slightly less interesting. I handled them every day but had never taken the trouble to look at one – at least, not until Bill pointed out a tiny box in the bottom left-hand corner headed 'Amount paid at end of Contract, including Interest payments and other fees'. Underneath, it read $27,848.

Of course it did: $359 multiplied by seventy-two comes to $25,848, plus $2,000 = $27,848. Simple arithmetic. I don't know why I was shocked, though I could quite easily understand why Bill looked like a man who'd just been sentenced to death for a crime he hadn't committed. After all, eight hours ago he was going to spend five thousand dollars on a truck, one hour ago he'd allowed himself to be seduced into spending $16,500 and now he was confronted with the preposterous idea that he was actually going to pay $27,848.

'What does it mean?' he said.

Somehow I summoned up the courage, no, make that effrontery, to look him in the eye. He was wearing wire-rimmed spectacles. I could see my reflection in the lenses but barely recognized myself. Was that horns I could see poking through my sweat-matted hair? I muttered something unintelligible about California sales tax and compound interest. 'Don't worry about it, it's the American car business. That's how it works,' I said, though I knew this wasn't the correct answer to the question.

What does it mean, Bill? I'll tell you what it means. It means that I'm a complete and utter bastard.

17

I went to see Tony at his new office and found him in good spirits. He really was indefatigable. This is what death must be like, I thought, as I looked around hamster-sized work-stations. It was easily the most cheerless spot in California, without natural light, laughter or any occupant who looked as if existing had been anything other than an unwelcome interlude between conception and death. I couldn't begin to describe how tedious Tony's new job was without falling asleep, so I'll make do with his title: Administrative Assistant (Customer Estimates).

'No, it's really interesting,' he said, sitting at his computer terminal. He punched up a spreadsheet. 'Say you want eighty feet of air-conditioning vent. All I do is put the dimensions into the program and the estimate order form comes out over . . . Ah, forget it. It's the worst fucking job in the world but the money's regular and I don't have to work weekends.'

Shunning the once-in-a-lifetime opportunity to tour a factory unit where air-conditioning vents were born, I drove the two of us to a shopping mall just off the nearby highway, where we joined the lunchtime queue at McDonald's. Three weeks had passed since he'd left the car lot and he had a thousand questions. Any news of Gerry? How was Mickey? Was A Crew being beaten again? Who had Tommy found as his, Tony's, replacement? How was I getting on? Was I going to win Salesman of the Month this month?

We grabbed a table at the back of the restaurant, where I did my best to bring him up to date. Yes, Gerry had called from a psychiatric unit. Alas, he was only allowed one two-dollar phone card per week and had been cut off before Frankie was able to tell him he could come back any time. Mickey was Mickey, hung-over and disobliging, but still selling more cars than anyone else. And no, A

Crew wasn't winning the Sales Team of the Month award, nor I the Salesman of the Month.

Curt the psychotic pizza chef – nominally Tony's replacement – had been fired after trying to strangle William the military reservist in an argument over the commission on a deal. The cops had been called in to escort him off the premises, their second visit in a week. I was just about to explain how the first involved one of the salesmen on B Crew, a hysterical customer and the miscounting of twenty-thousand dollars in hundred-dollar bills when two women who were sitting behind us got up to leave. 'Remind me not to buy a car at your place,' one giggled as they brushed past our table.

I cringed at the thought they'd heard every word but the embarrassment quickly gave way to relief. At least they hadn't heard the really bad stuff, the personal stuff. No one had until now, not even Maggie. Tony was different. He knew what it was like to sell used cars. There was no chance of him walking out on me, then appearing on *The Ricki Lake Show*, like the estranged wife of a serial killer, telling the world I wasn't the sensitive, caring man he thought I was.

I told him about the three-day sales contest and my growing realization that I despised the person I was turning into.

There had been further developments on that front, I reported sadly. No longer was I hateful only to customers who bought cars from me; I was hateful to those who didn't. The day before, confronted by a German couple who had politely asked me to let them have a look around the lot on their own for five minutes, I inexplicably metamorphosed into Basil Fawlty. 'Right, that's it. Off the lot, you two,' I barked, shooing them towards the exit.

'What d'you mean? We want to buy a car but we want to look around first,' the male said.

'I don't care. Be gone with you. If you won't let me talk to you, I won't let you look at my cars.'

As they backed off on to the pavement, I turned to the porch and gave the thumbs-up. I'm ashamed to say I was playing to the gallery. Even more shaming, the gallery consisted solely of Sunny, who'd only just finished explaining that the best way to handle uncooperative customers was to irritate the hell out of them. I was now seeking, and receiving, approval from the world's most objectionable man. He returned my thumbs-up.

'Absolutely disgraceful,' one of my startled German friends muttered, as they climbed back into their rented car.

'Well, if that's how you feel,' I replied, the last remaining vestiges of common decency finally leaving my soul, 'don't ever come back.'

Tony, good old Tony, thought this was hilarious.

'What are you laughing for? It's not funny, it's terrible,' I whined.

'Of course it's terrible, Scotty. You're selling used cars, what d'you expect?'

'I didn't expect to turn into this – this . . .'

While I went searching in the dusty recesses of my vocabulary to find a word that married the spivvery of Del-Boy Trotter to the darkness of Hannibal Lector, Tony swallowed a bear-sized bite of his Big Mac. 'What are you complaining about? No one made you do any of those things, did they?' he said, licking the sauce off his fingers.

He was absolutely right. I'd been at countless sales meetings and not once had I been instructed to lie and cheat for the greater good of Orchard Boulevard Pre-Owned Autos. Contrary to popular belief it *was* possible for a salesman to get through the working day with his integrity intact. After all, Tony had done it. Customers were always writing letters to Frankie praising his good nature and honesty, and rightly so. By depressing contrast, the postman never even rang once for me. The question was, why?

Either I was a lying, cheating scumbag, always had been, always will be, or some other force of nature was at work, which was beyond my control. It took me a while to come up with the correct answer but eventually I worked it out. In the world beyond the car lot I was just as good-natured and honest as Tony. It was only when there was a sales contest to win that I started to behave erratically. It was like the chemistry experiments we used to do at school: when you added water to some metals, nothing happened, but when you added it to others there was a loud bang and it took days to clean the mess off the ceiling. Obviously, Tony was the former and I the latter. In my natural state I was as harmless as he was, but pin a nametag to my tie then set me loose among 250 used cars and I became dangerously unstable. I didn't want to lie and cheat, I just couldn't help myself. It was a force of nature beyond my control.

That's why I had reached a momentous decision. 'I'm leaving. For good this time,' I said.

Tony shook his head. 'You're mad. It's the best job in the world.'

'Yeah, you loved it so much you're now filling in order forms at a ball-bearing factory.'

'Sheet metal.'

'Whatever.'

I sat in silence while he explained the myriad ways in which selling cars had indeed been the best job he'd ever had. Admittedly, the competition wasn't exactly strong – not unless you count selling hot dogs at San Francisco 49ers' games as the last word in career fulfilment – but for a moment he convinced me I was making a mistake. Wouldn't I miss the adrenalin rush of selling a car, the thrill of winning a sales contest (though sadly this experience would remain in the realms of fantasy for both of us), the challenge of having just a few minutes to make a customer like you, the tantalizing thought that the same person was about to pay you a thousand dollars' commission?

Before he became a car salesman the only goal in life Tony had ever had was to own his house by the time he was forty. 'Now I think anything is possible,' he said. 'The job showed me you've got to set yourself goals to go after. I told my wife, if you want something you've got to cut out a picture and stick it on the bathroom mirror so you can dream about it every day.'

Better than any of this, however, was the camaraderie. 'That's why I was always in such a good mood. I couldn't wait to get to work. It was like we were a family. There's none of that in this new job – you just kinda turn up, do your day's work and go home . . .'

His voice tailed off. He stared out of the window, as miserable as any man burdened with the title Administrative Assistant (Customer Estimates) ought to be. 'Tommy tried to talk me into staying. He even phoned my wife and begged her to let me stay. She told him to piss off,' he said wistfully, as we got up to leave. 'I wish she'd let me work there part-time or something.'

I looked at my watch. I was due at the lot in half an hour and for the first time in weeks I was actually looking forward to getting there. Tony had just made the most difficult sale of his life. He had made me want to be a car salesman again.

The journey took twenty minutes, enough time to make a list of resolutions, the most revolutionary of which revolved around selling cars to the general public at the lowest price possible. It would be easy: all I had to do was find out the minimum amount Frankie would sell the car for; then, in the privacy of the sales booth I'd tell the customers exactly how much to offer.

Who knows? I might have stuck around long enough to put this plan into action but I arrived at the lot to find a silver truck outside the office. It looked as if it had been parked by one or other of Starsky and Hutch, carelessly, with the doors left swinging open as they set off in pursuit of the villains. Ten days had passed since I'd sold it but I recognized it immediately. The adhesive price sticker was still on the top left-hand corner of the windscreen – *$16,500 – Automatic! Best Buy!*

My first instinct was to do a runner, perhaps drive up to San Francisco airport and catch a flight back to Glasgow, but something, at first I wasn't quite sure what, drew me into the office. One of the by-products of selling cars was the taste I'd developed for embarrassing confrontation, although the fascination was predicated on me not being involved in the confrontation. It was one thing to snigger like a schoolboy as Sunny tried to fend off an irate buyer whose back axle had snapped like a drinks straw after two days and twenty-six miles. It was quite another to have the guts and maturity to tackle such an encounter without being knocked unconscious.

I knew Bill Baldwin was waiting inside for me. I had no desire to be punched but neither in all conscience could I walk away from the prospect. If he wanted revenge, he could have it. Frankly, a good beating was nothing more than I deserved. In any case, his girlfriend Serena saw me through the glass doors before I had the chance to scarper.

As it turned out, they were more scared than angry. In fact, they were pleased to see me, as if I was the only friendly face they'd seen all day. There was a very good reason for this: I was. Tommy and Frankie had gone to San Francisco with their partners for the night to see *Miss Saigon*, leaving Al and Sunny – *Les Misérables*, so to speak – to run the store.

'Oh, hi there, Lawrence,' Serena said, smiling weakly as I went inside.

I nodded grimly, like a late arrival at a Mafia funeral. There was no need to ask what the problem was. Bill was standing in front of the sales counter, nervously explaining how he had never bought a used car in California before and hadn't understood that when the price sticker on the windscreen read $16,500 it meant he would eventually pay $27,848. From his body language and tone of voice – defeated, weary, apologetic – he appeared to be under the mistaken impression that this legalized mugging was actually his fault. 'Don't get me wrong, it's a really nice truck and all but we just can't afford it and that's why we've brought it back.'

More observant readers might have noticed by now that this book isn't an instruction manual on how to negotiate your way through the dangerous world of used cars. However, it should be noted that Bill's approach was absolutely perfect. It's pointless screaming at a car salesman: he's been abused every day of his working life and has developed an immunity to its effects. Calling him names is like punching Batman's washboard stomach; the only damage inflicted will be to your own fist. Politeness, however, always works. Disorientated, surprised, grateful not to have been mentioned in the same breath as a garden slug, the salesman will try to help the customer who confesses to his own stupidity and pleads for mercy. There is only one exception to this rule and that is when the salesman concerned believes with evangelical fervour that charitable acts are anathema to the American way of life. If you're unfortunate enough to find yourself faced with such a salesman, save your breath.

'I'm sorry,' Al said, once Bill had finished laying out his case, 'but you bought the truck. You can dump it back here if you want but you'll still be the owner. Your name is registered on the bank loan, and if you don't pay it, they'll repo your car and then they'll make you bankrupt.'

'But —' Serena tried to interrupt.

'I'm sorry, but that's just the way it is. I don't know how the system works wherever you come from but there is no cooling-off period in the state of California. Once you've written the cheque, that's it. Now, if you'll excuse me, there's something I've got to do.'

Believe it or not, this was Al at his customer-friendly best. He'd given up on the general public some time in the mid-eighties. Usually he responded to their pleadings with a blank, contemptuous stare. The strain of making this short, albeit spectacularly unhelpful speech had clearly left him in need of a rest. He brushed past the three of us and disappeared through the back door in search of a cigarette. There was no point in me chasing after him and begging him to reconsider because he would have given me the same answer, no doubt in its pithier form.

Bill and Serena looked helplessly at each other, and then helplessly at me, and I looked longingly at the floor, half hoping it would turn into a fast-flowing river and sweep me away in my shame. Suddenly Tony's enthusiastic words seemed like the ramblings of a drunken madman. The longer the silence went on the more convinced I was that somebody in the room was about to start crying and that the somebody would be me.

'Let's go,' Serena said eventually, pulling Bill's sleeve. Together they walked out into the afternoon sunshine, stood on the steps and stared at the truck for a minute or so, exchanging whispered intimacies. Bill sensed I'd followed them outside and swivelled round. 'Don't worry about it, Lawrence. It's not your fault, you were only doing your job,' he said, which I guess was supposed to make me feel better but made me feel worse. Not only had I screwed him, it was rapidly becoming clear I was about to get away with it.

I returned his weak smile, and because I'm an idiot who doesn't know that you should never speak unless whatever you have to say is going to improve the world as it might otherwise have been, I said, 'What are you going to do now?'

Bill shrugged. 'We're thinking about going home to the Virgin Islands,' Serena said.

See what I mean? It was bad enough knowing I'd saddled a decent young couple with a debt that threatened to impoverish them for the next six years. Now I would have to live the rest of my life knowing that I'd single-handedly ruined what ought to have been the greatest experience of their lives. The parallel between their story and mine was obvious and deeply, deeply uncomfortable. Like me, they had come to California in search of the American Dream, and like me they had finished up bankrupt. The only difference was that their bankruptcy was financial and involuntary, whereas mine was moral and self-inflicted.

'No, please, no – don't do that,' I said, desperately. 'I'll speak to Frankie – he's the real boss, not Al. Al just tells people any old crap so they'll go away. Frankie's different, he'll understand what happened, he'll help you, I promise he will.'

This might have been rash. Frankie was more reasonable than Al (so was Pol Pot, come to think of it) but the chances of him taking back the truck were slim. He'd made fifteen hundred dollars' profit on the deal and, as our resident Yale Law School professor had so helpfully pointed out before disappearing for a recreational smoke, the contract they'd signed was legally binding. Exactly why Frankie would tear up this document was a mystery to be solved later. For now, the wishful idea that he would was enough to sustain me for the two painful minutes it took Bill and Serena to climb into their cursed truck and drive it off the lot.

There's never a good time to confess your sins to a loved one but in my experience it's best to do it in a public place, preferably when you are both infused with the warm glow that comes from believing that life, at that precise moment, is good. Friday night at Los Gatos high-school sports field was absolutely ideal.

We went to watch an American football match featuring the local team, the Wildcats, against another school whose identity escapes me. Not that this mattered. The point about going to the Wildcats games was not who they were playing or even whether they were winning: the point was to bask in the communal experience.

My memory of school sports in Britain is distant and unpleasant. All I remember are cold deserted playing-fields and a bully of a PE teacher who used to slap the back of our legs if we lost. The idea of anyone other than a devoted parent turning up to watch us play was laughable. It couldn't have been more different in California. Friday-night ball games were much like church on Sunday mornings, part of the social fabric.

I don't know what such occasions were like in other places but in Los Gatos every effort was made to re-create the Superbowl, monetary and athletic limitations not withstanding. There were cheerleaders, a hilariously off-key marching band, giant banners through which the Wildcats' players would run (presumably in the hope that the opposition would think the banners were made of bricks rather than paper and get scared). I've no idea who the team's coach was but it should have been Jimmy Stewart, fresh from his role in *Mr Smith Goes to Washington*. Hundreds of people turned up, even paying to get in. For those who couldn't make it, recorded highlights were shown on the local cable access channel.

The matches were a fortnightly ritual for Maggie and me. It wasn't that we especially liked to watch football, it was more a feeling that we were taking part in a genuine, 100 per cent, stars-and-stripes, small-town American experience. We could shop at Gap, buy a Big Mac or watch one of Rupert Murdoch's stinking, overpriced TV channels anywhere in the world but sitting in the stands listening to 'The Star Spangled Banner' being beaten to within an inch of its life was something we would never have experienced had we not left Glasgow and washed up in Los Gatos.

We were walking home after the game when I told Maggie I'd

had enough of selling cars. I had no idea what she would say, except perhaps 'I told you so.' I suspected, deep down, that she'd been sceptical about the car business from the start. I can't say I blamed her; it had changed me for the worse (perhaps irretrievably). We hardly ever saw each other and the social cachet of living with a used-car salesman, even among her ironical group of friends, had to be negligible. We lived in one of the most exciting, interesting corners of the planet, yet the highlight of our social life was watching a bunch of high-school kids in shoulder-pads running around a football pitch on a Friday night.

'Good idea,' she said. 'I can tell it's been making you miserable for the last few weeks.'

I nodded, miserably.

'So what went wrong?' she said, squeezing my hand.

The question wasn't so much what had gone wrong, but where did she want me to start and how much did she really need to know?

I thought about lying – well, I was becoming such an expert – but it was football night and, as Frankie might have said after a particularly profitable Sunday afternoon on the lot, 'there was lot of love around'. I took a deep breath and started my story, from Tony leaving all the way through to my one-man attempt to reverse California's proud tradition of immigration by sending Bill and Serena back to the Virgin Islands. I left nothing out, not even the school librarian. I even told her about Andrea Catforth crying on the phone about the two thousand dollars I 'stole' from her and her son.

Here's why everybody in the world should have a Scottish girlfriend called Maggie: 'Don't blame yourself,' she said, when I finished. 'You only did those things either out of ignorance or because you were forced into doing them. It's not you that's terrible, it's the job.' I felt as if I'd just been absolved by the Pope himself.

My confession was going better than expected, well enough in fact to tackle the last remaining question, what do we do now? 'Why don't we go back home to Scotland? Fresh start and all that,' I said, speculatively.

These words didn't feel right when they were forming in my head and as soon as I let them out I knew they sounded ridiculous and cowardly. In my defence, I felt homesick. I missed my friends, my nephews and nieces, Saturday afternoons at Parkhead, the walk down to the newsagent's in the morning to buy a copy of the *Guardian*. There were other things too, petty things – like the way the barber just down the street from our flat in Glasgow cut my hair, for crying out loud – that I was too embarrassed to tell her about. But most of all I wanted to put as much distance as possible between myself and Orchard Boulevard Pre-Owned Autos. Six thousand miles seemed just about right.

It was pointless listing the reasons why Maggie thought going back to Scotland was a terrible idea there were many, some important, some trivial, all valid – so I'll stick with two that made me feel like an idiot for even suggesting it in the first place: (1) So much for the spirit of adventure. Eat your heart out, Christopher Columbus, etc., etc.; and (2) She didn't want to go back. I had dragged her here in the first place and just because I felt guilty about telling lies and selling a handful of overpriced wrecks that didn't give me *carte blanche* to disrupt her life all over again. 'Get over it. It's done. Move on,' she said. 'Why don't you ask Andy if he'll give you a job?'

'No way. That's why I ended up selling cars – remember?'

'Okay, not that – but something else. Go work in a record store, or play guitar in a band or write a Hollywood movie or be the next Sean Penn,' she said, and because she's the smarter, better-read member of the partnership she started quoting F. Scott Fitzgerald at me. 'This is America,' she said, '"a fresh green beast of the new world . . . for a transitory enchanted moment man must have held his breath in this continent . . . face to face for the last time in history with something commensurate to our capacity for wonder . . ."'

She was right, although not about jobs. I didn't want to do any of the things she had mentioned. I wanted to be the editor of the *New Yorker* or short stop for the San Francisco Giants or a lineman for the Wichita County electricity company (it was a Glen

Campbell/Jim Webb fixation in my early twenties). So what if lack of talent ruled out the first two and geography the third? This was California. I was allowed to dream.

18

Tommy was devastated. Who would have believed a Vietnam vet could have cried so much? And Frankie, too, the hardest man in the business – yet there he was, on his knees begging me to stay. Jason the owner refused to believe it at first. He offered me a new convertible Porsche Boxster like the one he drove to work every day if I would reconsider. When I declined he became frantic and upped his offer to 25 per cent of the company and . . . and . . . Who am I kidding?

I told Tommy as soon as I arrived at work on Saturday morning. 'Great, Scotty. Busiest day of the week and one of my best salesmen tells me he's leaving. Fucking fantastic,' he said, taking a long pull on his cigarette. 'You know that leaves me with three salesmen? How am I going to stuff Sunny's crew now?'

Frankly, I'd long passed the stage where I cared about beating Sunny's crew. However, Tommy's reaction to my going did make me feel warm inside: *one of my best salesmen tells me he's leaving* . . . The field was limited, admittedly, but he'd said this instinctively, as if he actually meant it. I'd seen enough salesmen leave to know I wasn't about to be presented with a gold carriage clock, in which case I was happy to accept a sincere compliment from an old pro as my leaving present. Unless, that is . . .

With some salesmen, like me, the insincerity is transparent. If I took someone on a test drive I always made a point of telling them they were 'a fantastic driver', even if they'd just ploughed through a bus queue. But with the real experts, like Tommy, you could never tell. They didn't make a fuss of complimenting you, they just did it and moved on, leaving the little seed of goodwill to flower into full-blooming acquiescence. Maybe Tommy really did think I was one of his best salesmen, or maybe he had just told me that in the hope it would help persuade me to work for another week while he tried to find a few more new salesmen. If so, it worked.

'One week and that's it,' I said, glowing with pride. In truth, I didn't mind staying on a few more days. It gave me time to talk Frankie into taking back Bill and Serena's truck.

'Good boy.' Tommy smiled and then, judging that he still had some goodwill in the bank, added, 'Now go blow up some balloons. I want this place looking like a birthday party when you're finished.'

News travelled fast. By the time I'd finished in the balloon room most of the other salesmen knew I was leaving. We talked about nothing else over breakfast. Modesty forbids me revealing at great length what was said, though most of it was flattering. I had been a pleasure to work with, apparently, though remembering a few of the social misfits who'd come and gone in recent months – Curt the strangler, Freddie the legal expert – this was less of a compliment than it sounded on first hearing. Touchingly, Sunny said I was the best Scottish car salesman he'd ever worked with, then went and spoiled the moment by saying I was the only Scottish car salesman he'd ever worked with. Who said American comedy died the day they stopping making *Seinfeld*? Mostly, everybody wanted to know why I was leaving and what I was going to do now?

I thought about making something up, like I was going back to Scotland, but knowing my luck I would probably have bumped into someone at the shopping mall the day after my fictional flight home. In any case I had nothing to lose by telling the truth. I was talking to car salesmen – they were used to people being rude to them.

Even so, I gave them an edited, heavily annotated* version: that I'd grown to hate the job and what it was doing to me. I couldn't sell cars unless I lied and cheated and took advantage of people's naïveté. It was a scummy business and I'd had enough.

* *But hey, guys, don't take offence. It's me I'm talking about, not you lot. Just because I ended up lying and cheating doesn't necessarily mean that all car salesmen do the same (despite strong evidence to the contrary in several cases) and, sure, we've all got to make a living but, well, I'd rather make a living doing something that won't make me scared to look at myself in the mirror.*

I was right about no one being offended. My little outburst even provoked a rare bout of introspection centring on the question, 'Can a car salesman go through life without lying to his customers?' (Some answers: 'It depends on what you call a lie'; 'If the customer lies to you, does that cancel out any lies you might have told them?'; 'Is a lie still a lie if you've got your fingers crossed when you say it?') For a few minutes it felt as if I was hosting a special Californian edition of *The Moral Maze* but then Frankie came charging out of the office and shouted, 'Customers,' and everyone scattered like wildebeest at a watering-hole when a lion wanders into view.

Because I wanted everybody to have fond memories of me after I had gone, I alerted another salesman whenever I spotted an unattended customer. It was a perfect arrangement. I didn't have to do any work, someone else was grateful to me for being generous and I got to feel good about myself for giving them the chance to make a sale. I almost got to the end of my shift without once leaving my seat on the porch when Mal from B Crew came rushing over and begged me to speak to some customers of his, saying, 'They're from England, they've got the same accent as you. I've told them you're our Toyota specialist.'

They were from Bosnia, with east European accents, and I told them the waitress who served us at the Mexican restaurant across the street knew more than me about Toyotas, just like I told them the car they seemed so keen on buying had an oil leak. 'Don't worry about that, my cousin could fix it,' the husband said.

Personally, if I wanted to buy a car that I could take home and have my cousin fix up I would have shopped at a scrapyard. I told them this too, but sadly a small proportion of the general public doesn't respond to candour. They think you're trying to lure them into a trap. As a salesman, you just have to let them believe what they want, and hope that you won't be around when they come back to complain. I wasn't going to be around after the end of the week so . . .

Mal closed the deal. At first they said the price was too high but then he pulled out a diamond engagement ring and started describing in lavish, flower-scented, violin-playing detail how he was going to propose to his girlfriend at an Italian restaurant later that night. The mood in the sales booth was transformed. Suddenly, it seemed churlish to argue over five hundred dollars with a salesman who was about to embark on life's greatest journey. They paid up.

Some familiar demons came to visit as I was listening to this heart-warming story. Not only was this the first I'd heard of any engagement, it was well known that Mal was capable of saying anything that might help him sell a car. Only afterwards, when he showed me the ring and I bit the stone and almost broke a filling, did the knot in my stomach loosen its grip a little. Even so, the last thing I wanted to do was celebrate selling another dud car but then Frankie came out of the office and made me give him a high-five.

'Good job, Scotty – those people bought that car only because they liked you,' he said, alarmingly.

'No, no, that deal was all Mal's work,' I replied, preparing my alibi just in case they came back with the car before the week was out.

I'd been avoiding Frankie all day. Call me delusional but I'd always felt I was one of his favourites. He'd invested a lot of his time in trying to turn me into a proper salesman. Even when his efforts conspicuously failed, he made up for it by spooning me deals or selling cars for less profit than he wanted – anything to make sure the board didn't look too embarrassing for me at the end of the month. I thought he might have felt betrayed. If he did, he hid the anguish convincingly. 'I hear you're leaving us at the end of the week.'

I nodded, guiltily.

He laughed. 'You were sucking the tailpipe for the few last weeks there, Scotty, weren't you?'

'Yeah, I dialled out of the dream, Frankie.'

'Never mind. You gonna sell a few cars for me – go out in a blaze of glory?'

'Sure.'

'You're welcome back any time you want. You're a good salesman, you know that?' he said, bathing me in a fatherly smile.

I could have explained at great length why he was wrong but it would have spoiled the moment. Anyway, Mickey butted in before I had a chance to reply. He hadn't turned up to work until three o'clock and had spent the hour since in the car park at the back of the lot smoking something, presumably not Marlboros judging by the similarity between his eyes and a pair of antique dinner plates. 'I hear you're leaving,' he said, gripping my shoulders and shaking me playfully. These were the first civil words he'd said to me for weeks. 'Just remember to settle our bet before you go.'

Of course, our bet. I'd bet him a thousand dollars that I'd be Salesman of the Month before the end of the year. Unless I sold eighteen cars in the next week, it looked as if he would win. 'What bet?' I said innocently.

I'd worked it out. Including my half of the sale Mal had just made, I was due a cheque for \$1,871 commission. It wasn't a huge amount of money but I knew exactly what I was going to do with it and my plan didn't involve subsidizing Mickey's gargantuan appetite for finest Californian hemp.

The blaze of glory I promised Frankie failed to materialize. The only incentive left to do any work was money and, as I sneeringly informed Sunny when he berated me for refusing to talk to customers, I wasn't going to sell a car for him, not even if he paid me. I came to work late and left early. When I turned up at all it was only to wallow in the certain knowledge that I would only have to do this for a few more days. There was one bright moment in the week. Frankie agreed to take back Bill Baldwin's truck, though only on condition he agreed to buy a cheaper one from us. It wasn't exactly what I wanted but an eight-thousand-dollar debt was better than \$27,848, and Bill was satisfied enough to cancel all plans to return home to the islands.

Tommy found my replacement. His name was Neil, a college drop-out who looked at least eight years younger than he claimed to be on the job application form. I don't think he'd even had his first shave. As usual no one told him where anything was or how anything worked. It was heartbreaking to watch him stand around, a schoolboy in every way bar a pair of short trousers, too petrified to ask questions or talk to anyone other than me. I decided he would be my final project. It took three days to coax him into approaching a customer and thirty seconds for him to come rushing back to me in a panic, saying, 'They told me they don't want to go for a test drive.'

Of course they wanted to go on a test drive, they just didn't know they wanted to, as I suavely proceeded to demonstrate.

'You're just shopping? Great. Collecting information? Very wise. I like customers who want to educate themselves. Now, tell me this, what's the most important piece of information you need to know about the car you're about to buy?'

'The price.'

'Right. The price, of course. Apart from the price, what's the other most important piece of information you need?'

'Nothing.'

'That's right! How the car drives. And how are you going to find out how the car drives?'

'Dunno.'

'That's right. By going for a test drive.'

'You think so?'

I was only showing off but afterwards, once I'd talked them out of taking the test drive I'd just talked them into taking, Neil said it was the most brilliant thing he'd ever heard. I blushed with pride. In five minutes I had talked two perfectly rational adults into doing something they patently didn't want to do. If required, I could just as easily have made a convincing case for buying a '98 Honda Accord, which we had for sale, rather than a '98 Ferrari Testerossa, which we didn't, without reference to notes or indeed any hard facts. Was this brilliance? Hardly. Was it something I could have done if I'd never worked at The Orchard? Definitely not, which made me think that in a small way my experience as a salesman hadn't been entirely wasted.

I needn't have gone to the weekly sales meeting but nostalgia got the better of me. Never again would I spend a Friday morning in a roomful of fist-pumping, white-shirted American males. Once Jason the owner started his sales talk – 'This week's theme, guys,

"How can you sell a car that you don't have?" ' – it occurred to me that never again would I want to. The agony lasted almost an hour. On the way out, Tommy handed me the cheque for the commission I was owed: $1,971. It was a hundred dollars more than I expected and only twenty-nine dollars less than perfect for my purposes.

I was supposed to start work straight away but I told him I had an errand to run, then jumped into my car before he had a chance to object. I cashed the cheque at the bank, then drove north on Highway 680 to small town called Vallejo.

She lived on a trailer park next to a small airport exactly seventy-three miles from Orchard Boulevard. It wasn't a Jerry Springer, I'm-sleeping-with-my-neighbour's-wife-and-she's-pregnant trailer park, but a neat estate with well-kept mobile homes, flower gardens and a communal swimming-pool. The house was on a cul-de-sac, with the '91 Honda parked in the carport. I knocked on the door, fingering the envelope full of cash. It occurred to me that $1,971 was a high price, even for moral absolution. But it was too late, the door opened.

She looked younger than I remembered her, cooler and less agitated – hardly surprising given the last time I saw her it was 100 degrees in the shade and I had successfully screwed her for six thousand dollars.

'Andrea, my name is Lawrence. From Orchard Boulevard, remember? You bought a car from me.'

It took a moment for her to recognize me and when she did she was understandably puzzled. 'Is there something wrong?'

'No, no, nothing's wrong. It's just that I've got something for you.' I handed her the envelope.

'What's this?' she said.

'Two thousand dollars, almost – the money you overpaid when I sold you the car.'

I'd played this scene a hundred times in my head on the drive up the freeway. What would I have felt if a used-car salesman had turned up at my door months after the event and said he was giving me a refund? Disbelief, confusion, gratitude, joy, pissed off that someone would play a practical joke about something so serious? At the very least I might have counted the money or smiled.

Andrea did neither. 'Thanks. Come in,' she said, quietly.

It looked like the kind of household where a two-thousand-dollar windfall should have met with more celebration than it had so far. The living room was small, the furniture dark and worn. Rubbish bags stuffed with old clothes were piled up in the corner. Felix, her son, was sitting on the settee watching the QVC shopping channel. Andrea told him to turn down the sound, then explained what I was doing there.

When she finished, I asked how the car was running.

'It's going great. You sold us a good car,' Felix said.

'Shame about the price, eh?'

His mother shook her head. 'No, it wasn't your fault. We'd been looking all day and we got a little bit excited when we saw your car and paid too much. It's happened to me before. You expect these things to happen when you go to buy a car in this country.'

'Well, you know what people in America say about car salesmen?' Felix said. I did, but he told me anyway: 'Sleazy.'

'We were angry at first,' Andrea continued. 'That was a lot of money for us but then we sat down and prayed together that everything would work out all right. Are you a religious person, Lawrence?'

Just then my eyes fell on a picture of Jesus Christ above the mantelpiece. I don't know why I hadn't noticed it before: it was big enough to hang in St Peter's.

'Not exactly,' I confessed.

'Well, maybe you will be now. We asked God to take care of us, and look – you're here. He sent you to our house. Our prayers were answered.'

At last she smiled, then walked over and gave me a hug. As she wrapped me in her arms I looked up and I swear I saw Jesus's lips move. 'Good job, Scotty,' he said. He was right. From sleazy salesman to the Second Coming and all for the discount price of $1,971 – how many times in your life do deals like that come along?

★

Ten pairs of envious eyes watched me hold open the office door for Richard and Dee. It was Saturday, my last day. No one had sold a car. 'You've got yourself a deal there,' Sunny whispered, as they went inside.

I nodded, regretfully. It was after five o'clock. My shift was over and I'd said my goodbyes. I'd been at the Coke machine, getting something to drink for the journey home, when I felt a tap on the shoulder. Somewhere in the dying embers the selling instinct glowed faintly.

Al was happy with the deal – thirteen thousand dollars for a two-year-old Toyota, two thousand less than the asking price. He didn't need to know they would happily have paid the full amount. 'Don't let them out of your sight until they've signed everything,' he said, handing me the paperwork. 'And whatever you do, don't tell them they could buy a new one down the street for less than they've just paid.'

'They can?'

I caught Richard and Dee kissing in the sales booth. They were excited. It was their first car. 'Where do we sign?' said Dee.

'Nowhere.' I ripped the contract in half.

Richard sat up straight, as if suddenly wounded. 'What are you doing?'

'Did you know you can buy a new car for less than this?'

'We can? Where?'

I stuffed the sheaf of papers in a drawer 'Follow me, I'll show you,' I said, as we walked towards the exit sign. 'And remember, if someone asks you what's wrong just tell them you've changed your mind. Tell them you know a better place to spend your money than this.'

refresh yourself at penguin.co.uk

Visit penguin.co.uk for exclusive information and interviews with
bestselling authors, fantastic give-aways and the
inside track on all our books, from the Penguin Classics
to the latest bestsellers.

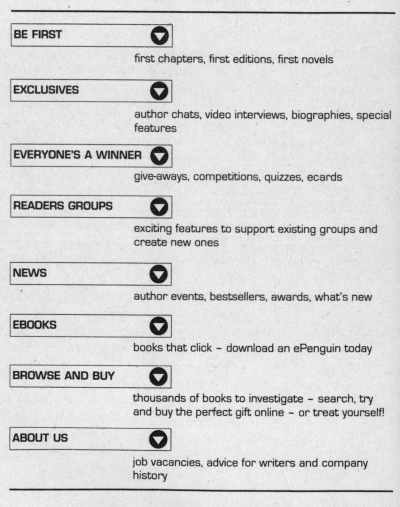

BE FIRST

first chapters, first editions, first novels

EXCLUSIVES

author chats, video interviews, biographies, special features

EVERYONE'S A WINNER

give-aways, competitions, quizzes, ecards

READERS GROUPS

exciting features to support existing groups and create new ones

NEWS

author events, bestsellers, awards, what's new

EBOOKS

books that click – download an ePenguin today

BROWSE AND BUY

thousands of books to investigate – search, try and buy the perfect gift online – or treat yourself!

ABOUT US

job vacancies, advice for writers and company history

Get Closer To Penguin . . . www.penguin.co.uk